ZERO POPULATION GROWTH— FOR WHOM?

Recent Titles in Contributions in Sociology
Series Editor: DON MARTINDALE

EDITED BY MILTON HIMMELFARB AND VICTOR BARAS

ZERO POPULATION GROWTH— FOR WHOM?

Differential Fertility and Minority Group Survival

CONTRIBUTIONS IN SOCIOLOGY, NUMBER 30

GREENWOOD PRESS
WESTPORT, CONNECTICUT • LONDON, ENGLAND

Library of Congress Cataloging in Publication Data

Conference on Population and Intergroup Relations,
New York, N. Y., 1975.
Zero population growth--for whom?

(Contributions in sociology; no. 30 ISSN 0084-
9278)
Sponsored by the American Jewish Committee.
Includes bibliographical references and index.
1. United States--Population--Congresses.
2. Fertility, Human--United States--Congresses.
3. Jews in the United States--Congresses. 4. Mi-
norities--United States--Congresses. I. Himmelfarb,
Milton. II. Baras, Victor. III. American Jewish
Committee. IV. Title.
HB3505.C66 1975   301.32'9'73   77-87966
ISBN: 0-313-20041-6

Library of Congress Catalog Card Number: 77-87966
ISBN: 0-313-20041-6
ISSN— 0084-9278

First published in 1978

Greenwood Press, Inc.
51 Riverside Avenue, Westport, Connecticut 06880

Printed in the United States of America

10 9 8 7 6 5 4 3 2 1

Contents

Preface

BERTRAM H. GOLD

Rousseau expressed the traditional view when he identified declining population with bad government. Today we take for granted the limits of growth. We know that population, like everything else in the world, cannot increase forever. In a recent United Nations survey, nations with a majority of the world's population said that their growth rates were excessive. This concern with population problems has given rise to a good deal of demographic research, which has focused on fertility, marriage, family size, and the effects of modernization. But few have paid attention to the effects of population change upon intergroup relations. That total population is growing too fast does not necessarily mean that all groups believe themselves to be growing too fast, particularly in comparison with even faster-growing neighbors, whether domestic or foreign. Some groups are not growing at all. The smaller ones, especially, may see the issue not as overpopulation but as survival. The large number of responses to the American Jewish Committee's invitations to a Conference on Population and Intergroup Relations in 1975, as well as the reactions of the participants, assured us that we had called attention to an important question.

This volume is the record of the conference. The papers by Bernard Berelson, Fred Jaffe, Charles Keely, and Etienne van de Walle were circulated in draft before the conference. That by Calvin Goldscheider was written after the conference to address an issue that had emerged with unexpected prominence. The dialogues were edited from the tape recording, thematically rather than sequentially, by Milton Himmelfarb of the Committee and Professor Victor Baras of the New School for Social Research.

We had not expected quite so much attention to be devoted to the Jews and their birthrate. Perhaps we should have, since the convener is a Jewish organization. But even a cursory examination of the proceedings will show intrinsic and not merely institutional reasons for the salience of the Jewish experience in the discussion. As far as groups go, the Jews are at once universal anomaly and universal paradigm. They are unique, and one feature of their uniqueness is that they are, as Jews themselves like to say, "like everybody else, only more so."

Are the Jews bound to experience continued low fertility and population decline? The Mormons, too, have a high average level of education and income, but their birthrate continues to be high. Questions both of fact and of policy are in dispute. We hope to examine them in future.

We are grateful to the scholars who took part. Above all, the conference was made possible by Sidney Goldstein's wise counsel, Fred Jaffe's indispensable help, and the Bixby Foundation's generous assistance. To further public understanding remains our goal.

BERTRAM H. GOLD
Executive Vice-President
The American Jewish Committee

April 1977

Postcript

Sadly, I must add that Victor Baras, a young man of great talent and promise, died in November 1977.

B.H.G.

December 1977

ZERO POPULATION GROWTH— FOR WHOM?

Introduction

SIDNEY GOLDSTEIN

The topics of our concern are not new. From time immemorial, societies and groups have been concerned with the adequacy of their population size, whether for purposes of war, for productivity and development, or for sheer survival. Such concerns are reflected in the Bible itself, both in the injunction "to be fruitful and multiply" (Genesis 1:27) and in the oft-cited practice of taking count of the population. The latter is exemplified both by God's command to Moses to "take . . . the sum of all the congregation of the children of Israel" (Numbers 1:2) and by the New Testament report of the Roman census, as a result of which Jesus was born in Bethlehem instead of Nazareth because of the de jure character of the census.

Between these biblical references to population concerns and the present, there are countless instances, some of them documented in the papers of this conference, in which nations as a whole or subgroups within nations have been concerned with rates of growth. More often than not, such national concerns have focused on the need for more people in order to maintain physical and economic strength vis-à-vis other nations. Within nations, demographic concerns have often focused on maintaining the comparative advantages of one or more subgroups. The majority group (whether judged by absolute numbers or economic and political strength), is characteristically anxious about its population size and growth rate in comparison to competing minority groups, while the minority group is often concerned lest it lose strength or eventually be swallowed up as a result of differential rates of growth, possibly coupled with assimilationist tendencies.

Today the rate of population growth has slowed significantly in the more developed world and come virtually to a standstill in some countries. Moreover, increasingly wide recognition is being given to the need for reducing growth rates in less developed countries as part of development efforts. Many of these countries have already adopted policies to reduce growth, and some already show signs of lowered fertility levels. Parallel with these developments, which have led or are leading to overall reduction in growth rates, is a growing concern in many nations with the differential rates of population growth among subgroups within countries. Such concerns have significance internationally, for world peace, as well.

Virtually no week (almost no day) goes by without some news event that relates either directly or indirectly to intranational imbalances in population composition and growth rates that have direct implications both for intergroup relations within a particular country and for international relations.

1. The bloodshed in Lebanon, while resulting from a complex set of factors, stems at least in part from the delicate demographic balance between the number of Christian and the number of Moslem Arabs in that country. Evidence for this point is seen in Lebanon's failure to take a census in the last forty years for fear that it would document a change in the balance between Christians and Moslems because of higher Moslem fertility and the fear that this would lead to a corresponding change in political power.

2. The situation in nearby Israel and the administered territories presents another case. In particular, the differential Jewish and Arab fertility levels and the impact they could have on the relative size of the Jewish and Arab populations is a major factor in discussions related to the future character and borders of the Jewish state.

3. A recent *New York Times* article on South Africa, "The End Is Inevitable, But Not Predictable," was subtitled, "The relentless arithmetic of the future: Already four blacks for every white; by the year 2000, five; by 2020, seven."

4. Research in Thailand clearly indicated that for a long time a major obstacle to a successful government population control was a strong concern on the part of the Thai majority, not founded on facts, that the economically strong Chinese minority would outpopulate the Thais if family-planning programs were instituted and adopted by the Thais.

5. In Nigeria, for the third time in twelve years, the results of a national census have been put aside because they did not show the population distribution among the regions, ethnic groups, and tribes to be what those in power preferred. Somewhat similarly, in Trinidad and Tobago, where the 1970 census found that the East Indians were the majority group, the government announced, after a long delay, that Negroes were still more numerous.

6. The *New York Times* has reported that the campaign to limit births in China had been intensified in line with the goal of making China a "powerful, modern socialist state"; but concurrently, members of ethnic minorities in China are being encouraged to take measures to increase their population. What groups and for what reasons is not specified in the article, but this decision obviously reflects a concern, for political or other purposes, with differential size and group survival chances.

7. Finally, here in the United States, with its current emphasis on pluralism, some persons have expressed concerns about the comparative demographic size and rates of growth of a number of subgroups. Such concerns have been sharpened by the approach to zero population growth (ZPG) in the United States, at the same time that group differentials in fertility levels still persist. Within the black community, a number of people have feared that advocacy of fertility limitation among blacks may be aimed at reducing their numbers and strength. Chicanos have expressed similar views. At the same time, a number of leaders of the Jewish community have voiced strong anxieties that Hitler's failure to exterminate the Jews will be largely reversed by the Jews themselves through a

form of "endogenous Jewish genocide" resulting from the combined effects of low fertility and high intermarriage rates. And on this basis, they advocate a return to higher fertility levels.

In all these demographic situations, at least three basic questions need careful review:

1. To what extent are the majority and/or the minority concerns valid with respect to the role of large numbers in group power and survival? What does history and what do the demographic facts really have to tell us about differential fertility and its relation to group continuation and power?

2. To what extent do these concerns on the part of the majority and/or minority leaders justify policies and programs to affect subgroup fertility levels and distribution patterns?

3. Assuming that changes in subgroup growth rates are desired, how successful has the past experience been with respect to achieving change? Is the reaction of the individual minority or majority group member, wherever he may live, similar to that of a Jew who wrote to *Time* (August 4, 1975), in response to an article reporting a plea for more Jewish babies: "As a Jew and a father, I don't feel it is necessary to design my family around the needs of my religion but rather around the needs of my economic status and the world at large. Any attempt at equating ZPG with antisemitism is frightening, Kafka-esque paranoia."

The AJC has planned this small conference to address issues such as these. The goals set forth, both for the background papers and for our deliberations during the next day and a half, are fourfold:

1. To assemble available information on national and international and intergroup problems related to population changes.

2. To assess the demographic realities underlying these problems.

3. To explore the need for and feasibility of a broader program of activities in this area, ro be undertaken by AJC and/or other organizations.

4. To yield an AJC publication, based on the prepared papers and the conference discussion, that will focus attention on these problems and their solutions.

1 The View from the Past: Population Change and Group Survival

ETIENNE VAN DE WALLE

In assessing the causes of the decline and fall of the Roman Empire, Edward Gibbon assigned part of the blame to the morality of the triumphant Christians.

It was their favorite opinion that, if Adam had preserved his obedience to the creator, he would have lived for ever in a state of virgin purity, and that some harmless mode of vegetation might have peopled paradise with a race of innocent and immortal beings. The use of marriage was permitted only to his fallen posterity as a necessary expedient to continue the human species, and as a restraint, however imperfect, on the natural licentiousness of desire. [1]

Indeed Saint Augustine toyed with the idea that mankind was striving toward moral perfection and that reaching it would mean the extinction of the species through the abolition of carnal desires. The admonition to "replenish the earth," however valid in the Old Testament while the genealogy of Christ was building up, was superseded by the cardinal concern to fill the City of God. It is no surprise then that the Christian ideal of chastity was seen by opponents throughout history as a factor of depopulation. The argument was invoked, for instance, by the French Revolutionaries when they voted the suppression of convents and religious orders, these "graves of population."

Modern scholars have debated the demographic causes of the fall of Rome and, before that, the decline of classical Greece. Many contemporaries were certainly concerned about low fertility, assumed or real, generalized or restricted to a small upper crust of society. The historian Polybius, writing in the second century B.C., claimed that "Greece suffers from such an interruption of procreation and such a shortage of men that cities are depopulated. The reason is that people today love opulence, money and laziness above all and don't want to marry; or married, to raise a family. At the most they accept one or two children, so that they can leave them rich and raise them in luxury." [2]

Similar indictments were formulated by Roman writers, and the opinion that Malthusian attitudes and practices contributed to the collapse of the empire is widely held today. In the 1930s, anti-Malthusian writers used the Roman example to argue that family limitation would lead to the decline of Western civilization. Today the best specialists of the demography of the ancient world incline to a more agnostic view. Infanticide and abortion were practiced widely in Greece. The surviving medical literature from the Greek and Roman writers contains many contraceptive and abortive recipes, although few of their methods would allow efficient control of fertility. Coitus interruptus, the main birth control technique of the European demographic transition in the nineteenth century, is not mentioned in the medical literature of Rome. Because of a total absence of statistical sources, it will be impossible to assess whether small families were widespread or restricted to a thin part of high society, the one that produces literature and moralistic treatises. It is likely that marital customs—late marriage of the men and a large age difference between the spouses—were not particularly favorable to high fertility. But no one can say whether the birthrate was particularly low. Fluctuations of mortality, especially because of epidemics, may have been more determinant in shaking the administrative and political order. But here, too, not enough evidence has survived to allow the barest quantitative assessment.

The view from the past on the subject of demographic factors in group survival, then, must begin in times and social groups where statistics are available. The earliest reliable evidence comes from elite groups. Shifting from the Roman Empire to the European aristocracies of the modern period represents a serious change of focus, and I must provide some kind of framework for this survey before going further.

THE SURVIVAL OF GROUPS

Many kinds of groups are threatened by extinction and loss of influence or, conversely, they can expand and flourish. For my purpose I shall distinguish between three types of groups: those that have in common a territory (a nation, province, village), those defined by a more or less indelible characteristic (such as race, language, religion), and those that share a common status or vocation (aristocracy and clergy, for example). Groups can gain or lose numerical importance and/or power and influence through natural increase, transfer from group to group, or qualitative improvement or decay. Table 1 illustrates the types of gains and losses more frequently sustained by various groups.

Most groups gain by birth (except the clergy) and lose by death, and they are usually subject to changes caused by migration, annexation,

Table 1

| | GROUPS DEFINED BY: | | | | | | | |
| | Territorial Criterion | | Physical or Cultural Trait | | | Social Function or Vocation | | |
	Country	Province	Race	Language	Religion	Aristocracy	Bourgeoisie	Clergy
GAINS								
Quantitative								
Births	x	x	x	x	x	x	x	
Immigration	x	x					x	x
Recruitment			x	x			x	x
Annexation	x	x					x	x
Qualitative	x	x	x	x	x	x	x	x
LOSSES								
Quantitative								
Deaths	x	x	x	x	x	x	x	x
Emigration	x	x				x	x	x
Defection			x	x				x
Loss of territory	x	x					x	
Qualitative	x	x	x	x	x	x	x	x

conversion, or defection. Some groups are not affected by border changes. A group identifiable by physical traits—such as color of the skin—can grow numerically only by the balance of births and deaths, although its influence may fluctuate independently of numbers. Qualitative gains by groups—that may well be more important in the long run for their continued viability—range from the gain of resources and technical progress, to their acceptability by the rest of society or even fashionability; similarly a group may perish because it could not adapt to changed circumstances or lost its raison d'être.

We assume that survival is a goal shared by all groups, although to a different degree and not necessarily with a high priority when in competition with other goals. Since my task is not to speculate on the dynamics of groups but to present some of the relevant historical experience, the above scheme is sufficient for my purpose.

THE SURVIVAL OF ARISTOCRACIES

Elites that are perpetuated by birthright obey very different principles of renewal than do empires and nations, even though birth, death, and migration are factors in both instances. The survival of an aristocracy is predicated on the individual survival of families, and there is no compensation when one family disappears and another has an overflow of sons. It is of no benefit to the last male La Rochefoucauld to know that the Montmorency have three sons. If one son is necessary to inherit the title and the manor, other sons will be no more than a hedge against high mortality risks. Cadets are an embarrassment as long as the eldest son is alive, and usually they will be accommodated in the army of the clergy as single men. Because they are not expected to marry, they do not offer a very effective defense against extinction of the name when an older son dies without offspring.

It seems a constant empirical fact that aristocracies have not been able to reproduce themselves, despite the vested interest in doing so that was stronger than in most other social groups. To survive in the long run, an elite group must allow the accession of selected individuals from the outside. In England, for example,

of the 63 noble families of December 1559, 21 had failed in the male line by December 1641, and 26 by December 1659. There is nothing unusual in an extinction rate of 40 percent per century, indeed it is probably rather low in comparison with other periods. This inexorable attrition destroyed any prospect of maintaining the peerage as a self-perpetuating closed caste. If the Crown did not bestir itself to plug the gaps, in 250 years or so there would be no one left to sport a title.[3]

The extinction of family lines is an unavoidable result of the distribution of infecundity among couples, chance variation in the sex ratio at birth, and high mortality before the age of reproduction. To show the interplay of these factors, I selected a population practicing little, if any, contraception: women married at twenty to twenty-one years before 1889 and still married to the same men, reporting the number of their live-born children in the Norwegian census of 1920.[4] The figures are shown in table 2. Large families are the rule in this population; the average number of children is 7.7, half of them boys. If 70 percent of them survive to the mean age of childbearing, there should be on the average almost three boys per family. But the point of view of individual families is different. Of these women, 2.6 percent bore no child at all; another 2.6 percent had only one child, and in about half of the cases it should be a girl. The probability of having all-girl offspring decreases with the number of children. Assuming for simplicity's sake that births are evenly distributed among the sexes, 6 percent of the Norwegian women would have had no son. And with 30 percent of the sons dying before the average age of paternity (a moderate mortality level corresponding to an expectation of life at birth of fifty years), about 10 percent of the families would die out per generation. It would take seven generations to reduce the number of

Table 2
CUMULATIVE LIVE BIRTHS REPORTED BY
NORWEGIAN WOMEN, 1920

Number of Live Births	Per 1,000 Women	Number of Live Births	Per 1,000 Women
0	26	6	78
1	26	7	95
2	36	8	111
3	41	9	131
4	55	10	132
5	66	10+	203

families by half, even under such favorable conditions of fertility and mortality, if only one son per family was entrusted with the function of perpetuating the family name and heritage.

In European aristocracies of the preindustrial era, the attrition seems to have been considerably faster, both because fertility was lower than in Norway and because mortality was higher. For example, of 177 families of the patriciate of Milan existing in 1650, only twenty-six were surviving in 1950.[5] In Florentine patrician families of the sixteenth and seventeenth centuries, "the marriage of only one son was such a common occurrence as to have been almost a general rule, and since 16 percent of the sons who did marry had no children. the chances were that family lines would be abruptly truncated within three or four generations, for lack of heirs."[6] Apparently when confronted with a choice between the risks of extinction and those of loss of prestige and social standing, the Florentine patricians were deciding for the former: "Given an unwillingness to divide estates permanently, and limited opportunities for making independent fortunes sufficient to provide patrimonies for second or third families, younger sons apparently resigned themselves to bachelorhood."[7]

In Florence at least, the erosion of the upper class was compensated by the continuous rise of bourgeois into the aristocracy. In Venice, the patriciate was closed. A law passed in 1297 restricted membership to the Great Council, and therefore access to important offices and committees, to an exclusive group of families. There were thirty ennoblements in 1381 and only minor exceptions thereafter. "For 265 years it was virtually impossible for even the wealthiest and most able nonnoble Venetian citizen to enter the ruling class."[8] When the economic fortunes of the city compelled the elite to change from commercial to landed sources of revenue, the preservation of family patrimonies became imperative. This gave rise to the general practice of restricted marriage. There was no custom of primogeniture as in Florence: "In most wills, possessions were left to all sons equally. . . . But since they usually remained under the same roof, and since the fideicommissum prevented them from alienating any of the 'immovable possessions,' and since unmarried brothers usually left their possessions to the children of the brother who had married, estates usually remained intact."[9] The patrician family of Venice functioned as an association of specialized brothers: one would participate in the government of the republic, one would administer the family's business, a third one would ensure the survival of the name by marrying.

James Davis has presented an illustration that admirably symbolizes the system. It is a family portrait; the mother is sitting in the foreground, holding four children; at the back, four elderly gentlemen stand, looking equally proud, with nothing to distinguish the genitor from his brothers. In Davis's words, "The Venetian experience becomes a fairly clear demonstration of the infeasibility in the long run of an 'aristocratic' or closed ruling class."[10] The nobility diminished by 55 percent between the middle of the sixteenth century and the Napoleonic conquest. The wealth of died-out families was redistributed among surviving related nobles or went to churches and monasteries. This demographic decline of the ruling class was translated into a shortage of manpower in the government, which greatly reduced its effectiveness.

The practice of restricted marriages was not the ony way by which aristocracies were limiting their numbers and apparently hastening their own extinction. The French dukes and peers started using contraception by 1700 (or perhaps even earlier). During the second half of the eighteenth century, among women married before they were twenty years old, 35 percent had no child, and another 46 percent had only one or two children.[11] In a social group where reproduction and survival must have been an important consideration, these figures cry for an explanation.

These facts have some relevance to one of the arguments in the theory of the demographic transition. In trying to explain why natural increase remains high in developing countries, despite the obvious problems caused by population pressure, some writers have argued that many cultures impose family sizes beyond what is necessary to reproduce the aggregate population because of the desire to have a son around during old age and the need to perpetuate the name. Heer and Smith, for example, constructed a model showing the rates of population growth and fertility implied under a series of mortality levels if it was assumed that parents desire 95 percent of certainty that at least one son would survive to the father's old age. Their computation suggested that a very substantial proportion of wives (up to 40 percent in some instances) would never bear the needed number of sons under conditions of high fertility and mortality. The authors concluded: "If . . . the degree of certainty for filial survival . . . is congruent with present day realities in the less developed nations, we can expect little reduction in the rate of population increase until we reduce mortality still further."[12] The paradox is that Western elite groups were putting a high premium on filial survival, but they nevertheless reduced their fertility and population increase either by restricting marriages or by using contraception before mortality had been reduced to levels reached by most areas of the world today.

To resolve the paradox, we must perhaps recognize that the imperative to reproduce has been ineffective at the very level where it counted most: the microcosmic level of individuals and families. The numerous wars of succession in history bear witness that even royal families could not count on male heirs, despite their advantages of wealth and the ability to influence law and religion for their purpose (demonstrated by Henry VIII of England). The intrinsic weakness of the survival mechanism in individual families explains perhaps in part why alternative systems of renewal have been devised and why reproduction has not been a more important imperative for larger social groups.

THE SURVIVAL OF LINGUISTIC, RACIAL, AND RELIGIOUS GROUPS

Heer and Smith argue that the preoccupation of individuals to have a living son when they are old leads them to overlook the collective interest in a lower growth rate. We are here turning the argument around and applying it to instances where the perceived interest of the group is a high growth rate and where that concern conflicts with individual benefit. Where groups are in competition, it has often appeared, rightly or wrongly, that a high rate of reproduction would further their collective aims. With the general decline of mortality, mortality differentials between social classes have tended to play a lesser role in the numerical importance of various segments of the population. Increasingly, therefore, high fertility has been identified as a sign of vital strength that would eventually ensure the triumph of minority groups. The term *revanche des berceaux* ("revenge of the cradles") has been used to characterize the higher fertility of the politically and economically disfranchised Francophone Canadians. Today's world is still full of such examples. It will be sufficient here to evoke the topic briefly to the extent that cultural differences have played a role in the history of the demographic transition.

There is a pervasive contemporary concern about differential growth by ethnic or linguistic groups. It is worthy of note that this concern appears quite late, either in public consciousness or in the literature. The idea seems to characterize the twentieth century for several reasons, the most important being that large differences in fertility are a recent phenomenon. And until recently there were no statistics to measure vital rates by subgroup of the population, both a consequence and a cause of the lack of interest in the subject.

In the nineteenth century, the modern State in Western Europe was concerned with nation building, unification, and, wherever possible, eradication of regional particularism. On the whole, the effort was highly successful. The Breton-speaking in France were estimated at 1.35 million in 1880; by 1930 their number had dropped to roughly one million, despite the large population increase in the Breton départements.[13] The Basque-speaking population fell from 150,000 to 100,000 during the same period. Other minority languages were not faring any better in Western Europe. In most instances, their very survival was threatened not by a failure of reproduction but because of the overwhelming strength of the languages of government, the towns, the schools, and the press. At the same time that powerful, unilingual States were forming, the main European languages were spreading out of national borders. French was the most important cultural language of Europe, and English spread widely overseas, while German minorities were expanding in Eastern Europe.

The early twentieth century, however, represented a radical change of trend:

The First World War resulted in the raising of most of the local languages of Eastern Europe to nationhood. . . . With the sanction of political authority and its institution as the language of instruction and higher culture all of the new national languages of Eastern Europe made gains as over against linguistic minorities within their national boundaries. Before they had the strength that comes from having roots in the soil, and, as predominantly rural and peasant peoples, higher birth rates than alien and more urban elements. Now these tendencies were reinforced by all the prestige and official sanction and use. In the face of this circumstance linguistic groups representing the old ruling elements retreated, in many cases the minorities being further weakened by emigration of some of their numbers to countries where their languages remained dominant.[14]

In Western Europe, too, there were clear cultural revivals illustrated by the conscious resuscitation of the Irish language, the new militancy of Flemish in bilingual Belgium, and the separatist agitation in the old Basque and Celtic marches. Thus by the twentieth century, there were new cultures acquiring nationalistic pretensions at the very time when fertility differentials were become large.

Linguistic statistics from censuses are notoriously unreliable because the central State has a stake in minimizing the extent of cultural dissimilarities. For example, the censuses of the Austro-Hungarian empire were classifying Yiddish as German, and the French linguistic censuses of Alsace-Lorraine were listing as "patois" what German censuses of the area had tabulated as High German. With the rise to nationhood of the

Versailles nations, the apparent linguistic makeup of Eastern Europe reported in censuses changed dramatically over what it had been—the result of a different phrasing of the question and of a different viewpoint on the part of census takers.[15] The absence or tendentiousness of the statistics on differential growth long contributed to a general ignorance of the problem that we are discussing here, and its recent accession to the forefront of public discussion coincided with a heightened sense of cultural identity.

In Europe during the last hundred years, the regional differences in fertility often tended to follow cultural lines. Ansley Coale tells the story of one of his students who showed a map of fertility by province in Spain to a professor of Romance languages and drew the comment that this was a linguistic map of Spain.[16] Regional differentials have usually reflected the time at which marital fertility started its steep modern decline—and therefore the onset of widespread contraception. While fertility was in its process of long-term decline, a lag in starting time would for long mean higher levels. In Belgium, the factor that accounts the best for the earliness of the fertility decline is on what side of the French-Flemish linguistic border a village lies.[17] During the last century, the Flemish have had a higher rate of natural increase as a result. In France, too, there is a relationship between the prevalence of minority languages and dialects and the nineteenth-century levels and trends of fertility. High birthrates continued to prevail in regions of Breton, German, and Flemish speech, and to some extent in the *langue d'oc* regions, after they had come down elsewhere.

The first explanation that springs to mind is that language is the vehicle for the diffusion of cultural traits, including the norm of the small family and the knowledge of birth control techniques; information is held up at linguistic boundaries. But a more insidious mechanism may be at work too. There is often a relationship between language and the extent to which a region has been drawn into the mainstream of economic and political life. Flanders no doubt, had suffered heavily from the process of industrialization and was economically depressed compared to Wallonia; French was the language of the elite. In France the regions where a language other than French was still spoken were areas that had long been isolated from the center because of a combination of ecological and political factors. The survival of dialects is an indirect measure of the failure of the educational and administrative systems in their efforts to integrate particular regions. There is a price to pay for being different, including higher mortality rates and unusually high migration. And if high fertility was the premium for relative backwardness, it also brought further problems and impediments in its wake. Nevertheless differential fertility does not prevail forever. The large differences in population growth that occurred as a result of the lags in the onset of the demographic transition in various groups were transitional phenomena. Today the fertility of the Bretons, the Flemings and the French Canadians is not standing out any more; in the two latter cases at least, it has decreased below national averages.

Religious differences sometimes operate much like linguistic ones. In the ongoing secularization process, the regions that preserved their traditional faith were often those sheltered from the inroads of administrative centralization, Bretons, Flemings, and French Canadians were all distinguished by their militant Catholicism. Maps showing religious practice in France during the interwar period look strikingly like maps of marital fertility for the mid-nineteenth century. That all religious doctrines do not accept contraception to the same extent may be relevant to some degree in explaining fertility differentials. But religion has acted as another barrier to the diffusion of information as much as it acted to indoctrinate its flocks; and the other barriers to cultural diffusion—distance, language, illiteracy—were protecting traditional belief at the very time they were impeding the transmission of new fertility norms. A student of religious sociology in France, Le Bras, pictured the nineteenth-century parish as "a defense post of Christian civilisation" and associated the decline of fertility with the spread of worldly influences:

Many novelties are contributing to loosen the hold of the Church on rural masses: the multiplication of contacts, social transformations, the persistent action of the lay State. There will soon be no village which will not be linked to the city by bus, no peasant who won't have his bicycle or his truck; Parisian fashions are implanted even in thatched cottages; newspapers, lecturers penetrate in the smallest hamlets. . . . The school and the army barrack transform spirits, the administration substitutes itself to the former leaders.[18]

Early explanations of the fertility decline were often cast in terms of the superior "civilization" and the greater spirit of restraint and foresight of the peoples who were able to improve their economic lot by curbing their impulses. It is not surprising, therefore, that the higher fertility of ethnic minorities was not usually seen as a strength but rather as a weakness, something that went with poverty, high mortality, low nuptiality, certainly with backwardness and perhaps with intemperance. To French authors of the nineteenth century, the high fertility of the minority areas was another of the quaint customs, to be classified with regional costumes, barbaric languages, and lack of hygiene. They were often opposing the Bretons and the Normands. About the latter, Pellegrino Rossi in his 1836 lectures at the Collège de France referred to "the welfare enjoyed by the laborious and prudent populations of the *departements* which have placed themselves in the lead of French civilisation."[19] In opposition, an English observer noted, "the Bretons seem by their very ignorance and the high mortality which it allows of, to be at once rendered insensible to consequences and freed from the necessity of placing any great restraint upon their inclinations."[20] The proliferation of the Irish was eliciting the same kind of scorn from Englishmen, who considered the high birthrate irresponsible.

It is only more recently that high fertility became a public virtue, under two sets of influences. First, the concern of States for the implications of vital trends reached crisis stage in the 1930s. Second, there was a resurgence of nationalistic movements in Europe with World War I. In the rhetoric of the interwar years, large families were equated with vigor and youth, and the constant progress of contraception was blamed on selfishness and "overcivilization" in the "senile" countries of Western Europe. The pockets of high fertility that had been left behind by the unequal diffusion of the demographic transition were seen as fountains of youth springing from the ancestral soil of the ethnic groups. And religion, with its opposition to contraception, was seen as a defender of the traditional virtues. Conversely the reproductive potential of the minorities was seen as a weapon in the fight for political dominance.

The long-term prospects implicit in the faster growth of ethnic or religious groups were noted in many contexts; numbers were often used to buttress particularistic viewpoints. But it would be wrong to picture these arguments either as very concerning or as shared by a large proportion of the very groups that were pictured as engaged in a struggle for dominance. Indeed they were part of a pronatalist propaganda that was notoriously unsuccessful. In Belgium for example, the higher birthrate of the Flemings was already obvious to observers at the beginning of the century. Jacquart, the head of the Belgian Statistical Institute, noted that

The extraordinary development of the Flemish race which fills the voids in the Walloon country prevents us from noticing the consequences of the decline in the Walloon birth rate. The colonies of Flemish workers who slowly invade Wallonia usually abandon the use of their mother tongue, so that the language census shows no observable change in the location of our linguistic border.[21]

Jacquart went on to observe that the Flemish bourgeoisie was contaminated by "the devastating germs carried by the French influence." Flemish writers, meanwhile, were congratulating themselves on the relative "health" of their people and discussing ways of protecting it against the French influence.

*Our people has long remained wholesome and healthy of heart and spirit, because
it was deeply anchored in the fertile soil of ancestral tradition. . . . Many [migrants]
have been attracted by and within the sphere of the superficial, frivolous French
mentality, and have abandoned the fundamental health of their own simplicity for
a French coating.*[22]

During the German occupation a Dr. J. De Roeck contrasted the biological strength of the "Vlaamsche Volk" with Latin degeneracy and produced population projections based on the continuation of prewar trends, which led to the quasi-disappearance of the Walloons: "The frightening fertility decline of the Walloons and the growth of the Flemish people's part raise in the mind the ghost of an almost complete netherlandization of Belgium within foreseeable time."[23] These predictions not only failed to recognize the parallel (although lagged) decline of Flemish fertility but also underestimated the cultural attraction of French.

Despite the higher reproduction rate in Flemish-speaking areas, the proportion of the population reporting that it spoke Flemish was 56 percent at both the 1866 and 1947 censuses. The latter was the last census to include a question on language because the linguistic border was fixed to prevent further encroachments of French on Flemish land.

Elsewhere projections have also been based on rather naive extrapolation and have failed to understand the transitional character of fertility differentials. In Switzerland, where it had been predicted that the higher fertility of Catholic cantons would necessarily lead to the spread of Catholicism, the proportion of Catholics evolved from 41 percent in 1860 to 42 percent in 1950 and 46 percent in 1960 (the latter rise mainly caused by migration). There was also very little change in the linguistic makeup of Switzerland over time.[24] In the Netherlands, some Catholics were seeing an opportunity "to outbreed the Protestants."[25] The high natural increase of the "healthy," noncontracepting faithful was seen implicitly as a "striking revenge of Divine Providence." Actually the percentage of Catholics went from 38 in 1849 (and 35 in 1909) to 40 in 1960. Although the Dutch Reformed church was steadily losing ground (in part to other Protestant denominations), the most remarkable increase was in the category "no religion," which increased from 0.3 percent in 1879 to 18 percent in 1960. Although the Roman Catholic had become the largest church by 1930, the trend was not leading to outbreeding. Finally in Canada, where the high fertility of the French Canadians has long been proverbial, the percentage of the population with French mother tongue has steadily gone down in recent years: from 29 percent in 1941 to 27 percent in 1971. Immigration of English speakers, or of other groups that were assimilated into the English community, has on the whole prevented the progress of the minority language. Conversely those who belonged to the less prolific segments of the population resented the threat of the fertile invaders. Thus, the socialist Sidney Webb in England said: "Twenty-five percent of our parents . . . is producing 50 percent of the next generation. This can hardly result in anything but national deterioration; or, as an alternative, in this country gradually falling to the Irish and the Jews."[26] Indeed, according to the 1916 report of the National Birth Rate Commission, the fertility of the Jews was above average in England.

Such differentials are subject to periodic changes, however. More-over the numerical advantages expected from differential growth are vulnerable to defections. It can be concluded, perhaps, that the social, economic, political, and cultural forces that lead to the survival or dominance of language or religion are worthy of more attention than the slow and unpredictable trend in the birthrate. This is indeed the position that professional demographers have assumed on the whole, and the opposite argument, with its racial and nationalistic overtones, has been restricted to partisan politics.

VILLAGES AND NATIONS

One of the questions raised by the organizers of this meeting was, Has any group ever bred itself out of existence? If the question refers to the single effect of low fertility, no well-documented example comes to mind among racial, religious, or linguistic groups. These groups, rather, are threatened by loss of identity through intermarriage and assimilation. The types of groups that have historically dwindled in size or influence, in part because of their low fertility, belong to the third category: those that are territorial in nature. There are many abandoned villages and dead towns, and low fertility usually accompanied their decline, either because the young people left early or because the population stopped reproducing itself.

Preindustrial village populations in Western Europe have often been remarkably stable over time. Dupâquier, who gives examples of this con-stancy over large numbers of years for the Basin of Paris, suggests that it results from a self-regulating mechanism having its origin in the social rather than in the physical world.[27] There are a limited number of slots in the village society — houses, farms, trades, jobs — and openings get filled as they occur by the single person waiting in the wings for this oppor-tunity to start an independent household. The numerus clausus of careers and opportunities determines the size of the system and regulates fertility through marriage as a consequence of the mortality level that created openings among the previous generation.

During the eighteenth century, in country after country, there was a clear tendency toward exceptionally large population increases. Although the controversy over the sources of the increase has not abated, it seems today that it can hardly be denied that mortality declined during the century—be it from the exceptional toll of epidemics and subsistence crises, or the "normal" deaths that yielded to improvements in economic welfare, hygiene, and public health.[28] The trend accelerated in the nineteenth century and gave rise to increased densities on the land. Toward the end of the century, an increasing proportion of the European population started to limit their marital fertility. (France had been engaged in this process much earlier.) The change in vital rates has been called *demographic transition*. It was accompanied—and to a large extent caused—by economic and social transformations, including a redistribution of the population over space. Economic competition and a growing reliance on the market favored certain regions endowed with resources and good communications. Remote areas that had been self-sufficient previously were emptied by migration. Over much of history, urban mortalities were probably high, and large cities were replenished by steady streams from the countryside. But with modernization and industrialization, the countryside started to lose population absolutely. Thus, the processes of differential growth of geographical areas by migration are commonplace enough to be excluded from the present discussion. More to the point is the regional role of fertility.

It is difficult to perceive the logic that determined the waning or the persistence of high levels of fertility in various regions of Europe. I am arguing that the numerical survival of established groups does not feature very highly among the priorities that regulate fertility; and this is more true for village communities than for any other type of group, perhaps because the identity of such a group is not very well differentiated and perceived by the component individuals. The map of rural Europe is full of examples of extreme family limitation that reduced numbers drastically over time. The "one-child system" adopted in Ormansag, a region of Calvinist villages in Hungary, by the mid-nineteenth century had led by 1970 to a take-over of the area by migrant families.[29] Philippe Ariès has coined the term *human evaporation* to characterize the steady decline in the Aquitaine region of France during the nineteenth and early twentieth centuries, a decline that was caused by low fertility without much migration.[30] Table 3 presents population totals (females only) for two départements in Aquitaine—Lot-et-Garonne and Tarn-et-Garonne—two départements in Normandy—Calvados and Eure—and, as a contrast, the Finistère département in Brittany, at three different dates. The four first départements are among those that adopted the practice of birth control on a wide scale at the time of, or before, the French Revolution; their birthrate had been under thirty female births per 1,000 women from the beginning of official vital statistics in France in 1801. In contrast, the decline of marital fertility does not seem to begin in Finistère before 1870.[31] In all instances, there is little net migration, and the growth or decline is mostly the result of the balance of births and deaths. (See table 3.) Finistère is the only département among the five that underwent significant, although moderate, out-migration.

The decrease of population must have appeared advantageous to individuals: it facilitated the access to land and the raising of the few children that were born. In 1911, Dr. Jacques Bertillon published the results of a survey of doctors' opinions in four départements of Aquitaine and Normandy.[32] He noted the association of low fertility with rural well-being ("the wealthiest cantons are those which are most sterile in men") and with the desire for land.

In Lot-et-Garonne . . . "a second pregnancy is considered as a shame" according to one of our respondents; "a man who has children is despised even by the women" according to another. Another writes that when a couple has a second child, he is presented not with congratulations, but with sympathies. . . .

Several of our respondents insist on the known fact that it is most of all out of fear to divide one's wealth that the peasant wants only one child. "He loves his land more than his family." "An only heir married to an only heiress, that is is his dream." "He accepts very well that his name disappears, and is easily resigned not to have another heir, even if his child is a girl."[33]

It is difficult perhaps to draw up a balance sheet of societal gains and losses resulting from this pursuit of individual reproductive goals. It may have depopulated the countryside—but the same result could have come about from migration to urban jobs and areas. It has been argued "that in the last century Aquitaine, declining in population, saw its agriculture stagnate, while Brittany, under constant demographic pressure, cleared the land, modernized its techniques, and branched out into entirely new products."[34] What if population pressure resulted in misery in the process? Is modern-day agriculture compatible with high rural densities? Thousands of noncompetitive Breton farmers are now compelled to leave the land and seek a living in the cities. On the other

Table 3
FEMALE POPULATION OF FIVE FRENCH DEPARTEMENTS,
1806, 1856, AND 1906

| | Lot-et-Garonne | | Tarn-et-Garonne | | Calvados | | Eure | | Finistère | |
	Number	Index	Number	Index	Number	Index	Number	Index	Number	Index
1806	166,731	100	122,973	100	262,349	100	216,131	100	229,944	100
1856	172,115	103	122,430	100	252,918	96	205,983	95	308,403	134
1906	137,391	82	95,032	77	209,678	80	164,765	76	397,482	173

hand, the Bretons have preserved their cultural identity to an extent impossible in the Garonne region, where a steady flow of foreign farmers has taken over the ownership of abandoned land.

The issue of competition between nations received a dramatic illustration while France was undergoing its fertility decline well in advance of that of other European countries. The wars of the Napoleonic period show that France could withstand the coalition of the other European nations by drawing upon its large population. "With a population exceeded in 1800 only by that of Russia, France saw her population outstripped in the nineteenth century by the population of Germany (1850), Austria-Hungary (1880), the United Kingdom (1900) and Italy (after 1930)."[35] The European equilibrium was displaced, and the colonial expansion of the English could not be matched. While large overseas nations were built on the emigration of prolific Europeans, France was becoming dependent on immigration to ensure the continued growth of its labor force; in 1927, 54 percent of the population were of foreign origin dating from the third generation or less.[36]

The nineteenth century and the first half of the twentieth represented a peak period of nationalism in Europe and intense competition among nations. The size of the military forces was a powerful argument in the resolution of conflicts. That the French resorted widely to contraception almost one century before their neighbors undoubtedly influenced the relative strength of nations. When this fact was realized, it became an important factor in national and international French policies.

The defeat of France by Prussia in 1870-71 greatly intensified the alarm of French social scientists and publicists at the low level of natality and population growth in France, in contrast to the levels prevailing in other large European countries. For this defeat not only diminished the military prestige of France and cost the country several millions of population; it altered significantly the distribution of demographic forces on the continent; it led foreign observers to conclude that the French race was decadent and that France had lost permanently her former position as the dominant continential power.[37]

Joseph Spengler, who wrote the classical *France Faces Depopulation* (1938), showed how the perception of a demographic weakness helped shape France's social and economic policies, diplomacy, colonial theory and practice, and migration legislation. In turn, a resolute attempt was made to influence natural increase. This effort illustrates the pitfalls in trying to impose collective goals on individuals by compulsion and repressive measures—although monetary incentives were present too. Alva Myrdal's indictment stands: "Population interest in France . . . never became sufficiently social-minded to care rationally for the economic fate of the large families it encouraged."[38] The law prohibited the sale of contraceptives, and doctors were prosecuted for giving advice on contraception. The effect was probably to entrust the poorest and least educated with the function of ensuring the reproduction of the country.

Meanwhile the international situation that gave rise to great concern in the early part of this century disappeared before the measures taken to correct national trends of population could have much effect. Today the rate of natural increase of most European nations is rather precariously balanced close to zero (Germany has a negative rate and France a positive one), the old military balances have lost their meaning, and developed nations import large labor forces from less developed ones. The conflicts between nations have changed in nature, and the argument of numbers is used today with a different twist: nations with an excessive rate of growth jeopardize their opportunities for economic and social development. Military might depends more on the quality of the hardware and the training of those who man it than upon the size of the battalions. The particular set of historical forces that resulted from time lags in the population transition and pitted nations with changing demographic potential against one another may never exist again in quite the same way.

CONCLUSIONS

An implicit assumption underlies much of the literature: reproduction is an important concern that will determine the behavior of populations, either directly, by the promotion of fertility-enhancing customs, or indirectly, by selection of societies that have proven fittest to reproduce. The existence of groups that behaved in ways that reduced their number or at least their relative strength therefore seems an aberration. But there are groups that bred themselves out of existence, and the historical record suggests that the survival instinct of a group may not be very strong. I suggest that there are different kinds of groups, with different types of motivations.

Where survival would count most—at the level of the individual family—the study of aristocracies shows that reproduction cannot be guaranteed even under optimum conditions of fertility and mortality. Villages, provinces, or even countries are not groups where survival should determine fertility behavior because their group consciousness is often not paramount and because migration (that is, deserting the group) is a more effective mechanism to adapt population size to resources. In ethnic or religious groups, the forces of assimilation compete with those of cultural identity.

In the groups reviewed here during the period considered, it is thus understandable that various forces that brought fertility down—economic advantage, land hunger, preservation of the patrimony—were more determinant than the elusive search for numerical survival.

When we discuss fertility differentials according to racial or cultural characteristics, it is essential to recognize that there is nothing intrinsic about religion, language, or race to explain the level of fertility. Although there is much that we do not know or understand about the levels of marital fertility before the long-term decline that occurred during the period for which reliable statistics exist, it is clear that those differentials that can be discussed intelligently must be attributed either to diverging norms about family size or to unequal access to efficient means of contraception. The desire and the ability to control family size account for a large proportion of the differences in growth rates among competing social groups in the Western world. Norms and contraceptive effectiveness may vary in function of cultural factors under given circumstances, but there is no reason why a particular ethnic, religious, or linguistic group would always be distinguished from others in a similar way. For example, France, "the eldest daughter of the Catholic church," was the first country where contraception was widely diffused and accepted. The Dutch Catholics were characterized by high fertility during the early part of this century. The French language is associated with low fertility in Belgium, with high fertility in Canada, and so on. In the course of the demographic transition, there have been lags in the onset of the decline of fertility. Many of the group differentials in fertility reflect that lag and are not a permanent feature of intergroup relations. Pockets of high fertility tended to be more rural and to have less income and less education, in addition to the fact that they were identifiable by their cultural characteristics. Dominant groups tended to be ahead of the others, whereas groups out of the mainstream had less access to modernity in the realm of reproduction. Hence high fertility became associated with traditional values and was visualized as part of a balancing mechanism that would ensure that certain minorities that felt wronged would prevail in the end.

History gives few well-documented examples of competition between ethnic or religious groups that were resisting assimilation and were bent on a collision course where numbers might become the deciding factor. Such examples unfortunately appear to exist in today's world. There are conflicting groups where one has a large technological advantage and the resulting degree of contraceptive knowledge and practice, whereas the less developed other will steadily accumulate overwhelming numerical advantages because of its uncontrolled fertility. History suggests that such differences are reduced in the long run but that vastly different accumulations of population can result before the process runs its course.

In Western societies, fertility differentials have tended to narrow, as have many other ethnic particularisms. Cultural groups are more threat-ened, however, by assimilation than by physical extinction. Assimilation and the preservation of one's cultural identity are both desirable in some respects, but the latter goal often requires the double-edged weapons of isolation and particularism. The advantages gained by maintaining a higher fertility have proven to be elusive historically, as defections and mixed marriages are nibbling away the temporary advantages of faster natural growth. Because of the high cost of excessive fertility, quantitative and qualitative advantages must be weighted carefully. Fertility is not a very good mechanism for the adjustment of society, and we do not even know how to manipulate it effectively. The social, political, economic, and cultural forces that lead to the survival or dominance of cultural groups are worthy of more attention than the slow and unpredictable trends in the birthrate.

NOTES

1. Edward Gibbon, *The History of the Decline and Fall of the Roman Empire* (New York: Fred de Fau and Company, 1906), 2:305.

2. Quoted in Marcel Reinhard, André Armengaud, and Jacques Dupaquier, *Histoire générale de la population mondiale* (Paris: Montchrestien, 1968), p. 37.

3. Lawrence Stone, *The Crisis of the Aristocracy, 1558-1861,* abridged ed. (New York: Oxford University Press, 1967), p. 79.

4. Quoted in Louis Henry, *Démographie, analyse et modèles* (Paris: Larousse, 1972), p. 47.

5. D. E. Zanetti, *La demografia del patriziato milanese nei secoli XVIII, XIX* (University of Pavia, 1972). The study is summarized in *Population* (July-October 1974): 923-931.

6. Burr Litchfield, "Demographic Characteristics of Florentine Patrician Families," *Journal of Economic History* (June 1969): 198.

7. Ibid., p. 202.

8. James Cushman Davis, *The Decline of the Venetian Nobility as a Ruling Class* (Baltimore: Johns Hopkins Press, 1962), p. 18.

9. Ibid., p. 71.

10. Ibid., p. 129.

11. Claude Lévy and Louis Henri, "Ducs et pairs sous l'Ancien Régime. Charac-téristiques démographiques d'une Caste," *Population* (October-December 1960): 820.

12. David M. Heer and Dean O. Smith, "Mortality Level, Desired Family Size, and Population Increase," *Demography* (1968): 120.

13. The estimates are drawn from E. Levasseur, *La population française* (Paris 1889): 392, and from Dudley Kirk, *Europe's Population in the Interwar Years* (League of Nations, 1946), p. 231. These figures do not take into account the intensity of knowledge or use of Breton (for example, as a second language only) in either period and may well underestimate the attrition.

14. Kirk, *Europe's Population*, p. 240.

15. Ibid., pp. 224ff., for the pitfalls in linguistic statistics.

16. Ansley J. Coale, "The Demographic Transition," in IUSSP (International Union for the Scientific Study of Population), *International Population Conference* (Liège, 1974), p. 63.

17. R. Lesthaeghe and E. van de Walle, "Economic Factors and Fertility Decline in France and Belgium," in A. J. Coale (ed.), *Economic Factors in Population Growth* (London: Macmillan, 1976), pp. 225-226.

18. Gabriel Le Bras, *Etudes de sociologie religieuse* (Paris: Presses Universitaires de France, 1955): 263-264.

19. P. Rossi, *Cours d économie politique*, 4th ed. (Paris, 1865), p. 329.

20. T. A. Welton, "Observation on French Population Statistics," *Journal of the Statistical Society of London* (June 1866): 267.

21. C. Jacquart, *Le problème de la natalité en France* (Brussels, 1904), p. 15.

22. Ward Hermans, *Het Bevolkingsvraagstuk in Belgie* (Brussels, 1926), p. 37.

23. Dr. J. De Roeck, *De Belgische Demographie en de Ongelijke Voortplanting van Vlamingen en Walen* (Brussels, 1944), p. 13.

24. W. Bickel, *Bevölkerungsgeschichte und Bevölkerungspolitik der Schweiz* (Zurich, 1947), pp. 139-140.

25. F. van Heek, *Het Geboorte-niveau der Nederlandse Rooms-Katholieken* (University of Leiden, 1954), p. 159.

26. Quoted by D. V. Glass, *Population Policies and Movements in Europe* (Oxford: Clarendon Press, 1940), p. 83.

27. Jacques Dupâquier, "De l'animal à l'homme: le mécanisme auto-régulateur des populations traditionnelles," *Revue de l'Institut de Sociologie* (1972): 177-211.

28. On this controversy, see D. V. Glass and D. E. C. Eversley, *Population in History* (Chicago: Aldine, 1965). More recently, P. E. Razzell, "An Interpretation of the Modern Rise of Population in Europe—A Critique," *Population Studies* (March 1974): 5-17.

29. Rudolf Andorka, "La prévention des naissances en Hongrie dans la région Ormansag depuis la fin du XVIIIᵉ siècle," *Population* (January-February 1971): 63-78.

30. Philippe Ariès, *Histoire des populations francaises* (Paris: Editions du Seuil, 1971), pp. 20-30.

31. The data are taken from E. van de Walle, *The Female Population of France in the Nineteenth Century* (Princeton: Princeton University Press, 1974).

32. Jacques Bertillon, *La dépopulation de la France* (Paris, 1911).

33. Ibid., pp. 108-109.

34. H. Mendras, *The Vanishing Peasant* (Cambridge: M.I.T. Press, 1970), p. 12, quoting Jean Chombart de Lauwe, *Bretagne et pays de la Garonne* (Paris, 1946).

35. Joseph J. Spengler, *France Faces Depopulation* (Durham, N.C.: Duke University Press, 1938), p. 22.

36. Ibid.

37. Ibid., p. 121.

38. Alva Myrdal, *Nation and Family* (Cambridge: M.I.T. Press, 1968), p. 8.

2 Alarums, Excursions, and Delusions of Grandeur: Implicit Assumptions of Group Efforts to Alter Differential Fertility Trends

FREDERICK S. JAFFE

Questions of population go to men's heads, and the
prospect of emptying cradles in particular is one
at which they look through reddening spectacles.

C. E. M. JOAD, 1947[1]

Differential rates of change have not only occupied a major place in the scientific study of population; they have also been a central, if not dominant, theme in the political consideration of population phenomena. Even a cursory reading of history shows that differential rates of population growth or decline often have been viewed with concern, and sometimes paranoia, by group leaders. Indeed, the implications of such differentials among nations and among ethnic, religious, and racial subgroups within nations have probably constituted the principal focus of political discussion of population matters in societies at differing stages of economic development and with very diverse social, religious, and cultural settings. The population question that seems to have gone most readily to people's heads has been the prospect that the cradles of one's own group are emptying more rapidly than those of one's neighbors — or conversely, that they are not being filled fast enough.

In a world in which the survival of nations and subgroups has never been certain and strategies to advance survival are more a matter of faith and ideology than of knowledge, this particular view of population change is hardly surprising. What is interesting is its persistence over time, regardless of historical experience, and its espousal by leaders who in most other respects represent very different, even opposing, philosophies and political forces:

1. In 1905, Theodore Roosevelt decried the declining birthrate in the United States as "race suicide" and condemned American women who limited their family size as "criminal[s] against the race."[2]

2. In 1917, When Margaret Sanger was prosecuted for opening a birth control clinic in the Brownsville ghetto of Brooklyn, the district attorney told the jury "the clinic was intended to do away with the Jews."[3]

3. In 1919, U.S. Catholic bishops attacked birth control as "the selfishness which leads to race suicide,"[4] an accusation that became a standard element of the Catholic literature on birth control in the 1920s and 1930s and was abandoned as "obsolete" only in 1963.[5]

4. In the face of projections in the 1930s that suggested rapid decline, if not actual depopulation, European leaders responded with actions characterized by one observer as "a panic that corresponded in the democratic countries to the blustering and population-boosting of the fascist states."[6]

5. In the mid-1960s, family planning programs in the United States were attacked as "genocidal" by some black males who advocated higher fertility as a means of increasing black voting strength, power, and/or fighting capacity.[7]

6. In 1975, the newly elected president of the New York Board of Rabbis warned that the American Jewish community faces "a threat to its existence" if it does not increase its population and urged Jewish couples to have a minimum of three children.[8]

These illustrations could be extended almost indefinitely to include not only the developed nations of Europe and North America but the underdeveloped nations of Asia, Africa, and Latin America and the socialist nations as well. Neither geography nor ideology seems to influence the exploitation of concerns over differential fertility for political purposes. Elites who lead nations and majority groups have typically expressed fear of loss of power or dominance as a result of the higher fertility of neighboring countries (some of which were historic adversaries), or of class, racial, or religious minorities within their borders. Not infrequently, these expressions have reflected explicit or thinly disguised racist, nativist, eugenic, or social Darwinist doctrines, as well as nationalist and imperialist ideologies. Leaders of minority groups often have accepted the assumptions underlying these claims and, in mirror-image terms, have advocated increased fertility to enhance their group's power or improve its chances of survival in hostile settings.

It seems useful to recall this background as the United States moves toward population stabilization and as population changes on a world scale command greater international attention. None of the jeremiads has come to pass, but the historical record is no guarantee against recurrence of the arguments. Not only does the persistence of the theme over time and in different settings imply that the issues are far from settled, but in the past few years when U.S. period fertility rates have dipped below replacement levels, we have begun to hear talk of a "birth dearth" and of the "dire" consequences associated with population decline. That there will continue to be national concerns over fertility decline and intergroup concerns and tensions over differential fertility seems highly probable. Whether these forthcoming debates are simply reruns of the earlier arguments remains to be seen.

These issues persist partly because the political consequences of population changes — of which the relationship between fertility and group survival is one — have been subject to "so many myths and so little research," as Myron Weiner has observed.[9] In the absence of systematic research, it is difficult to assess the validity of the claims and counterclaims. But the global assertions can be broken down into their component assumptions, which may be more amenable to examination in the light of available evidence, and the weight and direction of the evidence can be summed as a guide to policy making.

This essay attempts such an examination, an exercise that is inherently selective and to some degree judgmental. My principal purpose is to illuminate the relationship between fertility and the survival of minority groups in the United States. The available research pertains more to nations than to subgroups, however, and it will be necessary to draw on this literature. In my view, this is an appropriate procedure because the issues involved in the debate on the relationship between fertility and survival are essentially the same for nations or subgroups.

If the argument is focused on the ability of a group to survive or enhance its power in the face of real or imagined adversaries, the pronatalist position taken by leaders of many groups rests on three principal assumptions:

1. That a group's power to ensure its survival is dependent, to a significant degree, on its size.

2. That increased fertility constitutes an effective way to alter the group's size vis-à-vis its neighbors'.

3. That such increased fertility entails benefits to the group with few or no countervailing costs.

These premises appear to be accepted as self-evident by group leaders who advocate higher fertility as a key to group survival. The available evidence, however, suggests that not only are they not self-evident as generalizations but may in fact be wrong.

Studies on the relationship between population size and power deal primarily with nations, not subgroups. Among nations, size is obviously one determinant of power. But there are others that may be equally important: economic and technological development, human and natural resources, political structure and governmental efficiency, national morale, and so forth.[10] That the interrelations between these variables are complex is illustrated by David Heer in a simple table ranking the twelve nations with the largest populations, highest per capita incomes, and greatest production of steel;[11] only two of the nations with the largest populations are among those with the highest per capita incomes, and only six are included among the leading steel producers. Others point to the 1967 Israeli victory over Arab nations with vastly larger populations to make the same point.

Given the multiple determinants of national power, the policy issue for national leaders concerned with survival is to determine which of the malleable factors will most effectively yield the desired result of enhanced power. This would require a complex analysis of each nation's concrete situation. More than likely, neither the theoretical framework nor the empirical data exist for a definitive analysis, so the answers will be uncertain. What is certain, however, is that a simplistic effort to increase group size is not necessarily the policy option of choice, particularly when the effects of more rapid growth on such key variables as economic development and the quality of human resources are examined.

Among subgroups within a nation, there are analogues to most of the multiple variables affecting the power of nations. Size is, of course, one factor. Weiner suggests others: the group's cohesiveness and organizability, its skills (human resource development), its financial resources, its ability to deny goods and services to others.[12] Even within a representative political system based on one person, one vote, these other variables appear to be at least as important as size—and in some cases, more—in determining a group's overall power. It would be difficult to sustain an argument that the twenty-four million U.S. blacks are more powerful than the six million U.S. Jews. Before minority group leaders advocate higher fertility as one of the best solutions to their group's fears, a closer examination of the interrelations of these multiple factors is advisable.

The second underlying assumption—that increased fertility increases a group's size—also seems obvious, until it is set in a time frame appropriate to consideration of a group's ability to survive. Most political issues, including the international and intergroup conflicts that jeopardize survival, are relatively short term in perspective; in governmental circles, a time span of five years usually represents "long-term" planning. Presumably a group or nation feels threatened by what its enemies may do today, or in, say, the next ten to twenty years at most. In this context, how useful is fertility change in altering the balance between the group and its adversaries?

The answer will vary from case to case, but two recent analyses suggest its general direction. Dov Friedlander has examined the effects of a "return to the large family" represented by an average of 4.5 children per woman among Israeli Jews, which some Israeli leaders have advocated in response to high Arab fertility. Friedlander regards it as highly unrealistic that Israelis would choose to have such large families. Even if it were achievable, however, it would make a difference of only two to four percentage points, depending on the immigration policy pursued, in the proportion of Israel's population that is Jewish in the year 2000. From a current 86 percent, the proportion would decline to 78 percent if no further immigrants are admitted and the average number of children in each family remains at 2.6; under the same immigration policy, it would decline to 82 percent even if Israeli Jewish women have an average of 4.5 children. Since Israel's internal problems of survival would hardly be much different if Jews comprise 82 rather than 78 percent of the population, he concludes that higher Jewish fertility would have a negligible effect.[13]

Using a different methodology, Ernest Attah has projected the size and rate of growth of the white and nonwhite populations of the United States, employing alternative assumptions about the future course of fertility in each group. His assumptions include one set in which white fertility drops to replacement level immediately in 1965, while nonwhite fertility reaches replacement level only after seventy-five years. Even under these most extreme assumptions, it would take until 2005-2010 before nonwhites, who now comprise 13 percent of total U.S. population, reached 20 percent.[14]

Clearly increased fertility is of little use either to Israeli Jews or U.S. blacks who have reason to be concerned over their ability to survive in the next few years or decades. The slowness of demographic processes makes them notoriously inefficient for policies intended to affect short-term political problems.

It could be argued, however, that in the case of fertility policies as distinguished from other political issues, national and group leaders look to the long run; in a word, they act like statesmen when it comes to fertility. Of course, leaders believe they act like statesmen in protecting the long-run interests of their constituents on all policy matters, but there is no necessity for others to accept their beliefs uncritically. In light of the demagogic uses that leaders have made of differential fertility historically, such a claim is at least questionable. Nonetheless it is possible that political leaders may now understand that demographic processes take a long time; consequently they may be seeking solutions not for today's problems but for tomorrow's. In this context, examination of the third underlying assumption—that increased fertility entails benefits but few or no costs to the group—provides an opportunity to assess the statesmanship of leaders who advocate higher fertility.

As with other questions of social policy, balancing the benefits against the costs of higher fertility is not a simple procedure, especially if an effort is made to bring all costs and benefits, not only the economic ones, into the calculus. Assessment of cost-benefit ratios at the subgroup level is particularly difficult because most of the pertinent studies focus either on the macrolevel of nations or the microlevel of individuals. A subgroup would subsume the microeffects on individuals but not necessarily the macroeffects on nations. In the absence of systematic studies at the subgroup level, however, we can only try to infer conclusions from these studies that appear to be relevant to subgroups.

Perhaps the most general conclusion that emerges is that there is no universal answer to the question; the concrete situation of each nation, subgroup, and individual needs to be analyzed before a reliable cost-benefit assessment can be made. While population growth was traditionally thought to be necessary for national economic growth, many, if not most, Western scholars now believe that even from a macroeconomic perspective alone, the costs of greater size in many cases exceed the benefits. The excess becomes even greater when microlevel considerations are added to the calculation. Nor is the micro-macro distinction in the current state of the art entirely satisfactory. In essence, under the current highly selective conceptualization of costs and benefits and their interrelations, it is possible to reach the conclusion that the group receives a preponderance of benefits from a situation in which the individuals making up the group experience a preponderance of costs. Such a conclusion is peculiar enough to warrant the suspicion that the conceptual framework that permits it may be metaphysical.

At the macrolevel, high rates of population growth, which increase the ratio of dependents to earners, are considered to have adverse effects on the rate of capital formation and the growth of per capita output in developing countries.[15] In developed countries with more advanced economies, the relationships between population and economic growth are thought to be more complex.[16] After reviewing the evidence for the United States, the Commission on Population Growth and the American Future concluded in 1972 that "a reduction in the rate of population growth would bring important [economic] benefits" to the nation and to individuals.[17]

Subgroups are, of course, not nations; they do not encompass entire economies in the sense comprehended by macroeconomic analysis. It is nonetheless difficult to believe that U.S. minority groups would experience costs from a reduction of population growth if the nation as a whole receives benefits. It does not follow, however, that minority groups, particularly disadvantaged ones, would necessarily share equally in the benefits; whether they do depends not on population factors but on other policies. Slower population growth would make possible significant benefits but, as the commission noted, "the fruits ... will be denied to those most in need of them unless deliberate changes are made in distribution of income to those who lack it by reason of discrimination, incapacity, or age."[18]

The case is clearer at the microlevel: In the United States, the costs of high fertility to individuals generally outweigh the benefits. Systematic studies have shown that family size is negatively related to educational attainment and current occupational level—both significant measures of socioeconomic status.[19] They have also indicated that higher fertility among blacks in low-status occupations has a nontrivial adverse effect on future occupational achievement and upward mobility.[20]

In addition to economic costs, high fertility has other consequences for individuals. Bearing children at too young or too old ages, or too close together, or having too many children are major factors associated with higher rates of maternal and infant mortality and morbidity, prematurity, genetic defects, congenital malformations, and other handicapping conditions and adverse outcomes of pregnancy.[21] The social consequences have not been documented as well as the health or economic effects have been, but lack of documentation does not mean that they do not exist. In particular, high fertility is associated in the United States with early childbearing, which often results in precipitous marriage or out-of-wedlock birth, school dropout and low educational attainment, and higher probabilities of divorce. The impacts of these varied processes on the status of women have been studied very little, but their direction is reasonably clear. Almost all tend to reinforce the traditional maternal role and to diminish a woman's options to choose other roles or combine motherhood with a career.

This brief summary of some of the interrelationships is oversimplified, but it is sufficient to raise serious questions about the assumption that higher fertility confers only benefits on a nation or subgroup and exacts few or no costs. The costs are there: economic, health, social, and yet others that are invisible only because they have not been documented and monitored (in part because they have not been deemed important enough by policy makers and researchers). Friedlander states the trade-off exactly when he notes, in reference to Israel's low-income Asian-African Jews, that reduced fertility would contribute to improvements in their social and economic levels, even if it would reduce the overall growth of the Jewish population.[22] In the United States, the evidence suggests strongly that these varied costs aggregate to an inverse relationship between high fertility and a group's ability to invest in its future generations—the development of its human capital—which may be the decisive factor in ensuring its survival.

The American Jewish community offers a classic example of these processes. The impoverished immigrant Jews, whom the district attorney ostensibly sought to protect from genocide in 1917, crowded Margaret Sanger's clinics as soon as the authorities permitted them to function. In the next generation, they went on to become the "most careful family planners" of all U.S. religious groups.[23] In 1957—the last year in which Current Population Survey data are available by religious identification—U.S. Jews had a higher income and socioeconomic status than did either Protestants or Catholics, largely as a result of differential educational and occupational achievement.[24] The causal nexuses are not unambiguous, but it seems clear that effective family limitation was associated with greater investment in human resources, which in turn was associated with higher status (and, by inference, greater power).

When we turn to an examination of the measures employed by group leaders to implement higher fertility objectives, the balance of costs over benefits becomes even clearer. Historically three kinds of policies have been adopted by national and group leaders in an effort to elicit more babies from their followers: exhortation, positive inducements, and/or restrictions on the availability of the means of fertility control. The first two have proven largely ineffectual, and the third adds serious costs to the equation.

Pronatalist propaganda, comprising what David Glass has aptly described as "homilies on virtue, sacrifice, patriotism, social duty and all those sublime abstractions,"[25] has been employed by a variety of group leaders: Theodore Roosevelt, Charles de Gaulle, Benito Mussolini, Dick Gregory, and Rabbi Sol Roth (the president of the New York Board of Rabbis), to name only a few. Unlike the Pied Piper, however, leaders appear to have few followers when they summon their constituents to reproduce for the sake of the group. Clearly there seems to be a difference of perception. It is part of the ethos of leaders that they always act on behalf of their group's best interests, particularly when they solicit higher rates of reproduction. But their constituents evidently believe otherwise. There have been few studies of the costs of this disjunction to the morale of the group and its confidence in the judgment of its leaders.[26]

There is an extensive literature describing the various programs of positive inducements implemented in Europe and other countries in the 1930s and 1940s, which were justified, at least in part, on the grounds that they would lead to higher fertility,[27] and a number of studies have attempted to evaluate their effectiveness in achieving these stated objectives.[28] The results are inconclusive. Fertility levels have changed, but it is far from clear that family allowances, maternity benefits, and other similar measures have significantly influenced these changes. Perhaps this is because of the limited scope of most of these programs; as Glass observed thirty-five years ago, "However urgently governments may have declared their desire to increase the supply of births, they have nevertheless persistently tried to buy babies at bargain prices."[29] No nation seems to have been willing to carry out the fundamental redistributive policies implied in the restructuring of the conditions of reproduction advocated by Gunnar Myrdal in 1938.[30]

In contrast to the ineffectuality of exhortation and inducements, restrictions on the availability of the means of fertility control may have been somewhat more effective in some nations in increasing fertility. These efforts include various acts of commission and omission. Some nations enact laws to prohibit or restrict the dissemination of contraceptive information and services and make abortion illegal. Some subgroup leaders stigmatize fertility control measures and support restrictive legislation and policies. Even in nations that follow welfare-state principles, fertility control measures often are inexplicably omitted from socially provided national health services or provided only under conditions and restrictions that are not applied to other kinds of health care. (Is there a better explanation than a pervasive pronatalist bias for the fact that family planning was finally "integrated" into the National Health Service in the United Kingdom only in 1974, nearly three decades after the NHS was established, and the extent of its "integration" remains very uncertain?)

In these cases, national and group leaders demand more babies, whether their constituents want them or not. Sometimes they are successful but not always, because illegality or stigmatization does not deter all of their women constituents from finding ways to avoid compulsory motherhood. In almost all countries, one of the principal consequences of restrictive laws and policies is to reinforce differential fertility trends based on socioeconomic status; the poorest have the greatest difficulty in obtaining access to the services. Some of the costs of these processes are almost invisible (there are, for example, only two limited studies in the entire world of the effects on children of being unwanted by their parents,[31] and no one seems to have tried to measure the alienating effects of such policies on women. But others are plainly visible. The French leaders who opposed the legalization of abortion in 1974 could have done so only by shutting their eyes to the vast incidence of illegal abortion among French women, just as a U.S. black leader could oppose legal abortion only by ignoring the evidence of massive illegal and self-induced abortions among blacks that was to be seen daily before 1970 at Harlem Hospital in New York.

Rumania offers the best example of a nation that, by abolishing legal abortion, succeeded—at least temporarily—in reversing what was regarded as a disastrous fertility decline. A liberal abortion law was repealed in 1966, and restrictive conditions were once again legislated. In 1967, all fertility indicators nearly doubled, with the greatest relative increases occurring among women older than thirty who already had two or three children. By 1972, however, the birthrate had again declined (though not to 1966 levels), but the rate of abortion-related maternal deaths had increased three-and-a-half times.[32] Since Rumania also imposed restrictions in 1966 on oral contraceptives and intrauterine devices, investigators have concluded that the sharp fertility decline following the 1967 spurt and the rise in maternal mortality both imply that it took several years for illegal abortion facilities to become reestablished. Surely reestablishment of the illegal abortion industry was not the intent of the Rumanian leaders, but it is nonetheless a cost that has to be weighed against what appears to have been only a short-term increase in births.

In this analysis I have tried to set forth some of the elements of a more comprehensive calculus for assessing the costs and benefits of higher fertility for subgroups in the United States. Perhaps the attempt has succeeded only in demonstrating the very narrow calculus within which such questions are conventionally weighed, in part because of deep-seated biases of both policy makers and social scientists. The economic bias has been noted by many observers, but less attention seems to have been paid to possible sexist biases. When the subject is fertility, it seems clear that group leaders are demanding that their women constituents make greater sacrifices on behalf of the group against their own judgments of what is best for themselves and their families. It is questionable whether the leaders would treat such matters as prohibitions on fertility control quite so cavalierly if men bore the babies.

I hope my effort will also have suggested, as Bernard Berelson concluded in reviewing population policies of twenty-four developed countries, that "it is easier to lower birth rates by policy measures than to raise them."[33] If this is so, it is because the fertility levels even of developed nations—and of subgroups within them—include significant numbers of births that the parents would have avoided if they could, and it is easier through public policy to affect the supply of fertility control services than to modify the number of children that parents believe is best for them and their families.

It seems evident that there is no proven understanding of the relationship between population change and the survival of subgroups in the United States or in the world as a whole. Since the available evidence is not conclusive, each observer can add it up in his own way. In my view, the weight of the evidence suggests that in terms of the ability of U.S. subgroups to survive, higher fertility is the wrong issue. Factors other than size are more determinant of a group's status and power, particularly its capacity to invest more of its current resources in the development of its human resources. And higher fertility, for most subgroups, is counterproductive to this objective, particularly if it is to be purchased by forcing the birth of more unwanted children.[34] The survival of U.S. minority groups would seem to be served better by the continuation and acceleration of the recent trend toward diminished fertility differentials and convergence among all sectors of the U.S. population in fertility values and behavior; this rapid convergence has been associated in the last decade with greater access by all groups to modern means of fertility control.

Others may come to different conclusions but the evidence seems to me sufficiently consistent to sustain one basic conclusion. If group leaders are truly interested in advancing their group's capacity to survive, they will not automatically call for higher fertility. If the basic relationship between population change and group survival is at best uncertain, the weight that leaders attach to fertility in formulating survival policies is at least reduced. It goes without saying that they should also encourage and support systematic research that might reduce the level of uncertainty.

At bottom, the case of minority groups is part of a larger question of the relationship between the individual and society, which is a central issue of population and social policy and which, of course, has historically been a dominant subject of political debate and philosophic speculation. At one level of analysis, there is little but confusion. Myrdal and other European observers, contemplating fertility decline in Western democracies in the 1930s, found an inherent conflict between the individual's interest in maximizing his own welfare by limiting family size and society's long-term interest in reproducing itself.[35] Three decades later, Garrett Hardin (apparently proposing a universal truth), Kingsley Davis (in reference to less-developed nations) and Judith Blake (in reference to the United States) also found a basic conflict between the individual and society, only the terms are reversed: the individual is still determined to maximize his own well-being, but now he does this by having too many children for society's good.[36] The substantive differences reflect real differences in today's world compared to that of the 1930s. But the common features of both viewpoints are striking. Both pertain less to demographic matters than to human nature. The philosophic (and untestable) view they proclaim conceives of human nature as selfish and unadapting. They share a common elitist conviction that individuals cannot be trusted to perceive correctly the relationship between their own interests and those of the (presumably valued) groups to which they belong. Both positions espouse intervention and manipulation in the very personal area of family size decisions, a remarkable viewpoint to emerge in societies that still worship Adam Smith in the impersonal marketplace sufficiently to require that advocates of intervention bear a very heavy burden of proof.[37]

In terms of group survival and the ostensible conflict between the interests of the individual and the group, the basic resolution of the dilemma is given in this paraphrase of observations by Richard Easterlin (substituting in brackets *survival* and other terms pertinent to this discussion for the economic objectives to which he referred):

There is the question of what one conceives as the basic objective of social policy. Is the goal merely to maximize [survival] or to maximize individual welfare, broadly and democratically conceived? If it is the latter, then it is necessary to consider fully the ingredients of individual well-being. . . . If nothing is done to [increase group fertility], won't [the group] just go on [declining] until intolerable conditions result? The implication of this view is that human reproductive behavior does not voluntarily respond to environmental conditions. . . . Nowhere, I think, is this view called more into doubt than by American historical experience.[38]

Easterlin's essentially optimistic view includes advocacy of greater access to fertility control knowledge and services and public programs to assist U.S. men and women to avoid unwanted pregnancies. Such policies and programs are justified for welfare reasons alone and as means of ensuring that human reproductive behavior can voluntarily respond to environmental conditions. Presumably these same considerations of maximizing human welfare underlie the admonition of the World Population Plan of Action that nations "respect and insure, *regardless of their overall demographic goals,* the right of persons to determine, in a free, informed and responsible manner, the number and spacing of their children" (emphasis added).[39] Based on similar considerations of enhancing the well-being of their constituents (and thereby, the group's strength), leaders of U.S. minority groups should advocate full access for their constituents to the knowledge and means of ensuring reproductive freedom. For if survival does not encompass freedom in as fundamentally personal an area as reproduction, what does it mean?

NOTES

1. Introduction to J. C. Flugel, *Population, Psychology and Peace* (London: Watts, 1947).

2. Theodore Roosevelt, *Presidential Addresses and State Papers* (New York: Review of Reviews, 1910), 3: 282-291, cited by L. Gordon, "Race Suicide and the Feminist Response: Birth Control as a Class Phenomenon," paper presented at Berkshire Conference on the History of Women, October 1974.

3. M. Sanger, *An Autobiography* (New York, Norton, 1938), p. 226.

4. Pastoral letter of the archbishops and bishops of the United States, September 26, 1919, cited by J. Noonan, *Contraception* (Cambridge: Harvard University Press, 1965), pp. 423-424.

5. Noonan, *Contraception,* pp. 514-518.

6. Flugel, *Population,* p. 19.

7. See R. G. Weisbord, "Birth Control and the Black American: A Matter of Genocide?" *Demography* 10 (November 1973): 571.

8. *National Right to Life News,* February 1975. For similar statements by other Jewish leaders in other U.S. cities, see "Birthrate Lag Called Threat to Jewish Survival," *Washington Post,* March 17, 1975, and "Should Jews Have More Babies?" *San Francisco Chronicle,* April 2, 1974.

9. M. Weiner, "Political Demography: An Inquiry into the Political Consequences of Population Change," in R. Revelle, ed., *Rapid Population Growth: Consequences and Policy Implications* (Baltimore: Johns Hopkins Press, 1971), p. 612.

10. For reviews of the relevant literature, see J. J. Spengler, "Population and Potential Power," in M. Kooy, ed., *Studies in Economics and Economic History: Essays in Honor of H. M. Robertson* (Durham: Duke University Press, 1972), pp. 126-152, and D. Heer, *Society and Population,* 2d ed. (Englewood Cliffs, N.J.: Prentice-Hall, 1975), pp. 121-126.

11. Heer, *Society,* p. 123.

12. Weiner, "Political Demography," p. 595.

13. D. Friedlander, "Israel," in B. Berelson, ed., *Population Policy in Developed Countries* (New York: McGraw-Hill, 1974), p. 89, table 9.

14. E. B. Attah, "Racial Aspects of Zero Population Growth," *Science* 180 June 15, 1973: 1143, Table 11.

15. Cf. A. J. Coale and E. M. Hoover, *Population Growth and Economic Development in Low Income Countries* (Princeton: Princeton University Press, 1958).

16. For a comprehensive review, see A. Kelley, "Demographic Changes and American Economic Development: Past, Present and Future," in U.S., Commission on Population Growth and the American Future, *Economic Aspects of Population Change,* ed. E. R. Morss and R. H. Reed, Commission Research Reports, vol. 2 (Washington, D.C.: Government Printing Office, 1972). Also see A. R. Sweezy, "The Natural History of the Stagnation Thesis," in J. J. Spengler, ed., *Zero Population Growth: Implications* (Chapel Hill: Carolina Population Center, 1975), pp. 34-43.

17. U. S., Commission on Population Growth and the American Future, *Population and the American Future* (Washington, D.C.: Government Printing Office, 1972), p. 38.

18. Ibid., p. 41.

19. P. M. Blau and O. D. Duncan, *The American Occupational Structure* (New York: Wiley, 1967).

20. S. H. Preston, "Differential Fertility, Unwanted Fertility and Racial Trends in Occupational Achievement," *American Sociological Review* 39 (August 1974): 492.

21. For comprehensive reviews, see J. D. Wray, "Population Pressures on Families: Family Size and Child Spacing," in Revelle, *Rapid Population Growth*; A. R. Omran, *The Health Theme in Family Planning,* Carolina Population Center Monograph, No. 16 (Chapel Hill, 1971); World Health Organization, *Health Aspects of*

Family Planning (Geneva, 1970); and Dorothy Nortman, "Parental Age as a Factor in Pregnancy Outcome and Child Development," *Report on Population/Family Planning*, No. 16 (August 1974).

22. Friedlander, "Israel," p. 51.

23. P. K. Whelpton, A. A. Campbell, and J. E. Patterson, *Fertility and Family Planning in the United States* (Princeton: Princeton University Press, 1966), p. 252.

24. S. Goldstein, "Socioeconomic Differentials Among Religious Groups in the United States," *American Journal of Sociology* 74 (May 1969): 612.

25. D. Glass, *Population Policies and Movements in Europe* (Oxford: Clarendon Press, 1940), p. 204.

26. Recently the National Catholic Opinion Research Center reported on a study of a reasonable proxy measure of these processes: almost half of the decline in church attendance among Catholics was accounted for by dissatisfaction with the church's official position on birth control and another quarter by dissatisfaction with the position on divorce. See "Catholic Churchgoing Off; Birth Control Stand Cited," *New York Times,* October 15, 1975, p. 36.

27. Cf. Glass, *Population Policies,* and Berelson, *Population Policy.*

28. Cf. V. H. Whitney, "Fertility Trends and Children's Allowance Programs," in E. E. Burns, ed., *Children's Allowances and the Economic Welfare of Children* (New York: Citizens Committee for Children, 1968); A. L. Schorr, "Income Maintenance and the Birth Rate," *Social Security Bulletin* (December 1965); B. Madison, "Canadian Family Allowances and Their Major Social Implications," *Journal of Marriage and the Family* (May 1964); F. H. Hankins, "German Policies for Increasing Births," *American Journal of Sociology* (March 1937); C. B. Lloyd, "The Effect of Child Subsidies on Fertility: An International Study" (Ph.D. diss., Columbia University, 1972).

29. Glass, *Population Policies,* p. 371.

30. G. Myrdal, *Population—A Problem for Democracy* (Cambridge: Harvard University Press, 1940). Nor have the less developed countries been willing to carry out the opposite kinds of redistributive policies in order to induce fertility decline, perhaps because such policies usually penalize children already born.

31. Cf. H. Forssman and I. Thuwe, "120 Children Born after Their Mothers' Application for Therapeutic Abortion Had Been Refused," *Acta Psychiatrica Scandinavica* 42 (1966): 71, and Z. Dytrych, Z. Matejcek, H. P. David, and H. C. Friedman, "Children Born to Women Denied Abortion: Initial Findings of a Matched Control Study in Prague, Czechoslavakia," presented at Population Association of America, April 1974.

32. M. Teitelbaum, "The De-Legalization of Abortion in Romania," *Family Planning* 23 (1974): 38, and "Fertility Effects of the Abolition of Legal Abortion in Romania," *Population Studies* 27 (1972): 405; N. H. Wright, "Restricting Legal Abortion: Some Maternal and Child Health Effects in Romania," *American Journal of Obstetrics and Gynecology* 121 (1975): 246.

33. Berelson, *Population Policy,* p. 788.

34. This conclusion is shared by many U.S. black leaders who have supported programs to make fertility control more widely available. See, for example, Shirley Chisholm, *Unbought and Unbossed* (New York: Avon, 1970), pp. 124-136.

35. Myrdal, *Population,* pp. 33ff.

36. G. Hardin, "The Tragedy of the Commons," *Science* 162 (December 13, 1968): 1243; K. Davis, "Population Policy: Will Current Programs Succeed?" *Science* 158 (November 10, 1967): 730; and J. Blake, "Population Policy for Americans: Is the Government Being Misled?" *Science* 164 (May 2, 1969): 522.

37. Reports from the People's Republic of China imply that political pressures and exhortations, coupled with massive distribution of the means of fertility control, are responsible for China's presumed success in reducing fertility. In the absence of systematic data, it is difficult to determine how much success there has been and how much of it is attributable to the pressures and exhortations as compared to the distribution of the means. Nevertheless, it seems possible that in the context of a society in which all important aspects of social and personal life are subject to explicit planning processes, individuals would accept social decision making on reproduction. What seems impossible is that they would do so in the context of quite different societies, such as the United States, where there is little explicit social decision making even in impersonal areas.

38. Adapted from R. Easterlin, in *Economic Aspects of Population Change,* pp. 46-47.

39. United Nations Center for Economic and Social Information, *Action Taken at Bucharest* (New York: United Nations, 1974), p. 16, section 29 (a).

3 Demographic and Political Implications of Immigration Policy

CHARLES B. KEELY

The purpose of this essay is to review the historical and current contro-versies regarding U.S. immigration policies and their effects. This review is made in the context of trying to clarify the relationship between immigration policy and the demographic characteristics of the immigrant streams and the American population. This background should provide insights and raise pertinent questions about political and social implications of immigration for intergroup relations along a path to a stationary population in the United States. (I will interpret *population stabilization* in the more narrow sense of *movement to a stationary population*. The implications for immigration policy of stationary, stable, or quasi-stable populations would appear to be differ-ent, especially if different ethnic groups are not all in the same demo-graphic situation.)

The topic of population stabilization and intergroup relations is diffi-cult to handle for at least two reasons. First, it is a broad and extremely complex issue that affects the life of the nation from the bedroom to the boardroom. Examples can be multiplied endlessly illustrating the impact of slowing population growth and ethnicity (in the sense of racial, re-ligious and national origin background) on the economic, social, and political behavior of Americans. Second, it is a new topic of thought in this country. Serious consideration has not really been given to the effect of zero population growth on ethnic relations in the United States, a subject whose importance is clear. It is true that visions of being overrun by various groups of foreigners have been raised in the past and have affected policy. These nightmares are, unfortunately, also part of the American dream. The most recent example is the fear of a Latin American inundation, which resulted in the legislative jumble of current restrictions on Western Hemisphere immigration.

The complexity and newness of this particular topic apply also to the more narrow subject of immigration policy in a stationary population. To gain even a modicum of closure at this point is difficult indeed and even premature. My goal is more modest. It is to review the genesis and development of immigration policy, to trace its demographic effects, and to present the major policy questions currently raised about immigration. I will conclude by discussing some problem areas raised by immigration for intergroup relations.

IMMIGRATION AND POPULATION GROWTH: THE DEMOGRAPHIC ISSUE

Immigration was a fairly dead social, political, and academic issue until the interim report of the Commission on Population Growth and the American Future (1971). Perhaps it is too much to say that without the commission, people would not have become aware of the impact of immigration at its current volume and with its changing characteristics. It may not, however, have become such a live issue. Perhaps immigration would not have been the topic of a separate background paper at this conference but rather have been relegated to a subsection of the paper on differential growth rates. However, the commission did raise the question and raised it forcefully.

The interim report of the Population Commission (1971, 8-9) pointed out that about 20 percent of current population growth is the result of net immigration.[1] The commission also estimated that net immigration of 400,000 per year would yield an additional sixteen million persons in the population of the year 2000, and over the next hundred years, immigration at that volume would account for nearly half of the population growth from 204 million to 340 million.

This unforeseen situation aroused concern. News media gave coverage to the findings, members of Congress reacted in oversight hearings about the administration of immigration law (Keely, 1972b,2), and concerned citizen groups, like Zero Population Growth (ZPG), turned their attention to the impact of immigration.

The major issue that has been raised is the contribution of immigration (immigrants and their offspring) to population growth. There are some basic and serious methodological problems (which have policy implications) about the use of net civilian immigration rather than net alien immigration (Keely, 1972a), about estimates of the components of net civilian immigration (Warren and Peck, 1975), and about the use made of the balancing equation to arrive at the estimates of the relative contribution of the components of population growth (Keely, 1974b). However, the basic issue remains, What is a tolerable level of immigration? Is it the current level, zero net immigration, some number that takes into account the fertility and age structure of immigrants, or some other option?

A look at past and current data may illuminate this issue, although it will not provide a definitive answer since the issue is a question of values.

At its root, the issue of immigration and population growth requires balancing the costs and benefits of receiving immigrants. It seems obvious that people in the United States do not assign the same values to these costs and benefits or even consistently categorize an effect as a cost or benefit (for example, having a certain proportion of the population foreign born or of foreign stock; Aron, 1967, 29).

Census data on the foreign born and foreign stock (which includes foreign-born plus native-born persons, one or both of whose parents are foreign born) are available beginning with the census of 1870, and data on country of birth are available from 1850. Niles Carpenter's study *Immigrants and Their Children* (1927) examined the data on the foreign born and the foreign stock available in the two series. He drew four conclusions from his examination of the size of the foreign stock.

"*First,* the mere bulk of the foreign white stock has increased tremendously" (p. 7). The foreign born increased from about 2.3 million in 1850 to 13.7 million in 1920. In the fifty years from 1870 to 1920, the native-born whites of foreign or mixed parentage increased from 5.3 to about 22.7 million.

"*Second,* the proportion of the foreign white stock, both in the total population and the total white population, has not varied significantly during the period under consideration." (Tables 1 and 2 present the data Carpenter was summarizing).

"*Third,* in some respects, the proportionate size in the immigrant stock seems to be falling off slightly." Carpenter was referring to the decline between 1910 and 1920 in the percentage of foreign born (from 14.5 to 13.0 percent) and of foreign stock (from 35.0 to 34.4 percent). He interpreted this as the beginning of a declining trend resulting from

Table 1

**PERCENTAGE DISTRIBUTION OF U.S. POPULATION
BY NATIVITY AND PARENTAGE**

Class of Population	1920	1910	1900	1890	1880	1870	1860	1850
Native white	76.7	74.4	74.5	73.0	73.5	72.9	72.6	74.6
Native parentage	55.3	53.8	53.9	54.8	57.0	59.1		
Foreign parentage	14.8	14.0	14.0	12.8	12.7	10.8		
Mixed parentage	6.6	6.5	6.6	5.4	3.8	3.0		
Foreign-born white	13.0	14.5	13.4	14.5	13.1	14.2	13.0	9.7
All other[a]	10.3	11.1	12.1	12.5	13.5	12.9	14.4	15.7
Total population	100.0	100.0	100.0	100.0	100.0	100.0	100.0	100.0

a. Includes Negroes, Indians, Chinese, Japanese, and all other nonwhite.
Source: Carpenter, 1927, p.5.

restricted immigration, accelerated emigration accompanying World War I, and the effects of other factors, such as the exhaustion of free land.

"*Fourth*, the foreign-born element in the population of this country, while much larger, relative to the total population, than that in European countries, is, nevertheless, not such a large fraction of the whole as in certain other American nations" (particularly Canada and Argentina). Carpenter's conclusion was intended to underline the fact that the demographic impact of immigration in the United States was less than elsewhere and that the catastrophic results predicted for the United States by opponents of immigration were not a necessary result. Other countries with a larger relative impact showed social and cultural continuity.

Although Carpenter made this passing reference to the comparative perspective, his work shares the parochial outlook of much immigration literature. The reader is often left with the impression that U.S. policy and the size and composition of immigrant streams were only tangentially affected by what happened elsewhere and that U.S. immigration was not part of a world-wide population redistribution. Further, comparative studies of immigration policies and comparative studies of the effects of immigration are sparse. The approach parallels—perhaps affects or is affected by—the traditional congressional assumption that immigration is a purely internal matter and foreign policy or the wishes of other governments should not play a role in policy development in this area.

E. P. Hutchinson followed up the work of Carpenter in his 1956 study, *Immigrants and Their Children, 1850-1950.* He noted the rising trend in the number of foreign born until 1930 (14.2 million) and the beginning of the declining trend in 1940 and 1950, which continued through two subsequent censal periods. The proportion of foreign born has decreased since 1910. Table 2 presents data on the foreign born since 1850.

Hutchinson (p. 2) explained the declining trends as caused by immigration restriction, the depression, World War II, and the aging of the foreign-born population. Despite the increased alien immigration of the latter part of the 1960s, both the number and percentage of foreign born decreased between 1960 and 1970.

Patterns similar to the foreign born are apparent for the total foreign stock and native born of foreign or mixed parentage. The data in table 3 show that the number of foreign stock peaked at nearly forty million in 1930 and has been generally declining since that time to a level of thirty-two million in 1970.[2] The proportion of foreign stock began to decline in 1910 and was at 17.9 percent in 1970, the lowest level in the century for which data are available.

The native born of foreign or mixed parentage peaked in 1930 at about twenty-six million. The number declined during the 1930s only to rise again steadily until the 1970 Census, when it returned to the 1940 level. It

Table 2

FOREIGN BORN IN THE U.S. POPULATION, 1850-1970

Year	Total Population	Foreign Born	Percentage Foreign Born
1970	203,210,158	9,619,302	4.7
1960	179,325,671	9,738,143	5.4
1950	150,697,361	10,347,395	6.9
1940	131,669,275	11,594,896	8.8
1930	122,775,046	14,204,149	11.6
1920	105,710,620	13,920,692	13.2
1910	91,972,266	13,515,886	14.7
1900	75,994,575	10,341,276	13.6
1890	62,947,714	9,249,560	14.7
1880	50,155,783	6,679,943	13.3
1870[a]	39,818,449	5,567,229	14.0
1860	31,443,321	4,138,697	13.2
1850	23,191,876	2,244,602	9.7

Note: Continental U.S. for 1870-1950.

a. Adjusted for under enumeration.

Sources: Hutchinson, 1956, p. 2; U.S. Department of Commerce, 1970a, table 68.

Table 3

NATIVITY AND PARENTAGE OF THE WHITE POPULATION OF THE UNITED STATES, 1870-1950

					PERCENTAGE OF WHITE POPULATION		
Year (1)	Total White Population (2)	Total Foreign White Stock (3)	Foreign-Born White (4)	Native White of Foreign or Mixed Parentage (5)	Foreign Stock (6)	Foreign Born (7)	Foreign or Mixed Parentage (8)
1970	178,119,221	31,887,935	8,733,770	23,154,165	17.9	4.9	13.0
1960	158,837,671	33,978,380	9,294,033	23,784,347	20.9	5.9	15.0
1950	134,942,028	33,750,653	10,161,168	23,589,485	25.0	7.5	17.5
1940	118,701,558	34,576,718	11,419,138	23,157,580	29.1	9.6	19.5
1930	110,286,740	39,885,788	13,983,405	25,902,383	36.2	12.7	23.5
1920	94,820,915	36,398,958	13,712,754	22,686,204	38.4	14.5	23.9
1910	81,731,957	32,243,382	13,345,545	18,897,837	39.5	16.3	23.1
1900	66,809,196	25,859,834	10,213,817	15,646,017	38.7	15.3	23.4
1890	55,101,258	20,625,542	9,121,867	11,503,675	37.4	16.6	20.9
1880[a]	43,402,970	14,834,546	6,559,679	8,274,867	34.2	15.1	19.1
1870[a]	33,589,377	10,817,980	5,493,712	5,324,268	32.2	16.4	15.9

Note: 1870-1950 Continental United States.

a. Parentage data partly estimated.

Sources: E. P. Hutchinson, 1956, p. 3; U.S. Department of Commerce, 1970b, table 68, pp. 1-361

would seem obvious that the depression with its effects on fertility and the net loss in international migration to the United States affected these trends. Also it is to be expected that declining trends in the number of children of the foreign born would lag behind declines in the foreign-born population. The proportion of white persons of foreign or mixed parentage relative to the total white population has steadily declined since 1920 to the 1970 level of 13 percent, also the lowest level in the century during which data have been collected. The earlier decline in the proportion (as opposed to the number) of natives of foreign or mixed parentage should alert us to the question of the fertility of the alien population relative to the native population.

In short, the white foreign stock of the United States and its component parts have been decreasing numerically and, for a longer time, proportionately. Data on total foreign stock (all races) are available for 1960 and 1970 and are presented in table 4, which also shows the absolute and proportional declines between 1960 and 1970 in total foreign stock and its components, foreign born and native born of foreign or mixed parentage.

From these data, we can conclude that the country is not being overrun by immigrants and their children, although the United States continues to accept immigrants in generous numbers. The foreign stock is declining and is at its lowest level as a percentage of the U.S. population in a century, and the same is true of both its component parts.

The demographic significance of immigration takes on added importance with the cumulation of the streams. Information on the process of cumulation during intercensal periods is afforded by year-of-immigration questions. Such information was included in the censuses for 1890 through 1930 and again in 1970. In their study, *The Changing Population of the United States* (1958), Conrad and Irene Taeuber discussed the cumulative effects of migration between 1900 and 1930. Published data from the 1970 Census are not directly comparable with the Taeubers' presentation (periods of arrival differ), but there are some comparisons that can be made between the 1890-1930 data and the 1970 data in the two panels in table 5.

First, the number and percentage who arrived in the decade immediately preceding the census year declined during the period 1900-30. However, in 1970, 29.4 percent of the foreign born had arrived between 1960 and 1970. Second, in 1970, 31 percent of the foreign-born population had arrived before 1925 and was therefore forty-five years or older. In 1930, 32.5 percent was thirty years or older. Thus, as Hutchinson pointed out, the age structure and mortality play a significant role in the trends in the number and proportion of the population who are foreign born. In fact, in 1970, 32 percent of the foreign born were sixty-five years of age or older, and 59 percent were forty-five or older. This compares with 9.9

percent and 30.5 percent of the total U.S. population for the two respective age groupings (U.S., Department of Commerce, 1970b, vol. 1, part 1, table 49, 1-263).

Table 4

POPULATION OF THE UNITED STATES BY PARENTAGE, 1960-70

					PERCENTAGE OF TOTAL POPULATION		
Year	Total Population	Native Born of Native Parents	Foreign Born	Native Born of Foreign or Mixed Parents	Native Born of Native Parents	Foreign Born	Native Born of Foreign or Mixed Parents
(1)	(2)	(3)	(4)	(5)	(6)	(7)	(8)
1970	203,210,158	169,634,926	9,619,302	23,955,930	83.5	4.7	11.8
1960	179,325,671	145,275,265	9,738,143	24,312,263	81.0	5.4	13.6

Source: U.S. Department of Commerce, 1970a, table 68, pp. 1-361.

Table 5

YEAR OF IMMIGRATION OF THE FOREIGN-BORN POPULATION, 1970
(in Thousands)

	Total	1965-70	1960-64	1955-59	1950-54	1945-49	1935-44	1925-34	Before 1925	Not Reported
Number 1970	9,740	1,721	1,136	977	791	586	323	766	3,015	425
Percentage 1970	100.0	17.7	11.7	10.0	8.1	6.0	3.3	7.9	31.0	4.4

	Total	1920-1930	1911-1919	1901-1910	Pre-1901
Number					
1900	10,341				10,341
1910	13,516			5,098	8,418
1920	13,921		3,137	4,444	6,340
1930	14,204	2,948	2,652	3,986	4,618
Percentage					
1900	100.0				100.0
1910	100.0			37.7	62.3
1920	100.0		22.5	31.9	45.5
1930	100.0	20.7	18.7	28.1	32.5

Source: U.S. Department of Commerce, 1972, table 17 (5 percent sample); Taeuber and Taeuber, 1958, p. 65.

A longer-range view of the effects of cumulative immigration and immigrant fertility is offered by Gibson (1975) in his study on the contribution of immigration to U.S. population from 1790 to 1970. The 35.5 million net immigrants in that period contributed an estimated 98 million (48 percent) of the 1970 population. Although an increased proportion of annual population growth was brought about by immigration in the last decade, this has been caused by the decline in the amount and rate of natural increase in the United States. As Gibson (1975, 176) quotes from the Report of the Population Commission, "The increasing relative significance of immigration can be misleading for, if native births and deaths were balanced, [net] immigration would account for 100 percent of population growth," no matter how small net immigration was.

Gibson notes further that the number and percentage of contribution of immigration from 1790 has no obvious social, economic, or political implications because of the indeterminancy and variability of demographic and other variables. However, the cumulative effects of immigration from a more current date could indeed have policy implications. Such estimations, as well as projections of future cumulative impact, are possible using Gibson's methodology and Coale's (1972) methodology contained in his paper, "Alternative Paths to a Stationary Population." In each case, actual experience or different assumptions about various future characteristics of the immigrant stream can be substituted.

In this context, I feel more attention should be paid to the variables of the size of net immigration and immigrant fertility. Two points ought to be borne in mind regarding net immigration. First, net civilian immigration, as estimated by the Census Bureau, includes more than net alien immigration (that is, more than net total of foreign born intending settlement and possessing valid immigrant visas). It is clear that legal alien immigration, the other components of net civilian, and illegal alien immigration all affect future population size. It is not equally clear, however, whether or to what extent the impact of illegal immigration or the citizen components of net civilian immigration ought to affect policy to increase or decrease legal alien immigration. Second, the work of Warren and Peck (1975) calls into doubt recent assumptions about the amount of emigration. Their estimates of foreign-born emigration are well above the assumed level of total emigration (32 versus 10 percent of alien immigration). The amount of native-born emigration, independent of and related to this flow (for example, native children of foreign-born parents), could also be more substantial than previously suspected. In short, how one defines immigration and serious questions about the size of the emigration component lead me to the conclusion that the frequently used assumption of annual net immigration of 400,000 ought to be examined, and conclusions based on analyses of estimates and projections using that figure ought to be carefully stated, especially when policy on alien immigration is involved.

The fertility experience of immigrant groups is becoming the topic for an increasing amount of research. This development has been spurred on by the competing hypotheses used to explain differential fertility among subgroups in a population: the particularized theology hypothesis, social characteristics hypothesis, and minority group status hypothesis. Frequently analyses of subgroup fertility have dealt with broad comparisons, for example, among native white, Negro, and Spanish groups. More recently detailed comparisons among a larger variety of ethnic groups have been undertaken. Kritz and Gurak (1975), for example, have examined fertility differentials among eighteen ethnic groups in the United States to determine the contribution of ethnicity in explaining U.S. fertility patterns, to determine whether ethnic effects are additive or interactive, and to specify groups that have significantly different fertility processes from native whites. They conclude that, although the absence of ethnicity would not produce highly biased results in a study of general fertility processes, there are significant differences in fertility patterns across groups, with some foreign-born groups appreciably lower than native white. Such differences take on added significance on the local or regional level if a group is highly concentrated geographically.

Further, I have found after some preliminary analysis of completed fertility of older (forty-five and over) foreign-born women that their fertility is surprisingly low. However, I have not yet controlled for factors such as age at marriage, origin, and year of immigration and so do not draw any conclusions.

I raise these two examples to point out the need for more detailed analyses of ethnic fertility, especially in the context of ethnic relations in a population characterized as stable or stationary and especially given the findings of Kritz and Gurak on different patterns across groups. Such detailed analyses should also take into account ethnic concentration in order to evaluate localized effects on social and political relations.

One final word is necessary about future immigration. Clearly not only size but also characteristics of immigrants are important when considering their effects on society. Current proposals to alter immigration law, to say nothing about possible future action to reduce volume, could radically alter the composition of immigration. There seems to be no way to estimate future composition reliably, given the wide variety of proposals being discussed and contained in bills before Congress and the data available on immigrants, visa applications, and aliens resident in the United States (Tomasi and Keely, 1975).

It is clear that immigration as a demographic issue is developing as a policy concern. Most probably, the demographic impact of immigrants will become an increasingly important policy consideration, which has not been the case in the past. The major points of this section can be summed as follows:

1. The number and proportion of foreign born and foreign stock in the United States has been declining.
2. The increasing role of immigration in population growth can be misleading since it is a function of fertility decline.
3. Data on cumulative effects of past immigration reconfirm the "nation of immigrants" image but provide little insight for future policy.
4. There is serious question about the assumed level of emigration.
5. Ethnic fertility patterns need further study, especially when groups are highly concentrated in localized areas.
6. Future characteristics of immigrant streams cannot be reliably estimated.

I am led to the same conclusion stated previously: on the national level, the demographic issue is basically a question of values. How many people do we want in the society? Coale (1972, 599, 603) concluded that current levels of immigration are tolerable and that "it is *not* necessary to abandon the American tradition of welcoming immigrants." The president of ZPG, John Tanton, comes to the opposite conclusion on the basis of Coale's work. But neither of these conclusions deals with composition; they focus instead on volume. As we will see below, what kinds of immigrants the United States welcomes continues to be the major focus of controversy.

IMMIGRATION POLICY: THE BREAK WITH THE PAST AND ITS EFFECTS

The most important political factor in immigration policy has not been population size but ethnicity. Among the first federal laws on immigration were the Chinese Exclusion Acts of the 1880s. The development of congressional jealousy regarding its prerogatives in this area (now deeply institutionalized and supported by reelection concerns) has important roots in executive action relating to the Gentlemen's Agreement. In fact, up to and including the Immigration Act of 1965, ethnic considerations have been the chief ingredients in the formulation of law. The outlines of this history are fairly well known. I need only mention opposition to the "new immigrants," literacy tests, the forty-two volume report of the Dillingham Commission, national origin quotas, Oriental exclusion, and the Asia-Pacific triangle. These and other mechanisms were supported and justified by ideologies of racial superiority and hypotheses about assimilability.

After the passage of the McCarran-Walter Act in 1952 over President Truman's veto, those who rejected any scheme using national origin or ancestry as an immigrant selection mechanism (and the intellectual baggage supporting such schemes) regrouped for yet another assault against what some believed to be the cornerstone of U.S. immigration policy, the national origins quota system. As events developed, the opponents of the quota system were successful.

Until the 1965 act, the basic structure of immigrant selection was the quota system, which reserved a proportion of annual immigrant visas for countries based on the proportion of the ethnic stock of that country in the United States population as of 1920. Within each country's quota, immigrants were given preference on the basis of skills and family relationships. (see chart 1.) Certain immediate relatives of U.S. citizens were exempt from quotas. All countries had a minimum of a hundred. For natives of the Western Hemisphere (except those of Oriental ancestry), there were no quotas or ceilings. All immigrants had to meet certain health, moral character, criminal record, and past political affiliation tests. A special provision, the Asia-Pacific Triangle, applied to all persons with at least one-half ancestry traceable to an area defined by longitude and latitude in an area covering Asia and the Pacific. Such persons were counted not against the quota of their country of birth but of their country of ancestry. For those of mixed Asian background not predominantly from one country, a special quota of a hundred was established against which they would be counted. Although this provision was a break with complete Oriental exclusion, it was still clearly racial discrimination against persons of Asian ancestry.

The 1965 amendments to the immigration and nationality code made major revisions in U.S. policy (Keely, 1971, 1974a). The law eliminated the national origins quota system and Asian restrictions, introduced a new preference system (chart 1), added labor certification procedures for certain classes of immigrants, and put a ceiling on Western Hemisphere immigration for the first time. These changes resulted in increased volume and alteration of the origin and the demographic and labor characteristics of immigrants from various countries. These changes in the immigrant streams and the relationship of the structure and operation of the law and demographic changes have been discussed elsewhere (Boyd, 1974; Keely, 1971, 1974a, 1975a; Irwin, 1972). In the appendix I have included tables with some summary data on these changes.

There are two types of changes, however, that require discussion: geographic origin and labor force characteristics. The data are summarized in table 6.

First, there have been major shifts in origin (table 6, col. 1). European immigrants have proportionately declined. There has also been a decided shift to Southern European countries within Europe, with a resultant absolute decline for some Northern European countries, the previous recipients of high visa quotas (Keely, 1974a, 590). North and South

CHART **1**
PREFERENCE SYSTEMS
Immigration and Nationality Act of 1952
(McCARRAN-WALTER ACT)

1. First preference: Highly skilled immigrants whose services are urgently needed in the United States and the spouse and children of such immigrants.
   50 percent plus any not required for second and third preferences.
2. Second preference: Parents of United States citizens over the age of 21 and unmarried sons and daughters of United States citizens.
   30 percent plus any not required for first and third preferences.
3. Third preference: Spouse and unmarried sons and daughters of an alien lawfully admitted for permanent residence.
   20 percent plus any not required for first or second preference.
4. Fourth preference: Brothers, sisters, married sons and daughters of United States citizens and an accompanying spouse and children.
   50 percent of numbers not required for first three preferences.
5. Nonpreference: Applicants not entitled to one of the above preferences.
   50 percent of numbers not required for first three preferences, plus any not required for fourth preference.

Immigration Act of 1965

1. First preference: Unmarried sons and daughters of United States citizens.
   Not more than 20 percent.
2. Second preference: Spouse and unmarried sons and daughters of an alien lawfully admitted for permanent residence.
   20 percent plus any not required for first preference.
3. Third preference: Members of the professions and scientists and artists of exceptional ability.
   Not more than 10 percent.
4. Fourth preference: Married sons and daughters of United States citizens.
   10 percent plus any not required for first three preferences.
5. Fifth preference: Brothers and sisters of United States citizens.
   24 percent plus any not required for first four preferences.
6. Sixth preference: Skilled and unskilled workers in occupations for which labor is in short supply in the United States.
   Not more than 10 percent.
7. Seventh preference: Refugees to whom conditional entry or adjustment of status may be granted.
   Not more than 6 percent.
8. Nonpreference: Any applicant not entitled to one of the above preferences.
   Any numbers not required for preference applicants.

America also declined, especially after the imposition of the 120,000 ceiling in 1968. The other continents, most notably Asia, have an increased proportionate share of the larger volume following the 1965 act.

The proportions of persons intending to enter the labor force also changed. Europe and the Americas declined, and Asia and the other continents increased (table 6, col. 2). The proportion of professionals among those in the labor force by country (table 6, col. 3) and the geographic origin of the immigrant professionals (table 6, col. 4) altered radically. Asian changes in both cases are very notable. The declines in the professional categories in the Western Hemisphere are also worth noting.

CURRENT ISSUES IN IMMIGRATION POLICY: SELECTION MECHANISMS

At present, the major issues before Congress related to immigration revolve around immigrant selection, not volume. In short, the demographic concern is not yet mirrored to any large extent in congressional deliberations. I will consider four areas of policy: change to a worldwide selection system, illegal immigration, the brain drain, and legislative adjustments of a technical nature.

Worldwide Selection System

Experience under the 1965 amendments has led to a number of criticisms of the current law. The major criticism of the law's operation centers on the different sets of requirements for applicants from the Western Hemisphere and the rest of the world (Eastern Hemisphere). These hemispheric differences (in ceilings, applicability of the preference system, scope of labor certification, and adjustment of status) have resulted in a two-and-a-half year wait for a visa for Western Hemisphere natives; for most countries in the Eastern Hemisphere, all preferences are current or close to it. This situation is viewed as inequitable and has reinforced the dissatisfaction that existed with the involved legislative history, which led to the separate hemispheric provisions in the first place. That legislative history has been discussed elsewhere (Keely, 1972a). My purpose here is not to analyze the policy development process but to indicate that dissatisfaction with the longer waits for visas in the Western Hemisphere confirms a widely shared opinion about inequity in the hemispheric provisions.

The perceived inequity in treatment of natives of the two hemispheres has led to a number of omnibus-type bills to restructure immigration law once again. Their purpose is not so much to change policy goals as to devise a system whereby area of birth would not penalize a visa applicant. The desire is to ensure that, within the framework of family reunification and protection of U.S. labor (the preference system), discrimination on the basis of country of birth be eliminated from U.S. policy.

Three major bills were introduced into the Ninety-third Congress to develop a unified worldwide immigrant selection system: HR9409, an administration bill; S2643, introduced by Senator Edward Kennedy; and HR981, introduced by Congressman Peter Rodino, chairman of the House Committee on the Judiciary. These bills are representative of the general thrusts of changes suggested in this area. All three attempt to achieve uniformity in the application of immigration laws by having a worldwide ceiling of approximately 300,000 visas. All bills retain provisions for admitting immediate family members (generally parents, spouses, and children) of U.S. citizens outside the 300,000 limit. Each bill would have the preference system apply universally (and not just to the Eastern Hemisphere as at present). There are different proposed alterations within the preference system, such as eliminating married brothers and sisters of U.S. citizens from fifth preference, changing the proportion of visas reserved for each preference, and permitting the dropdown of unused visas in any category to meet excessive demands in the categories that follow (Tomasi and Keely, 1975).

A major point of contention in the different bills is the status accorded Canada and Mexico. Current law for the Eastern Hemisphere mandates that no single country receive more than 20,000 visas per annum in order to avoid domination of annual immigration by one country. No such limit currently exists for the Western Hemisphere. The House seems to favor treating contiguous countries as all other countries would be treated (20,000 visas). The Senate bill, however, would make an exception for Canada and Mexico and allocate 35,000 visas for these two countries on the basis of cultural, geographical, and political factors. The main argument on the House side was summed up by Congressman Joshua Eilberg, chairman of the House Subcommittee on Immigration and International Law, during debate on HR981: "We should treat all individuals regardless of place of birth on an equal basis."

Supporters of special treatment point to the sharing of borders as a basis of the two exceptions. Perhaps more to the point is the realization that the particularly difficult problem with Mexico over international migration could be exacerbated by reducing legal immigration to 20,000 per year. This whole problem of Mexican immigration, including illegal migration and temporary worker programs, is seen in the context of U.S. relations in the hemisphere. Mexican immigration and control of the Panama Canal are two potentially very explosive questions for the United States. The United States, unlike Russia and China, as James Reston (1975) pointed out, has not been paying attention to countries in its geographic area. The Western Hemisphere has not been a strong suit in U.S. diplomacy. Perhaps the Kennedy proposal reflects such concerns and uses the contiguous border concept to justify the effort to placate Mexico.

In sum, there is strong feeling, especially in Congress, that the dual-hemisphere approach to immigration is inconsistent and inequitable. There is general agreement on developing a unified worldwide system that maintains the goals of current policy but that better achieves the principle of equity (first-come, first-served regardless of birth) within the context of the family reunification and labor protection embodied in the preference system and labor certification procedures uniformly applied. The question of Mexican immigration remains unresolved. Changes to a unified system could result in major compositional changes of the immigrant streams.

Illegal Aliens[3]

Given the general consensus for a worldwide system, it seemed that some version of unified immigration procedures would pass the Ninety-third Congress. It did not, for two reasons. First, the Watergate affair and resultant change of administrations intervened. The Judiciary committees of both houses of Congress had major jurisdiction over impeachment hearings, and these are the same committees with jurisdiction over immigration legislation. Although the House did pass HR981, the Senate did not act. After the change of administrations, the crush of activity on the economy, energy policy, and Southeast Asia resulted in the Ninety-third Congress ending with no bill passed.

During 1974 and into 1975, the second factor, concern with illegal aliens, overshadowed immigration policy. Interest has focused on HR982, first introduced in the Ninety-third Congress and reintroduced in the House in the Ninety-fourth Congress under the same number. HR982 is designed to penalize employers of illegal aliens as a means to cut down on the volume of illegal immigration. It also contains an amnesty provision for aliens in the United States who entered unlawfully before 1968. The bill was favorably reported out of the House Judiciary Committee in July 1975 as HR8713. It does not appear that the Senate will accept the bill in its current form. It is a widely shared feeling, in fact, that the Chairman of the Senate Judiciary Committee has stymied all significant action on immigration reform because of opposition to the employer sanctions bill.

Illegal immigration into the United States is a social issue where concern outruns knowledge. President Ford appointed a Domestic Council Committee to study the problem, headed by Attorney General Levy in whose department the Immigration and Naturalization Service

(INS) is located. Commissioner Leonard F. Chapman, Jr., of the INS has spoken on numerous occasions about the size and economic impact of the situation. He variously estimates the problem to include from four million to twelve million persons and has indicated that with the proper resources, he could open up a million jobs for citizens and legal residents. The INS is feeling heavy pressure to control the flow of illegal aliens. The public statements of the assignments within INS toward more patrol and investigation (Chapman, 1974) reflect that pressure. The INS has also been funded for a major study of the number and flow of illegal aliens. Public concern is also mirrored in continuing congressional oversight hearings on illegal aliens beginning back in 1971 and the employer sanctions bill (HR8713). The news media and labor organizations have also evidenced interest.

The general label *illegal alien* applies to a number of subcategories, each with different information and problems of control. For example, seamen who jump ship and visitors who overstay their visas can be enumerated and often detected more easily than those who successfully enter clandestinely or violate the terms of their visas (for example, by working with a visitor's visa). Indirect information available from trend data on apprehensions and deportations indicates an increase in illegal entry and overstay. However, it is difficult to partial out the effects on the data of increased illegal entry and changes in law enforcement activity. Clearly apprehension data undercount the number of illegal aliens by an unknown amount, but this is at least partially offset by the large number of repeater apprehensions.

Characteristics of illegal aliens and their economic and social effects are obviously also difficult to determine. Although the major concentration seems to be Mexican nationals in the Southwest, other regions of the United States and nationals of other countries are also involved. New York City, for example, apparently has large numbers of illegal entrants among its various Hispanic ethnic groups.

In short, current information on illegal aliens is scattered and of variable quality. Nevertheless, concern and anxiety are high. Policy discussions at this point are in four directions: employer sanctions, increased law enforcement, control of social security cards, and national identity documents.

Hearings on an employer sanctions bill took place in the 93rd and 94th sessions of Congress. The arguments in favor of such a bill are that it would reduce the incentive to hire illegal aliens and thus reduce economic opportunities, which are assumed to be the major drawing factor. Arguments against such a bill revolve around enforcement procedures and unintended discrimination against "foreign-looking" or non-English speaking citizens and legal resident aliens. Although there is widespread support for the intent of the bill, there is still argument over the procedures for enforcement and legislative language to prevent unwarranted discrimination.

The second policy thrust is toward increased law enforcement by the INS. A set of revised priorities emphasizing patrol and investigation and reassignment of personnel was promulgated by the INS commissioner in September 1974 (Chapman, 1974). There is also pressure for increased INS budget for law enforcement manpower needs. Part of the redeployment of INS personnel included reducing the number of inspectors for overseas airline flights so that public inconvenience might be translated into increased funding for INS.

Increased enforcement does not involve a change of law, but it does intersect with an area of increasing policy discussion: temporary workers. There are numerous classes of temporary visas that are intended to permit the performance of work or that allow work to be performed as part of a "training experience" (Keely, 1975b). Such work encompasses not only lower-skilled and stoop labor but also the labor of skilled craftsmen in construction and highly trained professionals in medicine, academia, and business. The areas of temporary work and enforcement become intertwined when conditions of temporary visas are violated. Since many temporary visa holders are permitted to adjust status to permanent immigrant, there is also the problem of fraud involved in adjustment of status cases. Temporary visas and adjustment of status also involve the policy problems of the brain drain and international education. In short, increased enforcement is not confined to just border patrol and inspection of entrants; it involves the complex interaction of the whole range of policy areas that affect immigration.

The third policy thrust in controlling illegal aliens relates to control in the issuance of social security cards. Amendments in 1972 to the Social Security Act mandated passing of certain information by the Social Security Administration to INS regarding aliens applying for social security numbers. There has been much opposition to these procedures because of the clear legislative history surrounding the social security system. social security cards were not intended to be identity cards, and social security data were meant to be used only for social security administration, not in record matching for law enforcement. The expanded use of the social security number for a whole variety of purposes by all sorts of organizations (bank accounts, military identification numbers, personnel numbers in business and industry) has led to concern about record matching and unintended use of the social security number. The 1972 amendments to the Social Security Act went a step further in mandating passing of information gathered from applications for a social security number to a law enforcement agency. (Manpower shortages have led to recent cutbacks in the program for passing information from Social Security to INS.) Thus concern over the use of the social security number and information has led to opposition to the 1972 law, and the issue may eventually be adjudicated.

To carry out the 1972 amendments, there are plans (not yet instituted due to manpower shortages in the Social Security Administration) to issue social security cards to all children in first grade and to all permanent immigrants as part of their initial documentation. Such procedures would reduce walk-in applications for a social security number since citizens and eligible immigrants would normally receive a number. Thus, it would be administratively easier to check the eligibility of walk-in applicants.

A number of bills have been introduced to expand the use of social security cards to check legality of residence as well as right to work. This use of the social security card ties into the fourth policy as a means to control illegal immigration. During the 1975 hearings by the House of Representatives Subcommittee on Immigration and International Law on HR982, there was close questioning by subcommittee members regarding the idea of a national identity card indicating a person's legal status (citizen, permanent resident alien, and so forth) and right to take employment. The issue of an identity card is an emotional one in the United States because of a long tradition and deep feelings against such a document. The opposition involves constitutional questions about equal treatment, due process, and free movement among the states. There is also deep suspicion about government misuse, aggravated perhaps by questionable and illegal activities of members of the executive branch.

Given the long tradition opposing identity cards, that it is even brought up indicates the perception of the seriousness of the illegal alien problem. The members of the subcommittee and the executive and most persons testifying did not support such an extreme measure as an identity card. However, the problems of detection and enforcement of the law regarding illegal aliens are so difficult and the anxiety so high that even so controversial a measure is at least discussed.

In sum, the concern over illegal immigration has resulted in mandating changes in social security practices. There is pressure for increased funding for INS enforcement activities and wide support for the employer sanctions bill. The use of national identity cards, although a possible help in enforcement, receives little support currently because of the traditional opposition to the idea in the United States.

Illegal immigration clearly raises questions about ethnic relations. The political implications of methods proposed to control illegal immigration raise major questions about the type of society in which this and the following generations will live. The question of national identity cards or numbers and their use illustrate the broad range of implications of immigration policy.

Brain Drain

One of the most notable effects of the 1965 amendments to U.S. immigration law was the increase in the number and proportion of professionals and the changed areas of origin of such highly skilled people.

The changes illustrated in table 6 (especially columns 3 and 4) have led to concern about whether U.S. immigration law encourages a brain drain. It should be noted that the 1965 preference system lessened emphasis on skills as a basis of entrance. Under the McCarran-Walter Act (1952), persons who were highly skilled had first preference, and 50 percent of all visas were reserved for them. (See chart 1.) Second, the different effects of the 1965 law on the Eastern and Western hemispheres are also frequently overlooked in discussions of the brain drain. The provisions for Western Hemisphere immigrants (no preference system, the 120,000 ceiling, broad application of labor certification, no adjustment of status) and a two-and-a-half year wait for a visa resulted in a decline in the proportions of Western Hemisphere immigrants with a stated occupation (col. 2), who are professionals (col. 3), as a source of professionals (col. 4), and as a source of immigrants generally (col. 1). In short, a good case can be made that the most important change in the 1965 act that led to the increase in the proportion of professionals and in the change in the areas of origin of professionals was not the new preference system but rather the abolition of the quota system. If the 1965 act had contained all the changes it did except abolition of the national origins quota system, the number and proportions of professionals might well have remained steady or declined. If this is the case, the policy choice in retrospect would have been between retention of a discriminatory selection system based on national origin (and the attendant racial, religious, and nationality discrimination of the quota system) and the increase in professionals among immigrants, especially from Asia.

Of course, the policy decisions were not based on those considerations. The overriding concern in the congressional deliberations was elimination of the quota system. There was express consideration of the brain drain problem. What was not expected was the large demand for visas by professionals in some countries that removal of the quota system would generate, even with the downplaying of professional skills in the new preference system (third preference in the 1965 act versus first preference under the McCarran-Walter Act).

More focused concern has developed over the ability of Eastern Hemisphere applicants to apply for adjustment of status from a temporary to an immigrant visa. Adjustment of status was prohibited for exchange

Table 6

PROPORTION OF IMMIGRANTS BY AREA OF ORIGIN, WITH A STATED OCCUPATION, PROFESSIONALS AMONG THOSE WITH STATED OCCUPATION, CONTINENTAL ORIGIN OF PROFESSIONAL IMMIGRANTS, BY CONTINENT

	Proportion of Total Immigration from Geographic Region (1)	Persons with Stated Occupation (2)	Professionals as Proportion of Column 2 (3)	Proportion of all Professionals from Geographic Region (4)
Total[a]				
1961–1965	100.0	45.6	19.8	100.0
1966–1968	100.0	43.0	24.6	100.0
1969–1973	100.0	41.3	28.9	100.0
Europe				
1961–1965	41.9	50.5	19.5	45.9
1966–1968	35.3	46.1	22.8	35.2
1969–1973	27.3	45.2	18.7	19.4
Asia				
1961–1965	7.6	29.6	39.5	9.7
1966–1968	13.9	41.4	51.5	27.7
1969–1973	27.4	41.1	60.5	56.7
Africa				
1961–1965	.9	43.7	36.0	1.6
1966–1968	1.1	47.3	45.6	2.3
1969–1973	1.8	51.7	61.2	4.8
Oceania				
1961–1965	.5	36.8	41.1	.8
1966–1968	.6	37.1	48.6	1.0
1969–1973	.8	39.9	42.4	1.2
North America				
1961–1965	41.0	44.4	16.1	32.4
1966–1968	43.5	41.3	16.4	27.9
1969–1973	37.0	38.4	11.8	14.1
South America				
1961–1965	8.1	41.7	25.8	9.7
1966–1968	5.6	40.7	27.3	5.9
1969–1973	5.6	40.0	20.7	3.9

a. N for 1961–1965 = 1,450,314; 1966–1968 = 1,139,460; 1969–1973 = 1,887,131.
Annual averages volume for the three periods respectively are 290,063; 379,820; 377,426.
Source: U.S. Department of Justice, Annual Report of the Immigration and Naturalization Service, 1961-1973.

visitors, but a 1970 amendment limited that prohibition only to exchange visitors supported by their own or the U.S. government. The same 1970 law also instituted a temporary visa (L visa) for intracorporation transferees and restricted adjustment of status for them. The issue here is that some exchange visitors (H and J visas) and students (F visas), as well as other classes of temporary visa holders, can adjust status. Such procedures call into question the whole purpose of exchange programs and international education policy. It was feared that temporary visas would be used primarily as a means of early entrance, giving the recipient advantages for gaining U.S. work experience and finding employment. Thus, the temporary visa would not in fact be used to get training or experience for use in the home country but would increasingly become a mechanism to ensure permanent immigration.

Data do not lend support to the hypotheses of increased use of adjustment by students and exchange visitors (Keely, 1975b). The proportions of adjustees who were exchange visitors or students has remained steady.

However, there is the basic question about whether exchange visitors or students should be allowed to adjust status at all. To answer such a question involves complex problems about absorption capacity of developing countries, international education and exchange, the respective role of the sending and receiving countries in controlling and limiting manpower movement (skilled and unskilled), educational policies of sending countries, and opportunities for ethnic minorities and women in the United States.

At present, discussion in the United States over immigration and the brain drain is not focused on specific policy changes. There is still disagreement over such issues as the amount of drain versus overflow; the role of the United States in controlling immigration, especially if this requires singling out natives of only certain countries; the wisdom of curtailing the international flow of highly trained manpower; and the amount of federal government control of international education programs at state and private colleges and universities.

Obviously the brain drain issue intersects with many other complex policy issues. Indeed some are convinced that the generic term *brain drain* tends to oversimplify a complex phenomenon. At this point, discussion continues (some would say endlessly) with no resolution in the form of consensus over whether changing immigration policy would, on balance, be more beneficial to sending countries, the United States and the cause of Third World development and, if so, what changes should be instituted.

Other Policy Considerations

There are other immigration policy areas that would have an impact on the characteristics of immigrant streams and would therefore affect intergroup relations. Many are of a technical nature. That they are technical, however, does not necessarily mean they will be unimportant in their ramifications. The areas covered include proposals to expand temporary worker programs, to curtail labor certification exemptions for parents of minor U.S. citizens, to alter labor certification, to exclude from the Western Hemisphere ceiling Cuban refugees who regularize their status, and to alter provisions allowing temporary visa holders to adjust status.

Voluntary agencies, business groups, other private-sector organizations, and government officials have made suggests concerning all of these areas. Each of the subjects has been the object of discussion by those professionally involved with U.S. immigration policy and its administration.

Each of the major topics on current immigration policy has potential implications for intergroup relations or political implications for society at large. All center on selection mechanisms or control of illegal flows. The ethnic composition and other characteristics of those we welcome and those who enter illegally obviously will make an impact on the size, concentration, and effects of the foreign-born population and their offspring. At this point, I feel the resolution of these controversies is so unclear that to make any predictions or to draw any conclusions is presumptuous. But we must be aware that such policy questions are very live ones indeed and could have important implications.

Further, we should realize that important actors in these controversies include a wide variety of religious and nationality groups, as well as organized labor, and federations of such groups. Immigration is a major object of politics on the national level and in some areas the local level as well. Part of ethnic group relations now and in the foreseeable future is the cooperation and conflict over immigration policy. To date, there is no careful study of the role of such groups in policy formation and, equally important, policy administration. Such groups not only try to influence law, they are also the major watchdogs of congressional and executive action on immigration. Further, many such nongovernment groups are called upon to cooperate and aid government agencies in administration of the law through emergency resettlement (most recently in the Vietnamese situation). Finally, such private sector groups do much of the work of helping immigrant adjustment by means of social services in the absence of government schemes to help in adjustment, such as those that the Swedish government conducts.

Any proposal to alter immigration may affect not only future but also current ethnic relations in the political sphere. It is not easy to summarize how those relations would be affected in the absence of a specific issue. Most of the information on the stances, alliances, and presumed influence of such groups would be of the "inside-dopester" variety at any rate. To my knowledge, no one has tried to document who these actors are, their structural relationships, or their influence on actual decisions. The Population Commission, for example, soon became aware of their presence and the commission report, I think, clearly reflects the strength of organizations with a vested interest in immigration (Keely, 1972a).

The issues summarized here and the current and future ramifications for ethnic relations could change substantially. If, when, and how the demographic issue enters into immigration policy consideration is one example of how a significant new policy factor could change the current structure of ethnic relations. In a stabilized or stationary population, immigration policy will probably continue to be a stage of ethnic group interaction in a bid to achieve symbolic and substantive goals of various groups.

IMMIGRATION AND A STABILIZED POPULATION

Five topics are emerging as important issues in intergroup relations. Each of them would be further complicated by movement to a stable or stationary population, and each bears directly on immigration policy and its role in the future of ethnic relations in the United States.

The Hispanic Population

The rapid growth of persons of Spanish-speaking background has begun to raise doubts about the future of the U.S. culture and the political system. At their worst, these fears center on an Anglo-Hispanic version in the United States of the Anglo-French split in Canada or even a secessionist movement in the Southwest in territories that formerly were part of Mexico. The questioning, however, runs a whole gamut of cultural, political, social, and economic concerns.

The data in tables 7 through 10 summarize some of the characteristics and changes in the Hispanic population. Unfortunately changes in definition and types of data published by region do not allow meaningful comparisons of change in this group between 1960 and 1970 for the whole country and all states. (See U.S., Department of Commerce, 1971, for a discussion of the problem.) The concentration of Spanish surname and language in the Southwest states, as well as the number and percentages in some other states (table 10) indicate a potential for controversy, but the proportions are not so high yet that one would predict a problem as inevitable. The recency of some of the demographic trends, particularly

Table 7

PERSONS OF SPANISH ORIGIN IN THE UNITED STATES, 1970

Origin	Number	Percentage
Total	8,957,000	100.0
Mexican	5,023,000	56.1
Puerto Rican	1,450,000	16.2
Cuban	626,000	7.0
Central and South American	501,000	5.6
Other	1,356,000	15.1

Source: U.S. Department of Commerce, 1971.

Table 8

PERSONS OF SPANISH SURNAME FOR FIVE SOUTHWESTERN STATES, 1970 and 1960

State	1970			1960		
	Total Population	Spanish Surname (No.)	(%)	Total Population	Spanish Surname (No.)	(%)
Arizona	1,770,893	246,390	13.9	1,302,161	206,904	15.9
California	19,957,304	2,222,185	11.1	15,720,860	1,456,223	9.3
Colorado	2,207,259	211,585	9.6	1,753,925	152,039	8.7
New Mexico	1,016,000	324,248	31.9	951,023	275,731	29.0
Texas	11,195,416	1,663,567	14.9	9,581,508	1,422,787	14.8

Source: U.S. Department of Commerce, 1973, table 1.

Table 9

PERSONS OF SPANISH LANGUAGE AND SURNAME IN FIVE SOUTHWESTERN STATES, 1970

State	Number	Percentage
Arizona	306,609	17.3
California	2,738,513	13.7
Colorado	255,994	11.6
New Mexico	379,723	37.4
Texas	1,981,861	17.7

Source: U.S. Department of Commerce, 1970b, table 96 of Parts 4, 6, 7, 33, 45.

Table 10

PERSONS OF SPANISH LANGUAGE BY STATE, 1970

State	Number	Percentage
New York	1,455,941	7.9
Florida	451,382	6.6
Illinois	346,397	3.1
New Jersey	310,476	4.3
Michigan	120,687	1.3
Pennsylvania	106,634	.9

Note: State of 100,000 or more outside Southwest.
Source: U.S. Department of Commerce, 1970b, table 96 of Parts 34, 11, 15, 32, 24, 40.

migration, which are cited as the potential basis of a biculturalism conflict, as well as data problems, preclude any reference to effects of trends toward larger numbers and proportions of Hispanic persons.

The data in tables 7 to 10, along with amounts of migration and immigration (legal and illegal) of Hispanic persons, have contributed (with other events) to raising questions about the political and cultural future of the United States. There is, first of all, the question of the commitment to and the possibility of keeping English as the only official language. The use of Spanish in official documents, public notices, civil service tests, and business notices (for example, some utility companies' bills are in Spanish and English) are examples of language usage that goes beyond the use of a foreign language for personal communication by ethnics in their own community. This latter use is expected and has been part of the adjustment and assimilation of early generations in U.S. history. The wider use of Spanish goes beyond this traditional aspect of ethnic adjustment processes.

In addition, government programs such as bilingual education and ethnic heritage studies may have a latent function beyond the pedagogical purpose of aiding the learning of basic skills and building healthy self-images. Such programs may not only slow adoption of English as the mother tongue but also legitimize the official or quasi-official acceptance of bilingualism. Current practices are in that direction, although they fall short of Canadian policy. Further, Spanish was the native language of the "indigenous" (having established social institutions) Spanish population in the Southwest long before the Anglo conquest. Mother-tongue diversity seems to be largely derived from subordinate indigenous groups in long-standing, established enclaves (Lieberson et al., 1975, 54). Thus, the natural process of linguistic and cultural diversity in the region may be enhanced by national policy on education and new migration. Further, development of a national Hispanic federation may lead to demands for more widespread and legitimated use of a second language.

The situation is further complicated by the participation of persons of Mexican origin in the new ethnic consciousness. The Chicano and *la raza* movements add further to demands for cultural maintenance and abandonment of assimilationist policies and programs.

However, the Mexican-American group does not present a united front, for there are serious divisions within it that affect these processes. One is over illegal immigration. Cesar Chavez, for example, presented almost a classic case of the American labor leader torn between the needs of his followers in this country and the plight of their ethnic brothers seeking entrance. He had opted for U.S. citizens and residents and supported measures to curb illegal movement on the grounds of unfair labor competition until the August 1975 reversal of the UFW on the undocumented worker issue. Other Mexican-Americans have espoused views all the way up to a demand for virtually free movement over the border on the basis that the Southwest region is basically Mexican since it was taken by the United States. Mexicans, they argue, should have a right to enter the land that makes up part of their ancestral patrimony.

The questions of the cultural, political, and economic effects of Hispanic (and especially Mexican) migration are of national and regional importance. Information on developments may well be forthcoming from persons engaged in borderlands studies, a recently developed, interdisciplinary specialty. However, other regions also bear close scrutiny. The long-range effects of Cuban movement in Miami and the Hispanicization of New York City by a whole variety of Latin ethnics are two examples of localized impact of great importance, which even have national implications.

The questions concerning the Hispanic population need further attention to sharpen our focus on developing issues and to gather needed information. Such data collection can lead to informed decisions (even though they are ultimately choices of values) and can also function to define the issues. We may, in fact, be in the initial stages of such a process, which will have great national and regional import.

New Ethnics

Not only has the United States experienced a new ethnic consciousness but it has also been receiving new ethnics. As table A-1 shows, there has been substantial movement in the past ten years of previously slightly represented groups (often because of low quotas). Many of these groups pose new questions about ethnic relations.

There has been a movement of black West Indians as a result of the 1965 Immigration Act. This group, along with black Spanish-speakers, can raise problems for the black population, particularly in light of the split in the black group between West Indian and "American" (descendants of the U.S. slave population) blacks. A particularly interesting group are the Haitians, whose culture and French language set them even further apart. In 1974, immigrants from the Caribbean (except Cuba) made up 24.4 percent of Western Hemisphere immigration and 10.7 percent of the total. Both of these are in sharp contrast to the situation under the quota system when many Caribbean territories were colonies and had available 200 visas a year as a subquota of the colonizing country (for example, the above percentages were 5.4 and 3.0 for 1961 to 1965).

Asians have benefited greatly from the changed immigration selection system. The effects on traditional Asian ethnic groups (especially Chinese) and newly important groups (Filipino and Korean) need study. The special case of the large, one-time infusion of Vietnamese is also important, not so much for long-term impact as for knowledge of the process and result of large-scale resettlement undertaken by the United States from time to time (Hungarians and Cubans are two other examples). As is so often the case with ethnic groups, the Asian impact probably has greater regional impact (in Hawaii and on the West Coast especially) because of concentration.

I have previously discussed the Hispanic cases. Here, the question of integration or maintenance of sharp national difference is important. Other groups have transcended national identities for certain purposes, for example, using religion as the binding force. Catholics are a case in point, although nationality differences still have extreme importance within that group. There is also the case of the Jewish population transcending nationality for certain purposes. In short, there are examples in which nationality, while remaining a vital force especially in internal group dynamics, has been suppressed for certain broader group action and goals.

Whether Hispanic culture and identity can function in the way religion and peoplehood have in the two cases cited remains to be seen. If it does, ethnic relation dynamics will be obviously quite different for the United States in general and for internal dynamics of a Hispanic confederation.

Finally, a religious issue is involved in immigration and group relations. The immigrants in 1974 from predominantly Catholic cultures equaled about 206,000 or 52 percent of gross alien immigration.[4] Clearly not all these immigrants are Catholic themselves, and their Catholicism is not necessarily the same. Also, Catholics from other countries entered. My point here is that the number and proportion of Catholics (culturally and in practice) is high. This movement has generated a feeling of obligation and responsibility in the Catholic church, particularly the official organization. Thus, moves to reduce immigration or other policy initiatives seen as anti-immigrant can raise the question of anti-Catholicism. The point is not so much whether anti-Catholicism is intended. It is the perception and reaction to the coincidence of the religious background of immigrants and any anti-immigrant movement that may take place. Given U.S. history, it is not difficult to construct numerous scenarios of possible conflict, depending on immigration developments, especially as the population moves to a stable and stationary state.

In short, the composition of recent immigration raises important questions for and about the black, Hispanic, Asian, and Catholic groups. These questions not only focus on the results of current immigration law and policy but also center on changes in that policy and body of law. Once again ethnic relations in the United States have been, are, and probably will be played out in political arenas, and immigration law is part of the game.

For each of the cases cited, there is a basic need for demographic analysis of the potential impacts of these groups. For example, because black West Indians are coming in larger numbers, will their relative size and impact in the black community remain more or less constant? What may seem to be striking changes in immigrant composition will not automatically result in major changes in intragroup or intergroup relations. Obviously other variables will be involved.

POPULATION POLICY AND IMMIGRATION POLICY

Many people feel that the United States needs population and immigration policies in the sense of explicit goals or targets with rationally based and clearly articulated programs. Some even see immigration policy as a wedge to force the broader question of population policy. The current national debate in Canada on immigration is pointed to as a model of the process of using immigration to open up the population issue and apply pressure for the development of an integrated and explicit policy.

Berry's (1973) discussion of the problems of national urban planning is quite apposite. In analyzing the probability of the development of a national urban strategy in democratic nations, he states that the applied rationality of goal-oriented activity seems to be a threat to the traditional process of incremental adjustment characteristic of change in democratic societies. Manipulation of interest group politics, bargaining, coalition building and logrolling do not seem compatible with goal-oriented national planning. In fact, "the very utility of future-oriented planning is to provide a basis for decision-making more rational than that of interest-group politics" (Berry, 1973, 72). I think the same analysis applies to a national population policy.

In short, I do not expect the United States to develop an explicit population or immigration policy in the foreseeable future. Given the style of U.S. politics, the strong ethnic group interest in immigration and the interest in group survival, population policy may become (in fact already is to some extent), another forum for ethnic relations. The application of policy development studies to population is a potentially important source of information and can provide important insights into the course of ethnic relations.

Pluralism

Finally, the United States is probably in for another round of discussion on pluralism. It is perhaps part of the genius of American society (although intellectually untidy) that it absorbs new ideas and practices, even radical changes, and yet maintains the same labels. Tiryakian's (1975) recent discussion of U.S. society approvingly presents the work of such recent analysts of America as Revel and Servan-Schreiber. Both of the latter emphasize the American social system's flexibility and its ability to absorb profound change rooted in the personal and collective crises of the diverse and often contradictory "moral systems" (Tiryakian, 1975, 2-5).

One need not be sanguine about the United States' ability to absorb change or even to be in the state of constant revolution within the institutional structure of society. However, I think it is clear that in the area of ethnic relations, ideology has been shifting, and there is a continuing effort to redefine the ideology of ethnic relations. Even though pluralism is generally accepted as the norm, there are profound opponents of the idea and a great deal of disagreement about what it means. I see this as a continuing process with no ultimate resolution. Many who defend pluralism would oppose official bilingualism. There is a clear clash between pluralism and the values of individualism and universalistic criteria. The debate on pluralism represents another level of the contest of ethnic group interests and relations. However, I do not think the debate can be dismissed as just another ideological squabble having no impact on events. Whether we are a pluralistic society and what that means is part of the lives of many Americans. Ethnic institutional structures, political socialization of schoolchildren, career patterns and demographic rates are but a few examples of areas where pluralism (what we mean by it and do about it) affects us.

Immigration policy obviously is directly tied into the image of the United States as a pluralistic society. Do we want a continual infusion of persons of foreign culture? Is the declining proportion of foreign born and foreign stock a portent for the future? Does the citizenry still hold to a fear of non-Western cultures, which may be exacerbated by the current national origin composition? How does one react to the generally agreed upon need for opportunity for U.S. minorities and women and the high proportion of professionals among immigrants? The questions and the conflicts go on. They influence and in turn are influenced by our understanding of pluralism.

I do not think the question of pluralism will be resolved in a final and fixed way. I do think, however, that the debate on the issue is ignored at peril. Whatever the social sources of group positions on the subject and the dominant definition at any moment, the debate both affects and reflects ethnic relations.

This discussion of the Hispanic population, the new ethnics, population policy, and pluralism obviously does not exhaust the field of topics in which immigration intersects with intergroup relations, and I have only briefly outlined each topic as a starting point of discussion. It seems to me that these topics, along with immigrant selection mechanisms and their effects, will be among the major, if not the major, issues concerning immigration and intergroup relations.

NOTES

1. Net (civilian) immigration as estimated by the Census Bureau includes alien immigration, net migration from Puerto Rico, net arrivals of civilian citizens, conditional entrants (such as refugees), and emigration (Keely, 1972b, 2-3). It should also be noted that there are indications that estimated emigration at a rate of about 10 percent of alien immigration seems to be low for the 1960-1970 decade (Warren and Peck, 1975). Warren and Peck estimate emigration of the foreign born at about 1.06 million for the decade, or 100,000 per annum, which equals a bit more than 25 percent of net civilian immigration and about 32 percent of alien immigration. It should be noted that this is an estimate of foreign-born emigration only and does not attempt to account for native-born emigration. Since about 25 percent of Warren and Peck's estimated emigration were females aged twenty-five to forty-four, there is a possibility that substantial numbers of children who are native born emigrated. As Warren and Peck note, the possible sources of errors should lead one to regard their estimates, especially by age, as approximations. It is clear, however, that there was a large return migration of foreign born in the 1960s.

2. These data are for the white population only because of accessibility of data over time. In 1970, there were 801,765 persons of foreign or mixed parentage who were classified as Negro or other races. This was 3.2 percent of the total in that category. About 240,000 Negroes were included in that 801,765 and the rest were primarily Asian. This number of native Negroes of foreign or mixed parentage represented 1.1 percent of the 22.1 million Negro population. However, those classified as a race other than white or Negro totaled 2,552,575 persons, of whom 632,000 were foreign born and 561,000 are native of foreign or mixed parentage.

This amounts to over 46 percent of the (primarily) Asian population being of foreign stock. Thus, the Asian population, as part of the new ethnics (groups whose members increased rapidly after the 1965 Immigration Act) is in sharp contrast to the current situation of the white and Negro population.

3. There is opposition to use of the term *illegal aliens* because of the connotations of the concept. It is an example of "blaming the victim" in the sense that the concept ignores all the structural factors (including U.S. tolerance and even encouragement of illegal migration through enforcement procedures) involved in such international population distribution and focuses on the individual actor who may be reacting in a most rational way to factors beyond his or her control.

4. The countries of birth of the immigrants included are Ireland, Italy, Portugal, Spain, Philippines, Mexico, Cuba, Dominican Republic, Haiti, Costa Rica, El Salvador, Guatemala, Honduras, Nicaragua, Panama, and South American countries.

REFERENCES

Aron, Raymond. 1967. *Eighteen Lectures on Industrial Society*. London: Weidenfeld and Nicolson.

Berry, Brian J. L. 1963. *The Human Consequences of Urbanization*. New York: St. Martin's Press.

Boyd, Monica. 1974. "The Changing Nature of Central and Southeast Asia Immigration to the United States: 1961-1972." *International Migration Review* 8 (Winter): 507-519.

Carpenter, Niles. 1927. *Immigrants and Their Children, 1920*. Washington, D.C.: GPO.

Chapman, Leonard F. Jr. 1974. "Establishment of Operational Priorities, F. Y. 1975." *Interpreter Releases* 51 (October 23): 279-287.

Coale, Ansley J. 1972. "Alternative Paths to a Stationary Population." In Charles F. Westaff and Robert Parke, Jr., *Demographic and Social Aspects of Population Growth*. Washington, D.C.: GPO.

Commission on Population Growth and the American Future. 1971. *Interim Report*. Washington, D.C.: GPO.

_____. 1972. *Population and the American Future*. Washington, D.C.: GPO.

Gibson, Campbell. 1975. "The Contribution of Immigration to the United States Population Growth: 1790-1970." *International Migration Review* 9 (Summer): 157-177.

Hutchinson, E. P. 1956. *Immigrants and Their Children, 1850-1950*. New York: John Wiley.

Irwin, Richard. 1972. "Changing Patterns of American Immigration." *International Migration Review* 6 (Spring).

Keely, Charles B. 1971. "Effects of the Immigration Act of 1965 on Selected Population Characteristics of Immigrants to the United States." *Demography* 8 (May): 157-169.

_____. 1972a. "Immigration Recommendations of the Commission on Population Growth and the American Future." *International Migration Review* 6 (Fall): 290-294.

_____. 1972b. "Immigration Policy and Population Growth in the United States." Paper presented at the annual meeting of the Population Association of America.

_____. 1974a. "Immigration Composition and Population Policy." *Science* 185 (August 16): 587-593.

_____. 1974b. "The Estimation of the Immigrant Component of Population Growth." *International Migration Review* 8 (Fall): 431-35.

_____. 1975a. "Effects of U.S. Immigration Law on Manpower Characteristics of Immigrants." *Demography* 12 (May): 179-191.

_____. 1975b. "Temporary Workers in the United States." *International Migration* (forthcoming).

Krtiz, Mary M., and Gurak, Douglas T., 1975. "Foreign Stock Minority and Native White Fertility Differentials." Paper presented at the annual meeting of the Population Association of America.

Lieberson, Stanley; Dalto, Guy; and Johnston, Mary Ellen. 1975. "The Course of Mother-Tongue Diversity in Nations." *American Journal of Sociology* 81 (July): 34-61.

Reston, James. 1975. "U.S. Losing in Latin America." New York Times Syndicated Column (August).

Tanton, John. 1975. "Reply to Keely." *International Migration Review* 8 (Winter).

Taueber, Conrad, and Taueber, Irene B., 1958. *The Changing Population of the United States.* New York: John Wiley.

Tiryakian, Edward A. 1975. "Neither Marx nor Durkheim . . . Perhaps Weber." *American Journal of Sociology* 81 (July): 1-33.

Tomasi, S. M., and Keely, Charles B. 1975. *"Whom Have We Welcomed? The Adequacy and Quality of United States Immigration Data for Policy Analysis and Evaluation.* New York: Center for Migration Studies.

U.S. Department of Commerce. Bureau of the Census. 1970a. *Census of Population: 1970, General Social and Economic Characteristics, Final Report PC(1)-C1 United States Summary.* Washington, D.C.: GPO.

_____. 1970b. *Census of Population: 1970,* vol. 1: *Characteristics of the Population.* Washington, D.C.: GPO.

_____. 1971. *Comparison of Persons of Spanish Surname and Persons of Spanish Origin in the United States,* by Edward W. Fernandez. Technical paper no. 38.

_____. 1972. *National Origin and Language, Special Report PC (2)-1A.* Washington, D.C.: GPO.

_____. 1973. *Persons of Spanish Surname, Special Report PC(2)-1D.* Washington, D.C.: GPO.

U.S. Department of Justice. Immigration and Naturalization Service. 1961-1974. *Annual Report of the Immigration and Naturalization Service.* Washington, D.C.: GPO.

Warren, Robert, and Peck, Jennifer. 1975. "Emigration from the United States: 1960-1970." Paper presented at the annual meeting of the Population Asociation of America.

APPENDIX

This appendix contains summary data on the proportions and sex ratios of immigrants from various regions and countries. The goal is to provide a general overview of some effects of the 1965 Immigration Act, which amended the basic immigration code contained in the Immigration and Nationality Act of 1952 (the McCarran-Walter Act). The data are presented for three periods: 1961-65, the last five years under the McCarran-Walter provisions; 1966-68, the transition period during which the quota system was phased out; 1969-73, the first five years under the new provisions. (See Keely, 1971, for the details on the process of phasing out the quota system. For more detailed data on other characteristics, see Keely, 1971, 1974a, 1975a.)

These data are from a file in which published and unpublished aggregate data from INS for 1961 through 1973 were compiled for all countries from which 2,500 or more immigrants were admitted in any one year between 1961 and 1972. Support for the project in which these data were collected came from the Ford-Rockefeller Foundations Program in Support of Social Science and Legal Research on Population Policy (1973-74). The contents of the file are described in Tomasi and Keely (1975).

4 Ethnicity and Fertility: What and So What[*]

BERNARD BERELSON

This is a review of ethnic differentials in fertility in the modern world (*what*) and the policy-oriented concerns to which they give rise (*so what*). How common are they? How large? Where? By what ethnic characteristics? How "real"? How important? What difference do they make? Who cares?

The paper aspires not to technical analysis but rather to policy consideration, less to causes than to conditions and consequences. It consists of a descriptive survey, based on the available literature, of cases of differential fertility (and associated population growth) within countries that have resulted in public concern and/or policy determinations.[1] Ethnic differentials in mortality exist in today's world, though they are probably diminishing with the general decline in mortality, and occasionally some attention will be given here to mortality differentials.

That briefly covers the fertility side of the equation. What is meant here by *ethnicity*? For my purposes, this is the generic term designating groups characterized by distinctive origin. Members are identified as such at birth, share a common tradition and social life, and maintain their (usually irreversible) ethnic identity in one form or another from birth to death. There are three main ethnic differentiations: race: a common biological heritage involving certain, usually permanent, physical distinctions readily visible; religion: a common and distinct system of worship; and nationality: a common national or regional origin usually characterized by distinctive linguistic patterns. Often, perhaps typically, such differences are reinforced by residential segregation; that is, ethnic groups tend to live together in regions of a country or sections of a city and thus reinforce their ethnic character. In short, "the underlying idea is that of difference in some fundamental, readily visible, lasting, and socially reinforced way. Ethnic relations refer to interaction with 'unlike' people, to 'minority groups' on a 'we/they' basis."[2]

*I am glad to express both my appreciation and my gratitude for the invaluable bibliographic assistance of H. Neil Zimmerman, my colleague at the Population Council. Without his good help, this paper would have been even more difficult in preparation and would be less comprehensive in outcome.

So much for the stage setting. The first section summarizes a number of country examples of ethnic differentials in fertility that give rise to some degree of policy concern; the second section contains some conclusions and comments based on that array.

COUNTRY CASES

Most countries are pluralistic in that they contain groups of people recognized as ethnically different, both by themselves and by others. But ethnic homogeneity/heterogeneity is a relative matter, and on that continuum countries can range from the unity of, say, Poland or Sweden or Morocco to the bifurcated societies of Belgium or Lebanon or the multi-ethnic society of the United States. Even within the homogeneous countries, there are often little enclaves of the ethnically distinctive, but such situations are so quantitatively submerged as to be less problematic on grounds of fertility differentials even when the differential itself is large (for example, the Hutterites within Canada or the United States).

Beyond such homogeneity, what are some of the major fertility-related cases of ethnic differentiation? The following listing is presented not as a complete inventory of such cases, even less as a full examination of their demographic or social or political complexities, but rather as a representative set of cases that reveal the substance of the issues involved.

Africa

On this continent, the major cases are threefold: the black/white differences in the south, the special case of Mauritius, and ethnic differences in several other countries.

South Africa.   The basic ethnic distinction is between the Bantu (African) with 70 percent of the population and the whites with 17 percent (the remainder being "colored," 9 percent, and Asians, 3 percent). The (approximate) crude birthrates of Bantus and whites are 42 and 23, respectively, the crude death rates 15 and 9, and the natural increase about 2.7 percent and 1.4 percent (the latter comes to about 2 percent when immigration is added). Moreover, projections of population growth to the year 2000 envisage a Bantu population then of twenty-eight or thirty-five or even forty million, depending upon the assumed speed of mortality decline, as compared to the present fifteen million, and thus a sharply greater disparity in size.

The white governors of South Africa are reported to appreciate that their small minority, destined to be smaller still, cannot win a fertility race, but that was not always thus:

Table A-1

PERCENTAGE OF IMMIGRANTS ADMITTED BY COUNTRY AND CONTINENT OF ORIGIN

Area	1961–65	1966–68	1969–73
Europe	41.9	35.3	27.3
Czechoslovakia	.6	0.4	0.7
France	1.4	0.9	0.5
Germany	9.0	4.4	2.1
Greece	1.4	3.2	3.8
Ireland	2.1	0.8	0.5
Italy	5.7	6.6	6.1
Netherlands	1.3	0.6	0.3
Poland	3.0	1.9	1.1
Portugal	1.0	3.1	3.3
Spain	0.7	1.0	1.1
United Kingdom	8.7	6.6	3.2
Yugoslavia	0.8	1.4	2.0
Other	6.1	4.5	2.7
Asia	7.6	13.9	27.4
Hong Kong	0.2	1.1	1.1
India	0.2	1.0	3.2
Iran	0.2	0.3	0.6
Japan	1.3	1.0	1.2
Jordan	0.2	0.4	0.6
Korea	0.7	0.9	3.8
Philippines	1.1	3.0	7.4
Thailand		0.1	0.8
Vietnam		0.1	0.7
China	1.4	4.1	4.2
Other	2.1	1.9	3.7
Africa	0.9	1.1	1.8
Egypt	0.3	0.4	0.9
Other Africa	0.6	0.7	0.9
Oceania	0.4	0.6	0.8
North America	41.0	43.5	37.0
Canada	12.0	7.0	3.5
Mexico	15.4	11.5	14.5
Jamaica	0.6	2.7	3.7

Table A-1 (Continued)

Area	1961–65	1966–69	1969–73
Trinidad & Tobago	0.1	0.7	1.8
Cuba	5.3	13.1	5.1
Dominican Republic	2.4	3.3	3.1
Haiti	0.7	1.2	1.7
Costa Rica	0.7	0.4	0.3
Other	3.7	3.5	3.3
South America	8.1	5.6	5.6
Argentina	1.7	0.9	0.7
Brazil	0.7	0.6	0.4
Colombia	2.4	1.8	1.6
Ecuador	1.2	0.9	1.2
Peru	0.8	0.4	0.3
Other	1.3	1.0	1.3

Note: N for 1961–1965 = 1,450,314; N for 1966–1968 = 1,139,460; N for 1969–1973 = 1,887,131

Table A-2

SEX RATIO OF IMMIGRANTS BY CONTINENT

Continent	1961–65	1966–68	1969–73
Europe	68	77	91
Asia	63	86	80
Africa	98	106	125
Oceania	65	72	68
North America	97	77	90
South America	89	72	86
Total	80	78	88

Note: Sex ratio = number of males per 100 females.

In multiracial societies politicians may find themselves in the awkward position of desiring and even advocating, the encouragement of higher fertility amongst one ethnic group only. In South Africa, government leaders have frequently encouraged higher fertility amongst the white population alone. The most famous effort in recent years was somewhat anomalously carried out by M. C. Botha, Minister of Bantu Administration and Development. In 1967 he urged all white couples to have one more child than they had previously intended for the good of the nation, an effort which was greeted somewhat wrily by whites who nicknamed it the "Baby for Botha campaign" and which was hostilely received by non-white leaders who, evidently partly successfully, advocated the non-white boycotting of family planning services.[3]

The contention now is that neither can the Bantus win such a contest:

This group [the dominant white population] is less concerned that it will be increasingly outnumbered by the more numerous Bantu, colored, and Asian populations than that it will not be able to provide enough jobs for the growing population and thus avoid dissatisfaction and social unrest, which could lead to political revolt. Hence, the policy is one of highly selective immigration in order to provide managerial and entrepreneurial ability.[4]

Yet the Bantus welcome even a marginal decline in their increase as ameliorating their own situation, as well as contributing to the overall national prospects:

In some urban areas . . . many [Bantu] leaders appear to hold the view that in proliferating numbers the Bantu peoples have a potent political weapon which can be used to good effect. This is, of course, a delusion. They are already a majority group in a 7 to 3 ratio. They cannot lose their majority status. Insofar as political power is related to numbers, a rise in the ratio to 8 to 3 or 10 to 3 cannot add anything to it. Any marginal significance it may have will be wiped out by the erosion of their economic status. It will be greatly to their advantage to improve their bargaining power by way of economic progress, [partly] achieved through the reduction of the annual increments in population.[5]

As a matter of national policy, South Africa has instituted a family planning program designed for the entire population.

It is felt that any population control program should be non-discriminatory on ethnic or any other lines. A contributing consideration here was almost certainly that any discriminatory scheme or program, in spite of any justification offered by the differential nature of demographic realities among the various ethnic groups, would leave the white propagandists open to cries of selfish discrimination and racial superiority, if not deliberate genocide. Then, too, any scheme that was not non-discriminatory would constitute a poor strategy and be doomed to failure from the start.[6]

There is no available evidence to suggest that the program is making any difference to the current ethnic differentials in demographic measures. (And much the same overall demographic situation is true of Rhodesia as well.)

Mauritius.   This small island country, just under a million in population, is a complex ethnic community: 67 percent Indian, both Moslem and Hindu; 30 percent African-cum-European ("general population"), most of them Catholics; plus about 3 percent Chinese. These groups had the following gross reproduction rates in 1970: Hindu, 2.025; Moslem, 1.758; "General population," 1.595; and Chinese, 1.184. All are in substantially closer convergence now than earlier.

The population situation has been a matter of concern for at least a quarter of a century, first focusing on immigration and later, after concern about employment and welfare in the early 1960s, on fertility.[7] Some questions were occasionally raised about the potential of Hindu domination in the government, but the major differences over public policy on family planning arose on religious grounds in the face of strong Catholic opposition. The outcome, after some years of negotiated gestation, was government support to two family planning organizatons: the Mauritius Family Planning Association, later integrated into the Ministry of Health, and the Action Familiale, a Catholic agency offering only the rhythm method.[8]

Nigeria, Kenya, Ghana.   These countries are illustrative of ethnic situations in sub-Saharan Africa, both East and West, as related to population factors — included here not necessarily for their distinctiveness but because of the relative availability of information. In Ghana, fertility differentials have been identified but within a relatively small band at the high end of the continuum (for example, nine ethnic groups with total fertility ranging only from 5.3 to 6.6).[9] And even so, according to one expert,

[ethnic] differential fertility . . . may be attributed in part to education, degree of urbanisation, physical mobility, distorted sex ratios, and in part to factors like malnutrition, diseases and constitutional and aetiological sterility which tend to depress fecundity. Superstitions and differential reporting of vital events may also account for part of the differentials.[10]

In Kenya, when the family planning program was begun, "far more facilities were available to Kikuyo who were paramount in government; . . . it could be argued that these were the more urbanised and educated groups likely to employ such facilities first," as well as the politically dominant.[11] In Nigeria, with both ethnic differences (three groups of roughly equivalent sizes: Hausa, Yoruba, and Ibo) and religious

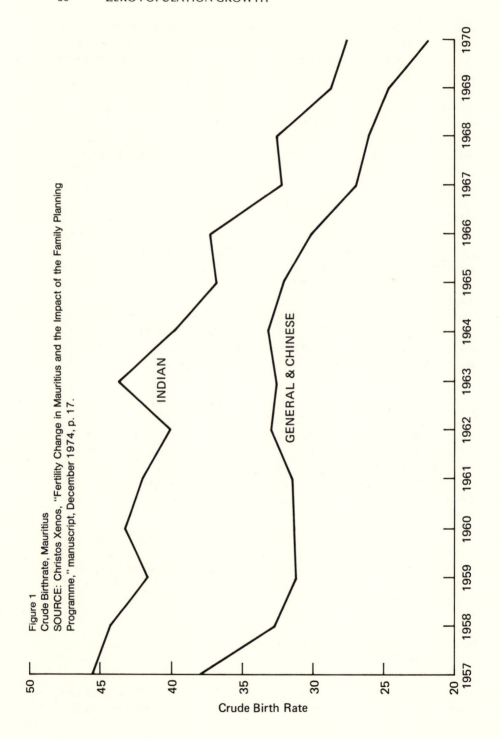

Figure 1
Crude Birthrate, Mauritius
SOURCE: Christos Xenos, "Fertility Change in Mauritius and the Impact of the Family Planning Programme," manuscript, December 1974, p. 17.

differences (Moslem about 50 percent, Christians 35 percent), the issue of population distribution as related to political representation has caused two censuses in the past decade to be put aside as incomplete, misleading, or otherwise incorrect—perhaps understandable in a country that at the same time fought a civil war on ethnic grounds.

Latin America

This area appears to have the fewest documented cases of ethnic differentials in fertility that are politically problematic. To a large extent, presumably, Central and South America have achieved sufficient assimilation of the various ethnic strains so that differential fertility is seen more as urban/rural or rich/poor than as ethnic in impact. The major exception may be in reverse—concern about mortality and morbidity among the Indian populations in several countries that has led to special health programs seeking a convergence on such rates rather than on fertility.

There appear to be no responsible reports on such issues in the Caribbean islands although they do contain populations in stress on other maters, both black/white and native/East Indian. The fertility matter does simmer beneath the surface, and occasionally a family planning program has apparently run into minor difficulties on this score. However, I found nothing in the literature.

Asia and Oceania

Here the picture centers on religion (and language) in the subcontinent and on national origin elsewhere.

India/Bangladesh. Each of these countries has a substantial minority of the other's religion: 11 percent Moslem in India, 18 percent Hindu in Bangladesh. The issue appears to be insignificant in the latter country, since Moslem fertility is no doubt higher in that Moslem country anyway, but there has been public debate in India to the effect that the family planning program will further disadvantage Hindu fertility relative to Moslem. Actually, the current practice of fertility control is higher among Hindus than Moslems in India (13.8 percent current users in 1970 to 8.8 percent); the ideal family size is larger for Moslems than Hindus (31 percent three or fewer children as against 41 percent);[12] and the population increase in the 1961-71 intercensal period was 31 percent for Moslems and 24 percent for Hindus.[13] That resulted in a shift in proportionate share of total population in the amount of about 0.5 of one point, that is, the Moslems rose in the decade from 10.7 percent to 11.2 percent.[14] "The differential growth rate was attributed to the differential adoption of family planning by the two major religious groups, and became a controversial issue for the family planning program," with a certain amount of press comment.[15]

Such differentials are particularly troublesome in areas of Moslem concentration, for reasons of political representation. The latter has also given rise to a kind of growth rivalry between linguistic communities identified with different states or districts ("the family planning program will be used against us," or, "we will take it up but they will not"). This has not become a key element in the program's performance, but it has not been completely absent either.

Sri Lanka. The major division here is between the Sinhalese-Buddhists (70 percent) and the Tamil-Hindus (20 percent). In the mid-1960s the government took an official position on reducing population growth and promoting family planning, but the policy was not vigorously pursued:

... official policy on family planning, for political reasons, tended to become ambivalent and cautious. Governments in power were peculiarly vulnerable to the charge that family planning could turn out to be a device which would inevitably turn the prevailing ethnic balance of population against the Sinhalese. ... It was argued [that] the Sinhalese population would be reduced to a minority or "would gradually disappear." A sustained attack on family planning campaigns was set in motion by members of the Buddhist clergy.[16]

The attack had an effect in diluting the program. Subsequently, special efforts were made to extend the program to the Tamil areas. Thus,

not unlike other multiracial societies where political power is based on contests within an organized multiparty system, attitudes to family planning in Ceylon have been determined to a considerable extent by political considerations. ... In such a context, it is surprising that family planning has not become a live party political issue of debate in Ceylon. Indeed, not a single parliamentary debate has been generated by the subject.[17]

The most powerful opposition came from Buddhist monk fraternities, partly on grounds of morality but mainly political in character: "the present programme of birth control endangers their future existence as an ethnic group."[18] In point of fact, the record shows at least an equivalent decline for the Tamils, but that did not eliminate political positions.

Thailand. Although the population of this country is 98 percent Thai born and 94 percent Buddhist, still there is considerable sensitivity about the ethnic Chinese despite their relatively small numbers: one to three million out of forty million (the uncertainty deriving from problems of definition and identification).[19] The sensitivity is probably based on their sharp difference from the Thai community: the Chinese are highly urban (and hence disproportionately visible in Bangkok and provincial capitals), better educated and better off, and especially prominent in the business world.

The issue arose, though subterraneously, at the outset of the national family planning program when it was argued, first, that the Chinese would not practice family planning while the Thais did; and then, after some experience, that the Chinese were not using the public clinics proportionately. Actually, as of the 1960 census, Confucianist fertility (not equivalent to Chinese) was about 12 percent below Buddhist, with Moslem lower still.[20]

In part, [such] research has reflected concerns expressed by policy makers in some multi-religious countries that if family planning was not uniformly adopted by members of all religious groups, the numerical balance among the various segments of the population would be upset. . . . Despite its small proportion of non-Buddhists, the Thai government, as part of its growing concern with the overall rate of population growth, has been increasingly interested in the extent of fertility differentials among religious minority groups within Thailand and their need for and receptiveness to family planning.[21]

The perception was troubling for a time. As late as 1969, 30 percent of a group of media professionals agreed that "with widespread family planning services, Thais will practice more birth control than minority groups," and another 19 percent were undecided.[22] However, it seems gradually to have declined, and now appears dormant, if not dead, partly because the Chinese are more integrated into Thai life linguistically, culturally, and occupationally.

West Malaysia.   This country has the same ethnic mixture as Singapore but in significantly different proportions: 50 percent Malays, 30 percent Chinese, and 11 percent Indians. As in other fields, this balance has been involved in the development of the Malaysian population effort particularly since the Chinese are more economically and educationally advantaged and more urban than the Malays. After a perceived electoral setback for the Malays in 1969, for example, "some Malay politicians and religious teachers raised the possible relationship between the extension of the family planning programme and the ethnic balance in the country."[23] At a subsequent national forum, the director of the National Family Planning Board, when

asked about possible loss of political power if Malays were to adopt family planning, [replied]: "Political power does not spring from sheer numbers alone. Being in

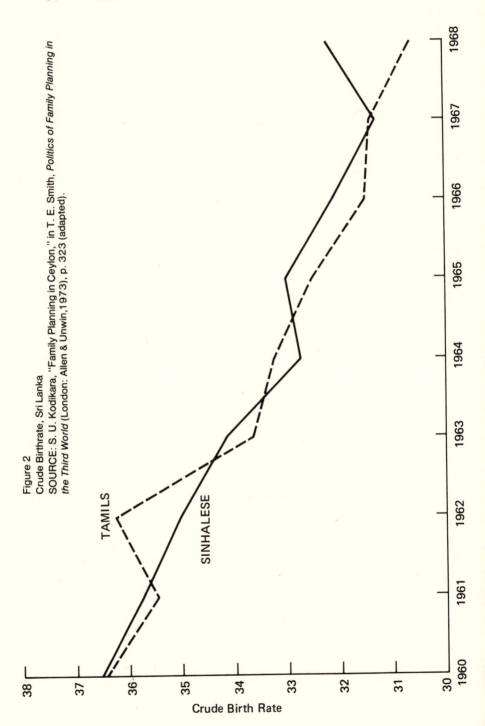

Figure 2
Crude Birthrate, Sri Lanka
SOURCE: S. U. Kodikara, "Family Planning in Ceylon," in T. E. Smith, *Politics of Family Planning in the Third World* (London: Allen & Unwin,1973), p. 323 (adapted).

a majority is not enough if others control the economy and are better educated. Hence the necessity to adopt family planning to catch up. In any case, even with family planning, Malays would remain a majority."[24]

At the same time, the national program placed its first clinics in the urban areas where the Chinese and the Indians lived and only later in the rural areas where Malays predominated—partly a strategic move to start where the task was easier but not without an eye to the political situation as well. However, the matter is now considered "not really a current issue in Malaysian politics. Non-Malays have not been drawn into a debate on family planning, and, indeed, the majority of political parties have little, if anything, to say about it," largely because respected leaders of several communities have supported the movement.[25] Moreover, fertility in the country has sharply fallen among all three ethnic groups—but always lowest among the Chinese (probably largely reflecting other social advantages), thus exercising a soothing effect.

Singapore.   This is another multiethnic society: 76 percent Chinese, 15 percent Malays, 7 percent Indians, and 2 percent other. In the eight-year period before the establishment of the National Family Planning Programme (1957-65), the total fertility rate fell by about 25 percent, almost all of it deriving from the Chinese community and suddenly leaving an ethnic disparity in fertility (measured in TFR, or total fertility rate) of about 50 percent in favor of the Moslems and the Indians. But in the following seven years (1966-73), when a strong family planning program was in full operation, the ethnic balance was restored: The TFR fell by another 30 percent, but by over half among the Moslems and the Indians. in 1957 there was a 15 percent spread in total fertility rates among the three groups; in 1973 that had fallen to 9 percent, but at a fertility level well below half (43 percent of 1957). As a high official observed, "Family planning had penetrated all ethnic, cultural and religious groups, though with differing timing, the Malays and Hindus being the last."[26] The acceptors in the national program were approximately proportionate in the three ethnic groups, but the Chinese were still marrying much later than the others (30 percent married among women twenty to twenty-four compared to over 50 percent for the other groups).[27]

Fiji.   This is another small island country with two major ethnic groups: Indian (50 percent) and Fijian (42 percent). About thirty years ago, the Indians exceeded the native population in numbers, and soon thereafter differential fertility became a persistent political issue. Indeed, the development of a family planning program in the early 1960s carried ethnic overtones from the start, including explicit calls upon the Indians

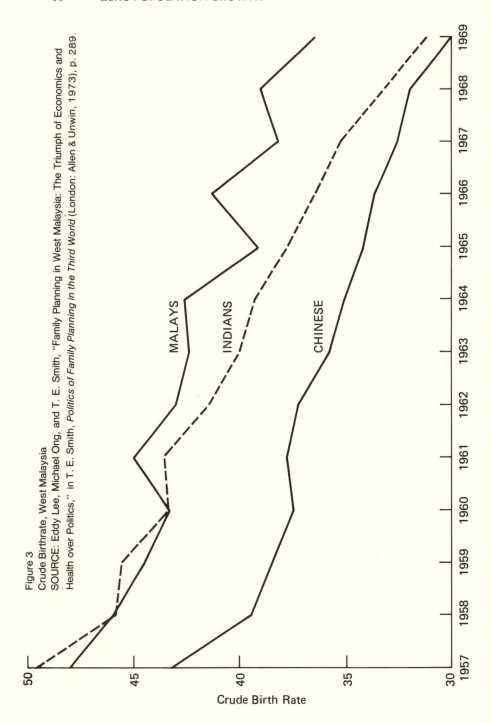

Figure 3
Crude Birthrate, West Malaysia
SOURCE: Eddy Lee, Michael Ong, and T. E. Smith, "Family Planning in West Malaysia: The Triumph of Economics and Health over Politics," in T. E. Smith, *Politics of Family Planning in the Third World* (London: Allen & Unwin, 1973), p. 289.

MALAYS

INDIANS

CHINESE

Crude Birth Rate

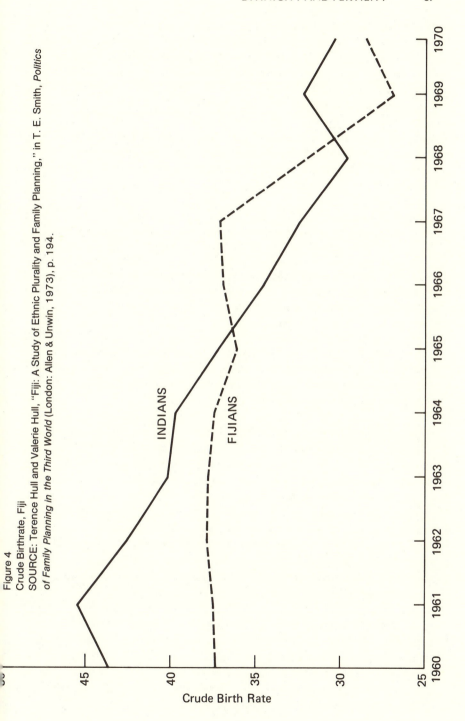

Figure 4
Crude Birthrate, Fiji
SOURCE: Terence Hull and Valerie Hull, "Fiji: A Study of Ethnic Plurality and Family Planning," in T. E. Smith, *Politics of Family Planning in the Third World* (London: Allen & Unwin, 1973), p. 194.

to control their population growth and expectations that the program would solve "the Indian problem" and "save" the Fijian race. At that time (around 1961), the crude birthrate (CBR) of the Indians was 45.5 and 37.4 for the Fijians, but about then the Indian rate began to fall sharply, with a remarkable decline by one-third by the end of the decade when it was within a point or two of the Fijian rate.

In the early years of the program, the Indians utilized the birth control services more than the Fijians did, though about half of the birthrate decline to the mid-1960s was the result of a rising age in marriage.[28] Throughout this period, a prominent part of the political debate about population and family planning was the concern about

the idea of a population growth race between the Fijian and Indian ethnic groups. The issue of whether or not Fiji is threatened by overpopulation has elicited state-ments which seem fairly clearly divided along racial lines. While Indians often contended that more people were needed to develop Fiji's resources fully and that redistribution of resources rather than population control would aid development, most Fijians and Europeans expressed concern that the resources of Fiji cannot support great increases of population.[29]

Not only was there concern about the numbers themselves but also about the related land tenure system and the voting procedures (based on com-munal rolls giving each group equal representation). By now, after the sharp decline in the Indian birthrate, there is much less political concern expressed on the issue than a generation ago.

Other.   There are a few other countries in the area where small ethnic minorities are given special treatment with regard to fertility- and mor-tality-related issues: *China,* where the government's efforts to reduce growth rates are applied in "national minority areas [where] appropriate measures are taken to facilitate population growth. . . ; in the national minority areas, a change has been brought about in the situation prevail-ing in the past, in which population grew at an extremely slow rate or even dropped sharply, owing to brutal persecution by the forces of reaction"[30]; *Taiwan,* where the family planning program was not extended to the aborigine population (250,000 out of fifteen million) for several years after it was provided to the general population in order to avoid any possible suggestion of impure motives; and *Australia,* where special consideration is required for the aborigine population: "they probably have the highest growth rate, the highest birth rate, the highest death rate, the worst health and housing, and the lowest educational, occupational, economic, social and legal status of any identifiable sec-tion of the Australian population," and what is needed is "a total pro-gramme of betterment" not limited to demographic measures.[31]

Middle East

Two of the world's major cases of concern are neighbors here: the Moslem/Christian issue in Lebanon and the Jewish/Arab issue in Israel, plus the probable case of Greek/Turkish tension in Cyprus.

Lebanon. The latest full census in this country was taken over forty years ago (plus a wartime count for rationing purposes, a "mini-census," over thirty years ago). The reason is well known: the system of political representation is delicately balanced between the two ethnic groups that make up the country. Given the sensitivity of internal politics (before the recent armed hostilities), there had been a tacit understanding not to risk the political consequences of the recalculation that would probably be required by a new census, in a system in which parliamentary seats are allocated by religion in the ratio of six Christians to five non-Christians (mainly Moslems). As was recently observed:

Policy makers have deliberately avoided this thorny issue because of the political implications and responses that may ensue. In fact, the fear of political repercussions is one reason why Lebanon has not had a census since 1932. The fundamental balance between sects is a principle that governs Lebanese political life. Any population policy that deliberately reflects on this balance is carefully avoided.[32]

According to a recent tabulation, Moslems have substantially higher fertility than their Christian counterparts at every age level (table 1).

At the end of World War II there were slightly more Christians than Moslems in the country. The estimates now are that there are slightly more Moslems, but the test was foregone by tacit agreement:

In general, the people of Lebanon do not think of themselves as having a population problem. . . . The primary concern is the fear on the part of the Christians that the Moslem birth rate will markedly alter the country's religious balance. There is uneasiness among the Moslems as well, over whether a Christian majority exists in the country. Religious groups watch anxiously the issuance of naturalization papers to people of various religions.[33]

Cyprus. Here too a census was involved. The 1970 census was postponed not out of concern over close balance—the Greeks are nearly 80 percent of the population, the Turks under 20 percent—but because of tensions and lack of communication between the two communities (soon to break into open violence). As the official Demographic Report for 1972 put it, "Due to the political anomaly prevailing in the island the Statistics and Research Department has been unable to collect detailed and up-to-date [vital] information."[34]

Table 1

**NUMBER OF CHILDREN EVER BORN TO LEBANESE WOMEN
BY AGE AND RELIGION**

Age of Women	Christians	Moslems
15-19	0.6	1.2
20-24	1.5	2.2
25-29	2.5	3.8
30-34	3.8	5.4
35-39	4.3	6.5
40-44	4.8	7.1
45-49	5.2	7.7
Total	3.8	5.1

Note: Data kindly provided by Joe Chamie; based on and adapted from 1971 Lebanese Fertility and Family Planning Survey conducted by the Lebanese Family Planning Association. The Moslem category includes Sunni, Shica, and Druze sects.

The crude birthrate is reportedly in the low 20s, with a growth rate of 1 percent or less, not because of high mortality but because of heavy emigration from the strife-torn island. Although no data are directly available, it would seem probable that the Greek birthrate is below the Turkish even though the latter are more urban: the district birthrates range between 24 and 14, far less than the range between the mother countries. In the 1950s the proportion of Greeks decreased by 1.9 percent and that of Turks increased by 0.2 percent, though migration was much involved. The two ethnic communities, particularly under the stress of events, are intensely loyal to their respective cultures, languages, and religions, and it would seem likely that their differential fertility has fueled the dispute, but I have been unable to find any documentation.[35]

Israel.   This may be the most dramatic case of all: a small country in a hostile region with an internal minority of the same ethnic stock as the hostile neighbors. Population size and growth (notably including immigration) relative to the region is of paramount importance, but differential fertility within the country is also of concern. This is indicated by various efforts to address the problem in recent years, culminating in the 1962 appointment of a national commission on the matter, the Natality Committee. In view of Israel's special circumstances, population has always been a political issue.

At independence in 1948, Israel was about 80 percent Jewish and 20 percent Arab; now, largely in consequence of the counterbalancing effects of Jewish immigration and Arab fertility, the population is nearly four times larger and 86 percent Jewish and 14 percent Arab. In the two decades from 1948 to 1968, just under 40 percent of the growth in the Jewish population of Israel came from natural increase (with over 60 percent from immigration), as against about 100 percent for the Arabs. But in recent years much more has come from Jewish natural increase as immigration has fallen. Throughout the country's history, Arab fertility has been much higher than Jewish; moreover, there has been a constant differential within the Jewish community itself, depending on national origin (see table 2).

Assuming the continuation of these patterns even for a limited period would imply that the less affluent, the less educated, the socially deprived section of the population would grow fast, while the affluent section would grow extremely slowly. . . . The Arab population in Israel . . . will increase rapidly and be equal in size to the Jewish population in less than three generations, assuming the continuation of current fertility and also assuming that no further substantial Jewish immigration takes place.[36]

Moreover, "family planning services are conspicuously absent from general public health services" though induced abortion is relatively available.[37]

Against this background, the Natality Committee advocated a pronatalist policy of psychological, economic, and monetary incentives, with this general tone: "If all families bore two children only, a dangerous demographic recession would follow. Families of three contribute just marginally, and only families of four or more children can make a real contribution toward the demographic revival of the nation."[38]

The opposing point of view, recognizing a rather rapid convergence of Jewish fertility toward the lower norms and considering a sharp reversal toward the large family to be most unlikely, concludes that the preferred policy would be twofold: encouragement of further Jewish immigration and spread of modern social conditions and fertility control throughout the country, especially to the disadvantaged groups. In this calculation, a net immigration of 15,000 per year is the rough equivalent of substantially (and unrealistically) higher Jewish fertility into the future (table 3). Moreover, in no realistically conceivable circumstance could even a successful pronatalist policy in Israel do much to increase the nation's share of the region's population (from 3.4 percent now to 5 percent by the end of the century under the most favorable assumptions) or to lower the proportion of Jews in the Israeli population (from 86 percent to 78 percent by then under the least favorable assumptions), let alone any consideration of high fertility in the homeland as a means for demographic revival of world Jewry (of which Israeli Jews are about 18 percent).[39] (See table 3).

Table 2

JEWISH AND ARAB NATALITY IN ISRAEL

	Gross Reproduction Rate (1966)	Crude Birth-rate (c 1970)	Rate of Natural Increase (c 1970)
Arabs	4.00	45.6	3.9%
Jews	1.65	24.2	1.7%
of European origin	1.19		
Israel-born	1.35		
of Afro-Asian origin	2.17		

Source: Gross reproduction rate from Dov Friedlander, "Israel," in Bernard Berelson, ed., *Population Policy in Developed Countries* (New York: McGraw-Hill, 1974), table 6, p. 50; data for crude birthrate and rate of natural increase from Dov Friedlander and Calvin Goldscheider, "Peace and the Demographic Future of Israel," *Journal of Conflict Resolution* 18, no. 3 (September 1974), table 1, p. 488.

Table 3

PROJECTED CONTRIBUTIONS OF FERTILITY AND IMMIGRATION TO GROWTH OF JEWISH POPULATION IN ISRAEL

	Jewish Population of Israel (in Millions)	
	1985	2000
Present fertility (2.6 children)		
No immigration	3.072	3.708
Immigration of 15,000	3.435	4.417
Fertility at level of large family (4.5 children)		
No immigration	3.252	4.623
Immigration of 15,000	3.633	5.426

Source: Adapted from Dov Friedlander, "Israel," in Bernard Berelson, ed., *Population Policy in Developed Countries* (New York: McGraw-Hill, 1974), p. 385.

Table 4

CRUDE BIRTHRATE IN IRELAND, 1960-62, BY RELIGION

	Northern Ireland	Republic
Catholic	28.3	22.0
Non-Catholic	19.5	13.2

Source: Adapted from Robert E. Kennedy, Jr., "Minority Group Status and Fertility: The Irish," *American Sociological Review* 38, no. 1 (February 1973), table 3, p. 89.

Europe

A number of countries in both Western and Eastern Europe are characterized by ethnic fertility differentials sufficient for public attention —
mainly religion in the West, nationality in the East.

Ireland. The fertility differences are substantial, and at different levels
in the Republic and in the North (or at least were over a decade ago).
(See table 4). By this measure (and the essential difference survives
the usual controls), religion makes a 30 percent to 40 percent difference
and residence about 20 percent to 30 percent. In the Republic, the religious
difference is less important politically; not only are the non-Catholics a
tiny proportion (about 5 percent), but they are older, have lower marriage
rates and birthrates, and are losing some population through intermarriage into the Catholic majority. The prime exception is the
imposition of Catholic-oriented beliefs with regard to the means of fertility control, though that too has recently been softened.

But religious differences do press hard in the North, to the point of
armed conflict. At the time of the partition in 1926, about one-third of
the population was Catholic; now it is barely one to two points higher.
That balance was not achieved through equivalence in fertility rates but
because heavy Catholic emigration (caused by low occupations) compensated over the years for higher fertility. Actually,

*in the creation of Northern Ireland from only six of the original nine counties of the
Province of Ulster, the link between religious composition and politics was a prime
consideration: if all nine counties had been included the Protestant majority would
have been only 57 percent instead of the 67 percent recorded. . . . Since the
partition, the relative size of the Catholic segment of the population, and the higher
Catholic fertility, have been widely recognized by both Catholics and Protestants
as having important political implications. For example, the former Northern Irish
Prime Minister, Capt. Terence O'Neill, made the following comments in a radio
interview following his resignation from office in 1969: "The basic fear of the
Protestants in Northern Ireland is that they will be outbred by the Roman Catholics.
It is as simple as that."*[40]

Given the strength of feelings, "in the last few years, the question of the
religious balance of the population in both parts of Ireland has been
raised in public debate. In the Republic, the idea that the non-Catholic
minority is being pressured out of the country is sometimes expressed,
while in the north, the notion of a *revanche du berceau* and an eventual
Roman Catholic majority is feared by some."[41] The question of contraceptive availability in the Republic is closely tied to religious position —
and indeed utilized as an argument against unification by some political

positions in the north as an indicator of what would happen under the majority's rule.

Belgium. The basic ethnic dichotomy is all the stronger for its reinforcing qualities: Flanders in the north: Flemish-speaking, Catholic, traditionally agricultural, and conservative; and Wallony in the south: French-speaking, less religious, long industrialized, and socialist. Flanders now contains about 56 percent of the population, up five points since 1930; Wallony 32 percent, down five points since then, a shift attributable largely to fertility differentials. Particularly over the past two decades, the linguistic problem in the relations between the two communities has been at the center of political life. The new constitutional amendments of 1970-71 recognize that officially in the formal governmental structure of the country, a kind of federalism.

From the fertility standpoint, the situation was eased in the 1960s by a sharper decline from the higher base in Flanders so that the differential in birthrates became only about one point in 1970 as against three points in 1963. About fifteen years ago, the matter was sufficiently alive to give rise to a special consultation for the French-speaking sector (the Sauvy report) that recommended various pronatalist measures (such as tax relief and child assistance on the French model), but that was unacceptable as a discriminatory proposal for one sector of the society. The government countered with its own commission (the Délperee report), which issued a wide-ranging document of a broad social security character like the Swedish model—not "population" but "quality of life"—but the report as a whole was never activated. The child allowances

were implemented without any relationship to population policy but rather in connection with the regional origin of the minister in charge. It is dubiously coincidental that increases in allowances for higher birth ranks were settled by Flemish ministers (Flanders having higher parity children than Wallony), with an inverse action taken when Walloon ministers were in office. [42]

Czechoslovakia. The basic regional differentiation, reinforced by religion, has a long demographic history as well. The Czech West (now 68 percent of the population) was historically part of Central Europe; not so the strongly Catholic Slovakian population of the East. Fertility differences between the two can be traced back two hundred years: Czech decline not long after the French, culminating in rapid fall in the late nineteenth century, Slovakian starting then and proceeding to the mid-twentieth century. In 1960 the birthrates were 13.3 and 22.1, respectively, with rates of natural increase ranging from 0.4 percent to 1.4 percent; but fertility fell in the decade, to a low point in 1968 and then slightly up (though with a convergence between the two communities) in 1971 to CBR 15.7 and 18.2. As close observers have concluded, "This historically constituted distinction . . . will require at least another ten years in order to even the fertility levels of the two Czechoslovak populations."[43] The differentials do not now appear to be of major policy concern, and certainly not of policy differentiation.

Yugoslavia.   This country contains a variety of nationalities differentiated regionally and theologically as well. And the differences find expression in birthrates too (table 5).

While, as regards particular demographic characteristics of the population of various nationalities (mortality, some structures, etc.), there are already tendencies toward equalization, differences with respect to fertility have remained exceptionally pronounced. We consider that it can be assumed that the different fertility rates in some nationalities are mainly caused by the factors of environment in which the population of these nationalities live or, in other words, by the impact of socio-economic factors. However, it is likely that the mentality, habit, tradition, customs and other elements, which characterize a given nationality group, constitute the cause of differentiation as regards the fertility of population.[44]

In the postwar period, birthrates have declined among all nationalities, but the differentials were not particularly narrowed. Note that Catholic fertility is on the low side and that the border provinces tend to reflect the fertility of their ethnic cousins across the border notably the highest (Kosovo/Albania) and the lowest (Vojvodina/Hungary).

In general, nationality issues are at the center of Yugoslavian politics. However, such fertility differences have not surfaced as a major issue though there is the usual grumbling in the industrial sectors (Serbia and Croatia) about their burden in carrying the less developed areas with their higher fertility and population growth.

U.S.S.R.   Here the differentials have also centered on national minorities — geographically dispersed, different in religion and language, widely diverse in birthrates. Broadly, concentric arcs centered on the Leningrad area show higher fertility the farther out toward the periphery (table 6). In a more detailed analysis of thirty-six ethnic groups (see table 7),

those below the median congregate in the European portion of the USSR and consist of traditionally non-Moslem groups speaking a language of East European origin, [whereas those above the median constitute] the Asian regions of the USSR . . . by and large inhabited by traditionally Moslem and some Buddhist groups whose indigenous tongue is related to either the Turkic, Mongolian, or Caucasian subdivision.[45]

Table 5
YUGOSLAV BIRTHRATES, BY PROVINCE

Province	Religion	Percent of Population	Crude Birth-rate (1966)
Serbia	Orthodox	25.5	18.2
Croatia	Catholic	21.6	16.6
Bosnia/Herzegovina	Moslem & Mixed	18.3	26.3
Slovenia	Catholic	8.4	19.1
Macedonia	Orthodox	8.0	26.9
Vojvodina	Catholic	9.5	14.7
Kosovo	Moslem	6.1	37.3
Montenegro	Orthodox	2.6	23.0

Source: D. Breznik, "Fertility of the Yugoslav Population," in Egon Szabady, ed., *World View of Population Problems* (Budapest: Akadémiai Kiadó, 1968), p. 64.

Table 6
BIRTHRATE DIFFERENCES BY REGION, USSR

	Percent of Population	Crude Birth-rate, 1973	CBR Range by Republics
Baltic (Latvian, Lithuanian, Estonian)	3	15.1	13.9–16.0
Western (Russian, Ukrainian, Belorussian, Moldavian)	79	15.2	14.9–20.4
Caucasian (Georgian, Armenian Azerbaidzhan)	5	22.2	18.2–25.4
Asian (Tadzhik, Turkmen, Uzbek, Kirgiz, Kazakh)	13	29.4	23.2–35.6

Source: United Nations, Economic and Social Council, "Post-War Demographic Trends and the Outlook Until the Year 2000," prepared by the Secretariat of the Economic Commission for Europe, July 1975; adapted from table V.17.

Thus with the U.S.S.R., at least until quite recently, there was a spread in fertility rates approximating that between the developed and the developing countries, though the extremely high rates now appear to be in process of decline (and within such ethnoprovinces are smaller ethnic groupings with even greater fertility differentials, for example, birthrates of 60 and 66 were reported around 1960 for the Ingush and Chechen, small Moslem groups in the Caucasian region).[46]

The large majority of the population of the U.S.S.R. (about 80 percent) lives in republics with relatively low birthrates. Nevertheless, concern has been expressed on the nationality differentials. For example, a symposium on regional features of population growth, held in May 1968,

Table 7

SELECTED CHARACTERISTICS OF 36 ETHNIC GROUPS IN THE U.S.S.R.

Geographic Region	Ethnic Group	Traditional Religion	Child-Woman Ratio	
			Below Median[a]	Above Median
Baltic states	Latvian (F)	Protestant	0.612	
	Estonian (F)	Protestant	0.638	
	Lithuanian (L)	Catholic	0.823	
Western U.S.S.R.	Karelian (F)	Orthodox	0.702	
	Ukrainian (S)	Orthodox	0.714	
	Belorussian (S)	Orthodox	0.836	
	Russian (S)	Orthodox	0.863	
	Moldavian (R)	Orthodox	1.190	
East European Russia	Mordvinian (F)	Orthodox	0.933	
	Chuvash (T)	Orthodox	1.037	
	Komi (F)	Orthodox	1.052	
	Tartar (T)	Moslem	1.105	
	Udmurt (F)	Orthodox	1.131	
	Mari (F)	Orthodox	1.146	
	Bashkir (T)	Moslem		1.431
Caucasus	Georgian (C)	Orthodox	0.905	
	Ossetin (I)	Orthodox	0.998	
	Armenian (C)	Orthodox	1.240	
	Avarian (C)	Moslem	1.334	
	Dargin (C)	Moslem		1.427
	Kumyk (T)	Moslem		1.504
	Kabardian (C)	Moslem		1.537
	Kaimyk (M)	Buddhist		1.646
	Balkar (T)	Moslem		1.698
	Azerbaydzhan (T)	Moslem		1.711
	Lezghinian (C)	Moslem		1.722
	Ingush (C)	Moslem		2.042
	Chechen (C)	Moslem		2.204
Southern and Northern Siberia	Buryat (M)	Buddhist		1.460
	Tuvian (T)	Buddhist		1.728
	Yakut (T)	Orthodox		1.494
Central Asia	Tadzhik (T)	Moslem		1.782
	Turkmen (T)	Moslem		1.809
	Uzbek (T)	Moslem		1.878
	Kirgiz (T)	Moslem		1.885
	Kazakh (T)	Moslem		1.896

a. Median fertility level estimated at 1,380 children age 0-9 per 1,000 women in the 20–49 age group (or roughly equivalent to the GRR of 2,330 daughters per 1,000 women). Capital letters in the parentheses refer to linguistic affiliations, such as (S) Slavic, (F) Finnic, (C) Caucasian, (M) Mongolian, (T) Turkic, (I) Iranian, (R) Rumanian.

Source: Based on data from the 1959 U.S.S.R. Census of Population and other sources.

under the auspices of the Coordinating Council for Population Problems of the U.S.S.R. Ministry of High and Specialized Secondary Education, concluded that "demographic policy can be differentiated in accordance with the peculiarities of individual areas. Depending on concrete conditions, it encourages births in some cases and is an influence for their reduction or stabilization in others. . . . At the symposium, measures contributing to an increase in the birth rate in certain of the country's republics and provinces were recognized as necessary."[47] This stance is taken to mean that the birthrate of the core republic should be increased somewhat. According to a recent review,

although no formal government policy has emerged, the majority of demographers promote a policy of raising the national birthrate through an increase in fertility in low-fertility areas. . . . The second major concern [of policy, after the decline in the rate of natural increase] is with the relatively high proportion of all births that occurred to the Muslim nationalities in the Soviet Union and the relatively low proportion that occurred to the Slavic groups. . . . Although I have never found any direct statement that too high a proportion of all babies are born to Moslem nationalities, one can note the effort by Soviet demographers to publicize the large territorial and ethnic differences in fertility that do exist. . . . The most frequently heard policy position is that the Soviet Union should seek to raise its birthrate but do so primarily by increasing the birthrate in the low-fertility areas. "It is necessary" (says a leading Soviet demographer) "to introduce a differentiated demographic legislation so that what is appropriate, say, for the Ukraine and the Baltic region is completely inappropriate in Central Asia or Azerbaidzhan."[48]

To date, to my knowledge, no such policies have been adopted, but the differentials appear to be diminishing somewhat, mainly because of a lowering of the higher birthrates.

Other.   There are other concerns about differential fertility by ethnicity in Europe, but on the whole they are less important than those cited above: *the Netherlands,* where the religious/regional difference — the Protestant north, the Catholic south — was accompanied by fertility differentials.[49] However, the 1960s brought a much faster fertility decline in Catholic provinces, so that a 16 percent differential in marital fertility around 1960 was more than eliminated by 1967. Although earlier non-Catholics widely believed that "it is the secret purpose of Catholics to 'outbreed' the Protestants," the issue is apparently not pressing at this time.[50] *Great Britain,* with regard to the fertility (as well as the immigration) of "colored" from the New Commonwealth countries, which "according to a recent estimate, may currently exceed the national average by 50 percent"[51] and, together with other ethnic immigrants, accounts for about 10 percent of all births in Britain.[52] Even so, the projections suggest that by the end of the century the "coloured minorities" would constitute from 4 to 6 percent of the population, as against 2.4 percent in 1968.[53] *Rumania,* where "natality is much lower in the western district than in the eastern part of the country (also reflecting ethnic differentials). But the gap is gradually narrowing because of the recent industrialization of eastern districts which, in the past, were primarily agricultural; while in the west, industrialization began many decades ago."[54] *Bulgaria,* where the celebrated peaking of child assistance on the third child is meant mainly to stimulate an extra birth among the dominant population but also, reportedly, to discourage high-parity births for welfare payments among the gypsies; and *Hungary,* where there is also some muttering about the high fertility of the gypsies.

North America

Both Canada and the United States have been marked by ethnic fertility differentials, which now appear to be narrowing.

Canada.   The ethnic differential from the outset has been nationality/religious/linguistic in character—the British (now about 45 percent) and the French (about 30 percent). The other segment of the population, from other European stocks, has assimilated to the British, and the dichotomy has been reinforced by the residential concentration of the French-speaking population in Quebec. Over most of the past century the French proportion of the population has stayed at about 30 percent, balanced similarly to the Irish and Israeli cases: high British immigration against high French fertility ("cradle revenge"), the latter not so much deliberate policy as the effect of religion and traditional values. Until quite recently the differential was substantial, "as great as fertility differences between developed and underdeveloped nations and account[ing] in large part for differences in family size between two nations."[55] However, as in other Western countries, the birthrate declined substantially in the 1960s (about ten points) and most sharply in Quebec (from 26.1 to 14.8), making it the lowest among the provinces:[56] "The overfertility of French Canadians has progressively been reduced and is now quite negligible."[59] That, plus a slow assimilation of French Canadians outside Quebec, has meant that the proportion of French-speaking people in Canada is slowly declining, down to 27 percent in 1971, and that drop in turn intensified the separatist tendencies of the province as a "survival" measure and led to national legislation about language usage throughout the country.

United States.   Here there are a number of ethnic communities with differential fertility patterns: blacks, Catholics (and differences by nationality within), Mormons, Chicanos and other Spanish-speaking, Indians, Hutterites (all on the high side), and Jews and Orientals (on the low side). In short, at least historically, differential fertility has characterized virtually all ethnic groups in the country, and the national figures are the resulting aggregate weighted by group size. Concern appears to arise under two conditions: when the minority group is large enough to "make a difference" (as nationally with blacks and Catholics or regionally with Chicanos and perhaps Mormons) or when the group itself becomes aroused to a perceived need for higher fertility for political or other reasons (as occasionally with blacks, Indians, and Jews).

To my knowledge, there is no single reliable source of comparable fertility measurements across the range of ethnic groups, but the broad picture can be pieced together to show rough orders of magnitude (table 8). And, just to establish an upper limit, the Hutterites serve as the current standard for sustained high fertility—about 8.5 children per married woman.

The broad picture emerges: the Indians, the Spanish speaking, and the Mormons substantially above the national average (say, 30-40 percent), blacks and Catholics[58] well above (15-20 percent), Oriental-Americans somewhat below (10 percent), Jews well below (25 percent). Indeed, in the United States, race and religion are key predictors of fertility, from the high of the Hutterites, Mormons, Chicanos, and Indians to the low of the Jews and the Japanese-Americans.[59] The ethnic groups with lower than national fertility are quite small (Jews under 3 percent and Orientals 0.6 percent), and two of those with higher fertility are relatively large (Catholics 20 percent and blacks 11 percent).[60]

As of 1970, those counties in the United States with substantial fertility (four or more children in the average family) were mainly characterized as rural *and* ethnic—and thus somewhat outside the mainstream of American life in fertility as in other respects. Figures 5 and 6 show how they are distributed across the country by ethnic and geographical status. But the situation has recently been changing, and there appears to be a convergence in progress. In the decade up to 1967-70, urban white fertility declined 27 percent compared to 30 percent for the Chicano and Spanish-surname group, 37 percent for blacks, and 45 percent for Indians:

The continuous decline in fertility in the United States since 1957, while affecting all elements of the population, has been most pronounced and most rapid among those groups which previously had the highest fertility—blacks, American Indians and Mexican Americans. . . . The decline was especially rapid for third and higher order births, suggesting a heavy concentration of completed fertility at two-child families.[61]

Table 8

RECENT ETHNIC DIFFERENCES IN FERTILITY, UNITED STATES

Average Children Ever Born Per Woman (35–44 years), June 1974[a]

White	2.89
Black	3.50
Spanish origin	3.59

Total Fertility for 1926–35 Cohort ("Baby Boom" Mothers)[b]

Jewish	2.13
Catholic	3.64
Mormon	3.52
White	3.10
Black	4.13

Cumulative Fertility Rate, Women 45 and Over, 1957[c]

Jewish	2.2
Protestant	2.8
Catholic	3.1

Crude Marital Fertility Rates, Wife under 40, 1967–70[d]

Japanese-American	0.385
Chinese-American	0.425
Black	0.436
Indian	0.510
Puerto Rico American	0.521
Spanish surname	0.550
Chicano	0.568

Total Children Ever Born, Women Aged 35–44, 1970 Census[e]

Japanese-American	2.2
Chinese-American	2.8
Black	3.5
Spanish origin	3.5
Chicano	4.2
Indian	4.3

a. U.S. Census Bureau, "Fertility Expectations of American Women: June 1974," *Current Population Reports,* Series P-20, no. 277 (February 1975), adapted from tables 17, 18, 19.

b. Charles F. Westoff and Norman Ryder, *The Contraceptive Revolution* (Princeton, N.J.: Princeton University Press, 1977), from table X-1.

c. Sidney Goldstein, "American Jewry, 1970: A Demographic Profile," *American Jewish Year Book* 72 (1971): 17.

d. James A. Sweet, "Differentials in the Rate of Fertility Decline: 1960-1970," *Family Planning Perspectives* 6, no. 2 (Spring 1974), p. 104, from table 2: rate based on average number of children under the age of three living in household with own mother (married, under age 40)."

e. U.S. Census Bureau, "Women by Number of Children Ever Born," *Subject Reports,* Series PC(2)-3a, July 1973; adapted.

HIGH FERTILITY AREAS IN THE UNITED STATES, 1970

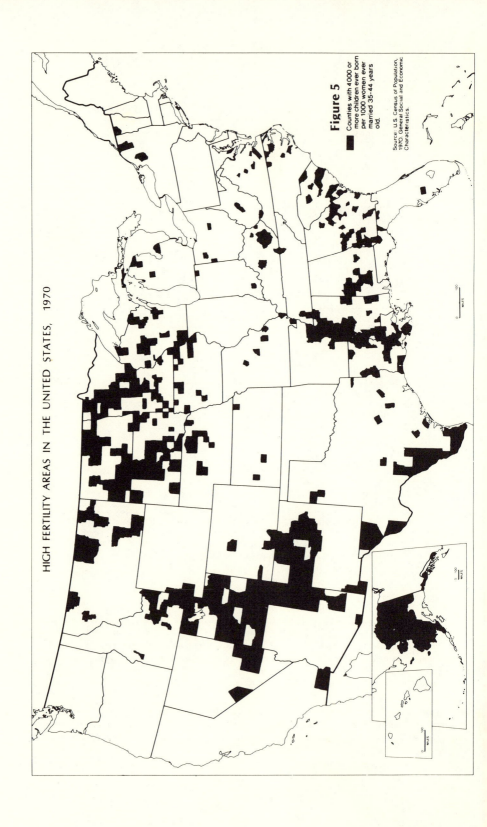

Figure 5

■ Counties with 4,000 or more children ever born per 1000 women ever married 35-44 years old.

Source: U.S. Census of Population, 1970 General Social and Economic Characteristics.

Children ever born per 1000 women ever married, 35 to 44 years old, 1970

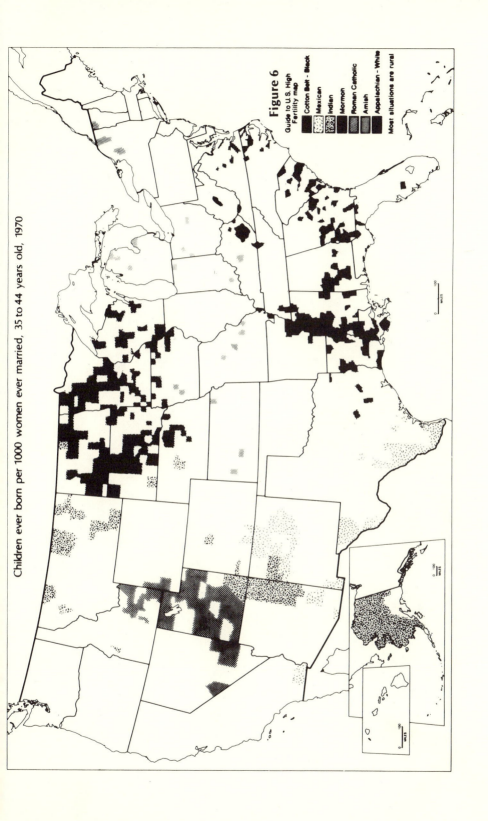

Figure 6

Guide to U.S. High
Fertility map

Cotton Belt - Black
Mexican
Indian
Mormon
Roman Catholic
Amish
Appalachian - White

Most situations are rural

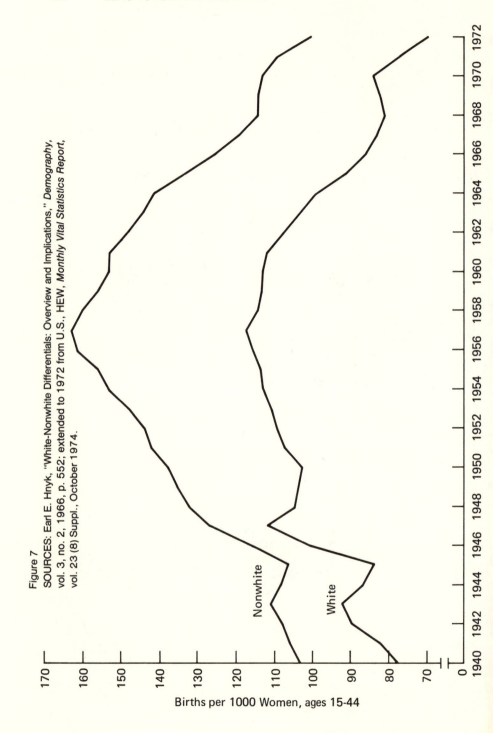

Figure 7
SOURCES: Earl E. Hnyk, "White-Nonwhite Differentials: Overview and Implications," *Demography*, vol. 3, no. 2, 1966, p. 552; extended to 1972 from U.S., HEW, *Monthly Vital Statistics Report*, vol. 23 (8) Suppl., October 1974.

Births per 1000 Women, ages 15-44

Similarly:

The declines, both absolute and relative, were twice as large for blacks than for whites, and twice as large for Catholics than for non-Catholics. As a result both the race and the religious differential closed by more than half a birth. The difference between white and black fertility as of the 1966-70 period was reduced to .53 births; and for Catholics-non-Catholics to .51 births. Since fertility has continued to fall very sharply since the 1966-70 period, these differentials today may be even closer together.[62]

The decline largely derives from decline in unwanted fertility rather than a shift in family-size norms. Says a leading expert in this field:

The greatest declines in unwanted fertility rates were observed among blacks and among white Catholics. The race differential still existed as of 1966-70 . . . but signs of rapid convergence were evident. . . . The Catholic-non-Catholic difference had virtually disappeared. . . . Nearly all of the excess of black over white fertility is due to the considerably higher unwanted fertility among blacks. Given the substantial reduction in the unwanted fertility rate among blacks across the generations, a rapidly increasing convergence of black and white marital fertility can be expected during the current decade. . . . Such a convergence was clearly evident during the 1960s in the trend of Catholic and non-Catholic fertility because of the greater decline among Catholic women. The remaining differential fertility in the period of 1966-70 (15%), is unlike the white/black difference, due to differences in the number of children wanted.[63]

Moreover, there is evidence that the improved contraceptive technology of the latter 1960s contributed to the fertility decline, and the same can be said in the case of the blacks for the publicly financed family planning programs of the period[64] and for the legalization of induced abortion in the early 1970s.[65] Thus the major high-fertility ethnic groups made considerable advances in the rational control of their fertility, moving in this respect toward their low-fertility counterparts.

Nonetheless, or perhaps hence, the family planning programs and the general concern about population stabilization—which requires more "sacrifice" of fertility from some than for others—gave rise to a certain amount of dissent within the black community, especially by its more militant wings:

In the black community, the deepest emotional source of this attitude is the apprehension that population policy and fertility control programs are genocidal attempts by the whites to eliminate the blacks. Such an attitude is reinforced by the appearance in ghettos of birth control clinics without pediatric or maternal health clinics or by occasional public proposals for compulsory sterilization of women on welfare having an additional child. Another related source is the concern that the dominant white community is trying to substitute population control for economic development—an attitude not dissimilar to that voiced occasionally by representatives of some developing nations. Still another expression takes the form of connecting increased population with increasing political power—a view strengthened by recent elections to office of black mayors and other government officials. . . . The picture of the attitudes of black leaders is diverse, ranging from indifference to animosity. In the black population at large, however, the average person, especially the woman, is just as anxious to regulate her childbearing as is her white counterpart.[66]

Finally, in recent years, as Jewish consciousness has again been raised by the political situation of Israel, there have again been calls for higher fertility in that traditionally low-fertility community (now with a birthrate approximating or below replacement), down from its high of 3.7 percent of the U.S. population in the late 1930s to under 3 percent today and falling, although still nearly half of world Jewry. In response to this situation, the newly elected president of the New York Board of Rabbis recently called for at least three children per Jewish family, which would amount to a substantial increase. Zero population growth, he said,

should find no application in the Jewish community. . . . Is it not obvious that in terms of Jewish survival, the European Holocaust of the war years and the Holocaust-size loss in Americans during the last three decades [by his reckoning, six million where there should be twelve million] produced the same result? [Without] an increase in population, it [the American Jewish community] will grow weaker and will face a threat to its existence. . . . Three children should be the minimum number for Jewish families, but the larger the better.[67]

But there is another view to the contrary:

This decline in relative numbers may not be very significant, since Jews have never constituted a numerically large segment of the population. If anything, it is noteworthy that, despite their small numbers, they are generally afforded the social position of the third major religious group in the country. There seems little reason to expect that this situation will change even though their percentage in the total population declines further, particularly since Jews, both as a group and individually, will undoubtedly continue to play significant roles in specific spheres of American life, such as cultural activities, education, and urban politics. From the demographic point of view, more important factors may be influencing the position of the Jewish community within the total American community, among them changes in the geographical concentration of Jews in certain parts of the nation as well as their disproportional representation in selected socioeconomic strata of the population.[68]

—to which could be added the political strength of Jewish residential concentration in New York and major cities.

SUMMARY

That is a highly compressed overview of ethnic differentials in fertility that have become politically problematic within countries—surely not an exhaustive exploration in any one case, probably not a complete set of such cases. Nevertheless, this overview is illustrative, perhaps representative, of the situation. This account has been limited to fertility differentials, without full regard to the differentials in migration, mortality, nuptiality, and age structure that would refine issues of population growth; yet omitting migration, the fertility differentials usually denote growth differentials of a similar order of magnitude.

CONDITION, CAUSE, AND CONSEQUENCE

The *condition* is present in many—perhaps most—pluralistic societies around the world. The condition is independent of type of country; it appears in large and small, in developed and developing, in capitalist and socialist, in religious and secular, in East and West, and in between. It involves all the major ethnic distinctions—race, religion, nationality, language. But although it is present, it is seldom manifest. There is "the existence of different demographic communities within the same society, with the consequent exacerbation of related social and political problems . . . although nowhere is it an explicitly pursued goal of national policy to equalize the vital rates of such internal divisions."[69] Still, in the very nature of the case, there may be more concern than gets expressed in formal doctrine, or for that matter in writing.

Indeed, an extensive study of European fertility has concluded that fertility norms and behavior were themselves diffused precisely through such "natural" communities.[70] In another view,

These examples point to a shift from concern with differential fertility rates among socioeconomic classes [an issue in much of Western Europe in the nineteenth century when conflicts were mainly along class lines] to a concern with differential fertility rates among populations having different cultural values, . . . or the changing proportions of racial, religious, or tribal groups [when] the difference is seen as having a significant political effect.[71]

Nor is there anything surprising here: perceived group differences have always presented difficulties of accommodation to human beings and particularly those of real or perceived permanence, fundamental and ineradicable.

At the same time, with only a few possible exceptions, the condition has not presented an issue of overriding importance to the body politic. It is mainly a limited affair. The differences, though present, are typically small and not very visible to the naked eye of social observance: a one-child differential per family is substantial. When the ethnic group is a small minority and not politically or economically powerful, even a large differential is primarily of only academic interest, as with the Hutterites in the United States and Canada. Moreover, in a number of countries—both developing: Mauritius, Singapore, Malaysia, Sri Lanka, Fiji; and developed: Belgium, Czechoslovakia, Netherlands, Canada, the United States—the differentials are narrowing:

The trend towards a diminution of the differential in a number of countries has been attributed to several factors: (a) a modification of traditional attitudes on the part of certain religious bodies towards ideals and practices which affect family size; (b) a weakening of the influence of religious doctrine and tradition; (c) a lessening in the nonreligious differences which appear in part to have contributed to the religious differential in fertility.[72]

Finally, within the demographic sphere, migration differentials by ethnicity are probably more visible, perhaps more telling; and in the political sphere generally there are many issues of much greater concern.[73]

Nonetheless, concern continues to be expressed, both nationally and beyond. A recent writer goes so far as to refer to the

critical problem of competitive breeding [as] in my judgement one of the world's central problems. . . . This topic, even more delicate than that of population control, rarely receives mention but it is a nettle which must sooner or later be firmly grasped. How can man ever control his overall population size within the carrying capacity of the environment whilst individual groups are remorselessly competing for numerical superiority, regardless of the consequences?[74]

—though this author was thinking of intercountry competitions as well as intra-.

The *causes* of such ethnic differentials are a matter of dispute within the scientific community: are they genuine (deriving somehow from the ethnic characteristics themselves) or are they spurious (reflecting merely some simultaneous other differences, in urban residence or education or income or occupation or socioeconomic status or some similar characteristic)? To any such complicated question the answer is seldom definitive, but the current judgment would appear to be that in most ethnic situations in most countries the difference is real.

Take the central case of religion. Across the world, three religious communities have distinctive and consistent fertility patterns: Moslems very high, Catholics higher than their national counterparts, Jews low. And such differences have some historical validity.

Over a long period of time Jews have had smaller families and have planned them more rationally—not just in the United States, not just recently, not just through social position.[75] Similarly "the cross-national pattern for Catholics is equally clear, and higher Catholic fertility has been observed in almost every 'developed' country where data are available."[76] In such countries "Catholic fertility exceeds that of non-Catholic in almost every country and socio-economic group," and especially where they are a distinguishable and self-defined minority.[77] As for Moslems, "within the important limitations of the data it may be said that Moslem natality (1) is almost universally high, (2) shows no evidence of important trends over time, and is generally higher than that of neighboring peoples of other major religions."[78]

In a review, the United Nations concludes:

... in any study of fertility differentials based on religion, it is important to consider to what extent the observed fertility differences between religious groups may be due to differences in income, occupation, education, urban-rural residence or some other non-religious factors. These studies have found, generally, that while socio-economic and residential factors often account for a substantial part of the religious fertility differential, they do not account for all of it.[79]

In sharp compression, whatever the full explanation, some of the reasons appear to be distinctive to each: cultural practices in family life and particularly the subordination of women among Moslems, doctrinal beliefs with reference to fertility norms and means of fertility control among Catholics (now weakening in the West), high social mobility combined with the historical "insecurities and marginality" of small-minority status among Jews.[80]

In the past five years or so have appeared a spate of papers seeking to explore the underlying causes of differential ethnic fertility through two competing hypotheses. First is the "assimilationist" or "characteristics" hypothesis that as ethnic groups become similar in social, economic, and demographic characteristics and thus assimilated into the mainstream, their fertility will also converge. The other is the "minority group status" hypothesis that fertility will remain low if the (small) minority group is after social mobility, has no pronatalist ideology ("particularized theology"), and suffers "insecurities and marginality" in its status (Jews in America); if not, it can be quite high as a matter of group preservation (Hutterites, Hasidim, and Black Muslims). This second hypothesis also holds that fertility will remain high if the group is large enough to challenge for political power (Catholics in Holland), if its chances for social mobility are not good (Catholics in Northern Ireland), or if its position in a heterogeneous society intensifies its religious feeling and the fertility norms that go with it (higher Catholic fertility in Australia, New Zealand, Canada, and the United States than in the Catholic majorities in Argentina, France, Italy, Hungary).

The outcome to date is inconclusive, as indicated by this conclusion from a recent article: "The findings of this study ... strongly suggest a minority group status effect. But they also suggest ... that with the assimilation of minority groups, the fertility of majority and minority groups converge."[81] In short, any narrowing of differences in subgroups is taken to support one hypothesis and any remaining difference to support the other.

So on the whole ethnic differentials in fertility appear to be real, not explainable away by reference to other social characteristics of the groups involved. But even if they are spurious, that is somewhat beside the point of policy-oriented concern, since the perception is also real in the sense that it leads to consequences and whatever the true cause, the fact remains that a clearly identifiable ethnic group has different fertility. In fact, the overlapping characteristics have been given a reverse twist, so to speak: "It would appear that rich/poor differences in fertility are mainly perceived as publicly troublesome only if simultaneously ethnic in character, as they typically are in non-homogeneous societies."[82]

Finally, the *consequences* of such differentials are considered to be mainly political — the power reflected in numbers:

In a democracy where one man has one vote it would seem obvious that groups with large populations would have more power than groups with a small number. Certainly many minority racial, religious, and ethnic groups have often assumed that they could relieve themselves of persecution only if they could increase their number sufficiently to gain greater voting power. In the United States it has been suggested that elements within the Roman Catholic Church may have encouraged large families among Catholic parishioners in order to gain the Church greater political strength. . . . In many cases a large population has provided a minority group with an increase in political power. In the early days of the United States, Roman Catholics suffered a great deal of political persecution at the hands of the overwhelming majority of Protestants. Eventually, however, as their numbers increased [through immigration as well as through fertility], the Catholics found themselves in an ever more favorable political position.[83]

This was particularly so when regional or local concentrations are considered: Catholics in Massachusetts, Jews in New York.

In any case, the road to political power through differential population growth is a long one. Consider these examples (based on simplistic assumptions of no migration or other demographic differentials, but suggesting orders of magnitude):[84]

With another child per family, when would U.S. Jews become
6 percent of the U.S. population?   111 years
. . . when would they total twelve million?   45 years

With a half-child differential in family size, when would U.S.
blacks become 25 percent of the U.S. population?   94 years

With the continuance of present birthrates in Northern Ireland,
when would the Catholics become 51 percent of the population?   82 years

With the continuance of present birthrates in Belgium, when would
the Walloons become 51 percent of the population?   200 years

With the continuance of present birthrates in Cyprus, when would
the Turks become 51 percent of the population?   143 years

With the continuance of present differentials in population growth,
when would the Moslems in India become 25 percent of the popu-
lation?   123 years

Policy does not usually get made, let alone applied, for such long-term prospects, and certainly not on such changeable matters as fertility rates. Moreover, as noted above, "an increase in population is not the only road to greater power for a minority group. . . . In all probability, Jews have increased potency in the United States not through an increase in number . . . but because so many individual Jews have gained influential positions in the society."[85] And the same situation obtains with regard to the small Chinese minorities in Southeast Asia.

Finally, in an economic consequence of differential ethnic fertility, felt on the individual level, the high fertility cohort is penalized by its own size in achieving educational and occupational mobility for succeeding generations:

The effect is to exacerbate a demand for government interventions if the economic characteristics and political opportunities of the groups are unequal. Among underprivileged groups, RPC [rapid population change] tends to increase differentiation and discrimination because their numbers increase faster than their opportunities. Demands for new opportunities could affect governmental services if politicians decide to respect rising group expectations, to capitalize on the awareness of group differences, or to respond to potentially effective organizational activity on the part of emergent groups.[86]

As for the effect of population growth in general upon ethnic tensions, there are as usual two sides to the question: (1) "In countries which do not have a homogeneous population, rapid population growth creates or aggravates political and economic conflicts between racial, cultural, religious, and linguistic groups."[87] (2) "There is less likelihood of ethnic conflict when all groups are growing than when some are growing and some declining. . . . Growth simplifies problems of accommodation and change."[88]

In any case, what is to be done if ethnic fertility differentials are "unacceptable"? What have these countries tried to do? The list is short: try to manipulate child assistance stipends (Belgium), try to manipulate family planning assistance (United States, Malaysia, Thailand), depend on migration in or out (Israel, Ireland, South Africa), exhort (Israel, U.S.S.R., South Africa), or look away (Lebanon, Nigeria, Cyprus). Given the conflict situation in which the ethnic groups are rooted to begin with, discriminatory policy of any strength is countraindicated at the outset short of repressive measures; and it may be that most governments are not particularly concerned not only by the substance of the matter, as suggested above, but also by two other considerations: acceptable policy interventions are not available, and the remedies are of such a long-run character as not to warrant much policy attention.

The issues, in short, lie deeper than fertility. If ethnic relations are poor, fertility gets caught up as an element in the conflict but cannot readily be addressed outside the arena; if they are good, the issue falls away. Like other problems, this one may be better solved indirectly. "As with so many other problems," Ryder says, "the solutions that seem plausible and effective and acceptable are non-demographic in character."[89] Or to put the matter more positively, large ethnic groups are not likely to achieve much more power in a matter of decades by differential fertility, and small minorities might best fulfill their perceived missions through the hold of internal doctrine or cultural identity rather than through an increase in numbers that in any case could only be marginal.

At the same time, fertility appears to be decreasing around the world. If that continues, as would seem likely, then given time there will be a much narrower band of fertility rates within which differentials can operate. Among other benefits of lowering fertility—and this is not the largest—should come a lowering of ethnic differentials, as the top falls toward the bottom. Although the data are by no means definitive, it begins to appear that policy can do more to decrease than to increase fertility. Thus over time there will be more of a convergence on the down side—not necessarily uniformity but less differential—and that may be the likeliest prospect both for the present transition and for ethnic differentials.

Hence in this as in other ways, it may turn out in the eye of history that the Jews got there early, if not first. This time, the wave of the future may be theirs.

NOTES

1. For a review of the intercountry situation, see Nazli Choucri, *Population Dynamics and International Violence* (Lexington, Mass.: Lexington Books, 1974).

2. This paragraph is adapted from Bernard Berelson and Gary A. Steiner, *Human Behavior: An Inventory of Scientific Findings* (New York: Harcourt, Brace and World, 1964), p. 494.

3. John C. Caldwell, "The Demographer and Political Intervention to Change Population Growth Rates," Conference on Population and Political Science, Population Council, October 1970.

4. L. T. Badenhorst, "South Africa," in Bernard Berelson, ed., *Population Policy in Developed Countries* (New York: McGraw-Hill, 1974), p. 385.

5. Ibid., p. 391.

6. Ibid., pp. 391-392.

7. For the early history, see James D. Greig, "Mauritius: Religion and Population Pressure," in T. E. Smith, ed., *The Politics of Family Planning in the Third World* (London: Allen & Unwin, 1973), pp. 122-167.

8. For a full review of the Mauritian situation, see Christos Xenos, "Fertility Change in Mauritius and the Impact of the Family Planning Programme," manuscript, December 1974.

9. United Nations, Economic Commission for Africa, "Review of Available Evidence on Fertility Differentials in Africa," November 1972, p. 7.

10. Ibid., p. 8, citing S. K. Gaisie, *Dynamics of Population Growth in Ghana,* Ghana Population Studies, no. 1 (Legon, Ghana: University Demographic Unit, 1969), pp. 37-49.

11. Caldwell, "Demographer and Political Intervention," p. 25.

12. Operations Research Group, *Family Planning Practices in India: The First All-India Report* [Baroda, Operations Research Group, 1971], tables 3.10, 8.13.

13. Pravin M. Visaria and Anrudh K. Jain, *India, Country Profiles* (New York: Population Council, 1976), table 5.

14. For a historical account of the differentials, see Leela Visaria, "Religious Differentials in Fertility," in Ashish Bose et al., eds., *Population in India's Development 1947-2000* (Delhi: Vikas Publishing House, 1974), p. 362.

15. Visaria & Jain, *India,* p. 12.

16. S. U. Kodikara, "Family Planning in Ceylon," in Smith, *Politics of Family Planning,* pp. 310-318.

17. Ibid., p. 318.

18. Ibid., p. 321.

19. For a revealing analysis, see T. O. Ling, "Buddhist Factors in Population Growth and Control," *Population Studies* 23, no. 1 (March 1969): 53-60, which concludes that Buddhist response to "population control policies will depend to a large degree on the communal situation, i.e., the reaction of Buddhist to non-Buddhist groups within the population"—for example, "the fear of Catholic power."

20. Sidney Goldstein, "Religious Fertility Differentials in Thailand, 1960," *Population Studies* 24, no. 3 (November 1970): 325-337.

21. Ibid., pp. 325, 326.

22. Ralph Thomlinson, *Thailand's Population: Facts, Trends, Problems, and Policies* (Bangkok: Thai Watana Panich Press, 1971), p. 90.

23. Eddy Lee, Michael Ong, and T. E. Smith, "Family Planning in West Malaysia:

The Triumph of Economics and Health over Politics," in Smith, *Politics of Family Planning*, p. 284.

24. Ibid., p. 285.

25. Ibid.

26. Goh Keng Swee, cited by George G. Thomson and T. E. Smith, "Singapore: Family Planning in an Urban Environment," in Smith, *Politics of Family Planning*, p. 254.

27. Data from Singapore Family Planning & Population Board, *Eighth Annual Report 1973* (Singapore: National Family Planning Centre, August 29, 1973), tables 9, 10, 37.

28. Norma McArthur, "Fertility and Marriage in Fiji," *Human Biology in Oceania* 1 (1971): 10-22.

29. Terence Hull and Valerie Hull, "Fiji: A Study of Ethnic Plurality and Family Planning," in Smith, *Politics of Family Planning*, p. 207.

30. "Speech by Head of the Delegation of the People's Republic of China at the World Population Conference," Bucharest, August 1974, p. 14.

31. *Population and Australia: A Demographic Analysis and Projection*, First Report of the National Population Inquiry (Canberra: Australian Government Publishing Service, 1975), 2: 455, 738. For a full analysis, see "Part C: The Aboriginal Population," pp. 455-539, and "The Aborigines and Population Policy," pp. 737-740.

32. Adnan Mroueh, "The Population Explosion: Urgent Need for Control and Planning," *The Arab Economist* (September 1974): 13.

33. Juliette Sayegh and Charles Churchill, "Lebanon," manuscript, 1975, p. 32.

34. Republic of Cyprus, Ministry of Finance, Statistics and Research Department, *Demographic Report 1972*, p. 3.

35. This information is from *Area Handbook for Cyprus*, prepared by Foreign Area Studies of the American University (Washington, D.C.: U.S. Government Printing Office, 1971), pp. 74-75.

36. Friedlander, "Israel," p. 52.

37. Ibid., p. 60.

38. Ibid., pp. 64-65.

39. Ibid., from table 9, p. 90.

40. Robert E. Kennedy, Jr., "Minority Group Status and Fertility: The Irish," *American Sociological Review* 38, no. 1 (February 1973): 91-92.

41. Brendan M. Walsh, "Ireland," in Berelson, *Population Policy*, p. 37.

42. Louis Lohle-Tart, "Belgium," in Berelson, *Population Policy*, p. 214; the data are also from this source.

43. Zdenek Pavlik and Vladimir Wynnyczuk, "Czechoslovakia," in Berelson, *Population Policy*, pp. 319-354.

44. D. Breznik, "Fertility of the Yugoslav Population," in Egon Szabady, ed., *World View of Population Problems* (Budapest: Akadémiai Kiadó, 1968), p. 64.

45. D. Peter Mazur, "Fertility Among Ethnic Groups in the U.S.S.R." *Demography* 4, no. 1 (1967): 177.

46. D. Peter Mazur, "Relation of Marriage and Education to Fertility in the U.S.S.R.," *Population Studies* 27, no. 1 (March 1973): 114.

47. Reproduced in "U.S.S.R.: Views on Population/Family Planning," *Studies in Family Planning*, no. 49 (January 1970): 15.

48. David M. Heer, "Recent Developments in Soviet Population Policy," *Studies in Family Planning* 3, no. 11 (November 1972): 257, 259, 263.

49. Philip van Praag and F. Louis Lohlé-Tart, "The Netherlands," in Berelson, *Population Policy*, p. 304.

50. For an interesting historical analysis, see F. van Heek, "Roman Catholicism and Fertility in the Netherlands: Demographic Aspects of Minority Status," *Population Studies* 10, no. 2 (November 1956): 125-138; the quotation is from p. 135.

51. John Simons, "Great Britain," in Berelson, *Population Policy*, p. 612.

52. Ernest Krausz, *Ethnic Minorities in Britain* (London: MacGibbon & Kee, 1971), p. 49.

53. Ibid., p. 54.

54. Petre Muresan and Ioan M. Copil, "Romania," in Berelson, *Population Policy*, p. 361.

55. Larry H. Long, "Fertility Patterns Among Religious Groups in Canada," *Demography* 7 (May 1970): 148.

56. Andrew Kantner et al., *Canada, Country Profiles* (New York: Population Council, 1974), p. 5.

57. Jacques Henripin and Hervé Gauthier, "Canada," in Berelson, *Population Policy*, p. 415.

58. Not to mention the nationality differences within the Catholic community—Irish, Mexican, Italian, Polish, French, and so forth. See Thomas K. Burch, "The Fertility of North American Catholics: A Comparative Overview," *Demography* 3, no. 1 (June 1966): pp. 174-87.

59. United Nations, Department of Economic and Social Affairs, *The Determinants and Consequences of Population Trends: New Summary of Findings on Demographic, Economic and Social Factors* (1973), 1: 102. "Religious differences have emerged in recent years as perhaps the strongest of the socio-economic determinants of fertility"; and Vernon C. Pohlmann, "Longitudinal Study of Demographic Variables Associated with Differential Fertility of Whites and Non-Whites in the United States," paper prepared for presentation at the annual meeting of the Population Association of America, New Orleans, Louisiana, April 26, 1973: "race *per se* is a key predictor of fertility."

60. The Mormons are an interesting special case, especially in comparison with the Jews: both are small, with high education and income, plus strong consciousness of religious and social differentiation from the majority. Yet they are close to the extremes of American fertility, high and low. In the past thirty years or so, Mormon fertility (as indicated by birthrates in Utah) has consistently been from 25 percent to 40 percent above U.S. fertility as a whole, though it has closely followed the U.S. trend up and down. See Judith C. Spicer and Susan O. Gustavus, "Mormon Fertility through Half a Century: Another Test of the Americanization Hypothesis," *Social Biology* 21 (1974): 70-76. While high fertility may have been necessary in the early historical circumstances of Mormon life, in surviving against hostile neighbors and subduing a frontier farmland, it is apparently promoted at present by Mormon doctrine applied through a cohesive social organization and a strong sense of family life. The biblical injunction to "be fruitful and multiply" is taken seriously in the theology; as in Catholic doctrine, the primary aim of sexual intercourse is taken to be procreation, and both contraception and abortion are

disapproved. The theological rationale "is based upon the belief in three worlds — a pre-earthly existence, an earthly existence, and an after-life. Until all unborn souls existing in the pre-earthly existence have had the opportunity of an earthly life, there will be no 'second coming' or millennium. Further, because life extends beyond the earthly existence, *as a family*, marriage and the formation of a family with children is only the beginning of a continuing pattern of existence." Lee L. Bean, personal communication, September 1975. For further material on Mormon fertility, see Donald W. Hastings et al., "Mormonism and Birth Planning," *Population Studies* 26 (1972): 19-28, and Thomas F. O'Dea, *The Mormons* (Chicago: University of Chicago Press, 1957), pp. 131, 140-141.

61. James A. Sweet, "Differentials in the Rate of Fertility Decline: 1969-1970," *Family Planning Perspectives* 6, no. 2 (Spring 1974), table 2, p. 107.

62. Charles F. Westoff and Norman Ryder, *The Contraceptive Revolution* (Princeton: Frinceton University Press, 1977), p. 7.

63. Charles F. Westoff, "The Yield of the Imperfect," Presidential Address, Population Association of America, Seattle, Washington, April 1975, pp. 9, 11. For a similar conclusion with regard to unplanned fertility, see Westoff and Ryder, *Contraceptive Revolution*, p. 28: "The decline in unplanned fertility accounts for just about all of the decline in total marital fertility," 1961-65 to 1966-70. (Unplanned includes both timing and number failures.)

64. Frederick S. Jaffe, "Family Planning Services in the United States," in *Aspects of Population Growth Policy*, ed. Robert Parke, Jr., and Charles F. Westoff, Commission on Population Growth and the American Future, *Research Reports*, 6 (Washington, D.C.: U.S. Government Printing Office, 1972).

65. Marcia J. Kramer, "Legal Abortion Among New York City Residents," *Family Planning Perspectives* 7, no. 3 (May-June 1975): 128-137.

66. Charles F. Westoff, "United States," in Berelson, *Population Policy*, pp. 749-750. For some extreme examples, see J. Mayone Stycos, "Opinion, Ideology, and Population Problems — Some Sources of Domestic and Foreign Opposition to Birth Control," in *Rapid Population Growth: Consequences and Policy Limitations* (Baltimore: Johns Hopkins Press, 1971), pp. 551-554. For two recent reviews, see Robert G. Weisbord, *Genocide? Birth Control and the Black American* (Westport, Conn.: Greenwood Press, 1975), and his "Family Size and the Black American," *Population Bulletin* 30, no. 4 (1975).

67. "Rabbi Deplores Small Families," *New York Times*, January 24, 1974, p. 40. Actually, the U.S. population increased in those three decades by just over 50 percent, not 100 percent.

68. Goldstein, "American Jewry, 1970," p. 12.

69. Berelson, *Population Policy*, p. 787.

70. A. J. Coale, "The Demographic Transition," IUSSP International Population Conference, *Proceedings* (Liège: Derouaux, 1973) 1: 62-63.

71. Myron Wiener, "Political Demography: An Inquiry into the Political Consequences of Population Change," in *Rapid Population Growth*, pp. 597-598.

72. United Nations, Department of Economic and Social Affairs, *Determinants and Consequences*, p. 102.

73. For example, two recent reviews of population policy in Western and Eastern Europe say nothing about the matter: Massimo Livi-Bacci, "Population

Policy in Western Europe," *Population Studies* 28, no. 2 (July 1974): 191-204, and Milos Macura, "Population Policies in Socialist Countries of Europe," *Population Studies* 28, no. 3 (November 1974): 369-379.

74. Jack Parsons, in book review of *Population and Its Problems: A Plain Man's Guide,* ed. H. B. Parry, in *People* (IPPF) 2, no. 2 (1975): 45.

75. Calvin Goldscheider, "Fertility of the Jews," *Demography* 4, no. 1 (1967): 196-209.

76. Calvin Goldscheider, *Population, Modernization, and Social Structure* (Boston: Little, Brown, 1971), p. 277.

77. Gavin Jones and Dorothy Nortman, "Roman Catholic Fertility and Family Planning: A Comparative Review of the Research Literature," *Studies in Family Planning,* no. 34 (October 1968): 3.

78. Dudley Kirk, "Factors Affecting Moslem Natality," in Bernard Berelson et al., eds., *Family Planning and Population Programs: A Review of World Developments* (Chicago: University of Chicago Press, 1966), p. 567. See also Oladele Olawuji Arowolo, "Correlates of Fertility in Moslem Populations: An Empirical Analysis" (Ph.D. diss., University of Pennsylvania, 1973), table 2.1, p. 47, showing birthrates of nineteen Moslem countries in Asia and Africa with a median of 47.

79. United Nations, *Determinants and Consequences,* p. 102.

80. Calvin Goldscheider and Peter R. Uhlenberg, "Minority Group Status and Fertility," *American Journal of Sociology* 74, no. 4 (January 1969): 372.

81. P. Neal Ritchey, "The Effect of Minority Group Status on Fertility: A Re-examination of Concepts," *Population Studies* 29, no. 2 (July 1975): 257. The other major titles are Goldscheider and Uhlenberg, "Minority Group Status"; David S. Sly, "Minority Group Status and Fertility: An Extension of Goldscheider and Uhlenberg," *American Journal of Sociology* 70, no. 3 (November 1970): 443-459; Robert E. Roberts and Eun Sul Lee, "Minority-Group Status and Fertility Revisited," *American Journal of Sociology* 80, no. 2 (September 1974): 503-523. Goldscheider, *Population,* pp. 270-298 and Kennedy, "Minority Group Status." There are at least two earlier titles of relevance: Lincoln H. Day, "Natality and Ethnocentrism: Some Relationships Suggested by an Analysis of Catholic-Protestant Differentials," *Population Studies* 22, no. 1 (March 1968): 27-50, and Van Heek, "Roman Catholocism." One additional title to consult is Douglas T. Gurak and Mary M. Kritz, "Sources of Ethnic and White Fertility Differentials: Minority Status Reconsidered," paper presented at Eastern Sociological Society meeting, New York City, April 1975.

82. Berelson, *Population Policy,* p. 772.

83. David M. Heer, *Society and Population* (Englewood Cliffs, N.J.: Prentice-Hall, 1968), p. 98.

84. I am indebted to my colleague Dorothy Nortman for these calculations, as well as for other assistance.

85. Heer, *Society,* p. 99.

86. John D. Montgomery, "Planning to Cope: Administrative Consequences of Rapid Population Growth," in Warren F. Ilchman et al., eds., *Policy Sciences and Population* (Lexington, Mass.: Lexington Books, 1975), p. 102. The analysis proceeds:
In the abstract formulation of the four extreme demand situations, (I) would describe a case of equal growth rate among the different ethnic groups where opportunities are restricted to

a preferred elite community; (J) where growth rates are uneven and the opportunities are differentiated; (K) with even growth rates and undifferentiated opportunity, and (L) unequal population growth in communal situations of undifferentiated opportunity.

		ETHNIC GROUP FUNCTIONS	
		Restricted Opportunities	**Undifferentiated Opportunities**
Distribution of RPG Rates Among Ethnic Groups	Even	I	K
	Uneven	J	L

Situation I. The ethnic groups that are restricted to low productivity or marginal economic functions will be disadvantaged by RPG and will agitate for education, employment preferences, and unemployment and other social benefits. (Examples: Canada, Rhodesia.)

Situation J. If the increase occurs in economically marginal ethnic groups, a highly volatile situation arises (if rural, the group will demand urban access; if urban, they will demand increased welfare services or equivalent amenities); in more favorably situated ethnic groups, the possibility of volatile responses would still remain if they lose their preferred status because of excessive growth rates. This situation is common because restricted opportunities tend to relegate certain groups to below-average socioeconomic levels, which in turn leads to above-average birth rates. For the same reason, Situation I is rare. (Examples of Situation J: Lebanon, Egypt, Sudan, Kenya, S. Africa, Congo, Bolivia, U.S., U.S.S.R., Yugoslavia, Malaysia.)

Situation K. RPG does not magnify ethnic conflict as a source of demand for government services. (Example: Tanzania.)

Situation L. Foreshadows possible future ethnic specialization leading to Situation I or J because fastest growing groups may gain control of certain occupations. Differential cultural compatibility with requirements and opportunities of modernization in either Situation K or L could also lead to Situation I or J. (Examples: China; Zaïre; the southern Nigerian states.)

87. Roger Revelle, "The Population Dilemma: People and Behavior," *Psychiatric Annals* (September 1971): 14-15.

88. Norman Ryder, "Two Cheers for ZPG," *Daedalus* (Fall 1973): 61.

89. Ibid.

5 Demography and American Jewish Survival

CALVIN GOLDSCHEIDER

It has long been recognized that population factors have important implications for the nature and quality of human society. One of the master themes of demography has been the analysis of the relationship between population growth and economic development, historically and comparatively. The examination of whether population change generates or impedes economic growth in less developed countries and the investigation of how population factors relate to the changing quality of life in the more industrialized nations have been major areas of demographic inquiry. An interrelated theme in population studies is the analysis of differential growth. The relative population growth and size of different societies, of groups of societies, and of subpopulations within societies have been studied extensively.

Although a great deal of research, planning, and policy have been directed to reducing the quantity of population expansion so as to improve the quality of human life, much less attention has focused on the issues of differential policies for subpopulations or small nations that experience population declines and shortages of manpower. Indeed, these issues of population change, socioeconomic development, and differential growth may be examined in the context of the demography of ethnic minority groups.[1] The vitality, quality, and survival of ethnic minority groups are related directly to population processes and demographic parameters. To the extent that differential growth of ethnic populations characterizes pluralistic societies in less and more developed areas of the world, differential social consequences — including conflict, tension, and inequalities — will result. The analysis, therefore, of the demographic patterns of ethnic and minority subpopulations may be of critical significance in understanding the changing intergroup tensions and conflicts in the world.

In what ways is the study of demographic factors in minority group survival different from the analysis of the demography of whole societies? What are the implications of shifting the unit of demographic analysis from the nation or total society to the subgroup, the subsociety or ethnic-religious-racial minority populations? Several major differences emerge as critical.

First, a systematic examination of the role of demography in the continuity of minority groups involves an analysis of the entire range of population elements and processes. The study of population size, growth, distribution, structure, and composition is integral to demographic analysis regardless of the unit of analysis. This is also true for the population processes of mortality, fertility, and migration. However, when the unit of analysis is a subgroup, an additional process of "entering and exiting" must be examined: in- and out-marriages. The study of the gains and losses through intermarriage is a central feature of the demography of minority groups. Minority populations increase through births, in-migration, and in-marriages; they decrease through deaths, out-migration, and out-marriages. The demographic balance is a product of these entering and exiting processes.

A second feature of minority group demography is the need to select among a wider range of comparisons for analysis. The population processes of a minority group may be compared to the majority population and/or to other minority groups. The central analytic question in the sociology and demography of minority groups is whether there are differences between minority and majority populations that go beyond the particular matrix of socioeconomic characteristics differentiating these populations. These differences may relate to some cultural or structural differences or to the fact of minority group status per se. The centrality of this question requires that comparisons be made between minority and majority populations, controlling for socioeconomic and related characteristics.

Another important type of sociological and demographic analysis associated particularly with the study of minority subpopulations relates to the question of residential clustering. There is a series of complex issues associated with residential segregation and integration of minority groups and the implications of the changing population concentration, dispersal, and density of subgroups within society.

Although minority subgroups tend to be smaller and relatively more homogeneous units of analysis than total societies, there remains sufficient subgroup variation within minority ethnic groups to allow for detailed examination. This is of particular importance for minority groups undergoing sociocultural change. The analysis of heterogeneity within minority groups provides clues to the direction in which these groups are moving vis-a-vis other minority groups and with regard to the total society. Through the examination of subgroups who are in the forefront of change, some hints as to the future direction of the total minority group may be revealed.

Finally, the implications of demographic patterns for minority and majority populations may vary. Rates of growth, distribution, composition and levels of mortality, fertility, and migration may have different consequences for minority populations. Zero population growth has a set of consequences for a total society, for example, that cannot be applied uniformly to every subpopulation. Policies to control, regulate, or channel population growth and processes applied to total nations do not necessarily fit the goals, needs, and aspirations of selected ethnic segments. Indeed there are a variety of socio-political-economic consequences of differential population growth of majority and minority ethnic populations. Minority populations that are rapidly increasing in size within a society whose rate of demographic growth is stable are as problematic as minority populations that are declining or are stable while the total population is expanding rapidly.[2]

An interesting illustration of the role of demographic factors in minority group survival in modern society is the American Jewish population. As a case study and as one model that may foreshadow the future patterns of other American ethnic minority groups, the examination of Jewish demographic patterns in the United States reveals some of the major analytic issues associated with minority group survival.

A series of basic questions will serve as background to the ensuing discussion. Is there a problem of Jewish demographic survival in America? What role do population factors play in the quality of American Jewish life? How viable is Jewish ethnicity in American society? How do the current patterns of Jewish American demography indicate the future quantity and quality of Jewish life? What are the major demographic trends characterizing the evolution of the American Jewish community, and what do they imply about the future? What may be inferred from the analysis of these patterns about intervention and policies?

As a first step in clarifying the issues underlying these questions and placing in a general context the demographic problems of American Jews, two alternative views or perspectives on the American Jewish dilemma are outlined.

OUTSIDER AND INSIDER PERSPECTIVES

To an outsider, the concern about the disappearance of American Jewry or the vanishing American Jew appears exaggerated or alarmist, if not ludicrous. At best the issue appears rhetorical or artificially created, to be rejected with the obvious retorts about the strengths of American Jewish life. One does not have to go beyond a regular reading of the press to know that Jews are conspicuously present in a wide range of political and social activities. Hardly a week goes by without some report of a Jewish organization's attempt to influence American policies in the Middle East, reacting to the subtlest shift in politics about Israel, Zionism, Jews, or Arabs, or linking détente issues with Jewish emigration from the Soviet Union. Similarly national American politics have always raised the visibility of American Jewry. Jews have been viewed as supporters of particular candidates and as an important voting interest group. In a cruder but no less revealing way non-Jewish candidates appear at Jewish organizational functions, pose with Hasidic rebbes, eat "Jewish" delicacies on the Lower East Side of New York, or wear a yarmolke.

These and related macropolitical indicators of Jewish vitality and presence are convincing and reassuring; the third religious subgroup in America after Protestants and Catholics is vibrant and visible. Surely a vanishing breed is rarely a source of such conspicuous sociopolitical power and influence. Indeed it has often been suggested that the Jewish group in America epitomizes the fact that power is not necessarily a function of demographic size, larger and more are not synonymous with better and powerful.

Jewish vitality in America is reflected not only in secular political indicators. Since the mid-1960s there has been an enormous growth in Jewish activities, and new forms of Jewish identity have emerged. These have been particularly concentrated among those age segments in the Jewish community that in the past have been the least Jewish-committed— the teenage, college, and young adult populations. The impressive growth of Habad houses, Jewish consciousness among college students, kosher facilities, Jewish studies, the wearing of the skullcap, and Israel-Zionism-Soviet Jewry activities, among others, have been revolutionary forces in American Jewish life that few if any social scientists imagined or predicted ten or fifteen years ago.

A silent but significant revolution has occurred in American Jewish life. American Jewry thirty to forty years ago was relatively "silent" about the Holocaust and Israel. Institutional heterogeneity and organizational disarray characterized the American Jewish community structure in the immediate postwar era. The religiously committed Jews of the 1940s and 1950s were either older, foreign-born persons, or marginal within the Jewish community. For the Jews of the 1960s and 1970s, being "noisy" about Jewishness has become the norm. Jews and Jewish institutions have become vocal about Israel, the Palestine Liberation Organization, Soviet Jewry, Jewish life in America, Jewish women and Jewish students, and, to a lesser extent, the Jewish aged and Jewish poor.

Committed Jews have come out of their silent closets; some of the uncommitted appear to be searching for new forms of Jewishness, rooted in tradition but reflecting America of the 1970s. The increasing use of the public media by religious, committed, and searching Jews has raised the level of Jewish conspicuousness in America. The Protestantization of Judaism is much less characteristic of America in the 1970s than succah building, hallah baking, and Passover seder preparations. Young women are more likely to be interested in teffilin wearing, minyan participation, and active Jewish commitments than sisterhoods, "donor" luncheons, and passive homemaker Judaism. Ethnic Jewish pride appears to have replaced the semiembarrassment associated with the retention of Jewish culture and consciousness.

In many ways, it seems that the issue has become how "unvanishing" American Jewry is. The questions that are raised tend to be addressed to the sources of Jewish American ethnicity, whether ethnic pride among Jews is only an imitation of black, Chicano, and other ethnic movements in America and whether there are inner sociocultural strengths to American Jewry beyond the external issues of Zionism, Israel, and oppressed Jewries around the world. Certainly, the outsider would argue, there appears to be little basis for the question of whether Jewish life will survive in America in the foreseeable future and no grounds for positing an "end" to Jewish Americans in the ethnic-conscious United States of the 1970s.

An insider who knows the strengths and weaknesses of the Jewish community goes beyond the superifical indicators and below the surface, however. Other signs appear, more powerful and challenging, subtle and destructive, which provide an alternative perspective to the one focusing on the positive, revolutionary changes in Jewish life in the 1960s and 1970s. To balance the indicators of strength and renewal, the insider sees assimilation rather than Jewish consciousness, acculturation not Jewish identity. The signs of renewal and searching are viewed as marginal and transitory, reflecting the failure of Jewish organizations and the dismay and frustration of Jewish youth. From the insider's perspective, there is lack of depth in Jewish commitments and a general absence of rich Jewish content. Ineffective, inadequate, and unsuccessful Jewish education (measured in continuation rates and eventual adult commitments and knowledge) combined with pervasive ignorance among the middle-aged and older segments of the community about things Jewish and Israeli are emphasized. The decline in temple and synagogue participation, empty synagogue schools, unused facilities, and the growth of Hebrew day schools for some of the wrong reasons fit this general pattern of decline and irrelevance. The increasing growth of secularism among Jews, the emphasis on and acceptance of minimum Jewish commitments, and the mobilization of energies for fund-raising devoid of Jewish content as a goal in itself represent substitutes for creative Jewish commitments and have become the major character of Jewish activities in organizational and community life.

Given this context, the insider stresses the high rates of intermarriage among Jewish youth and bemoans the apparent attraction of a variety of exotic non-Jewish spiritual alternatives among high school and college students. Without a crisis in Israel, a problem of Soviety Jewry, or new forms of ethnic discrimination and insecurity in America, there appears to be insufficient depth or commitment internally for American Jewish cultural or social survival. The insider sees the pockets of renewal and vibrance located in specific areas where Jewish population concentration is high, or he dismisses it as characteristic of a vocal minority.

To the many critics of American Jewish life, secularism, universalism, and an open opportunity structure are direct challenges to the future survival of ethnic Jewish particularism.

Are these outsider and insider views simply reflections of optimistic and pessimistic perceptions of the same phenomenon? Are we only dealing with the question as to whether the glass is half full or half empty? Do the outsiders emphasize only the good in the Jewish situation while the insiders see the bad even in the good?[3]

In large part, I suspect that these two views focus on different aspects of American Jewish life in the 1970s. Basically the argument to be presented is that to understand the social dynamics and variations in the emerging American Jewish community, three complex issues must be clarified: the growing polarization within the American Jewish community and the "shrinking middle," the changing Jewish demographic balance, and the implications of Jewish demographic patterns for the question of polarization and for the broader issues of the quality and continuity of Jewish life in America.

It seems clear to most serious students of American Jewish life that American Jewry is not about to vanish in either the demographic or sociological sense. However, American Jews are becoming more polarized than ever before—more secular and more Jewish in different subsections of the community. The American Jewish population is slowly shrinking in size, but, more important, it is changing in composition, characteristics, and distribution; concerns about quantitative survival nationally are much less real than the problems of the growth, size, and structure of local Jewish communities. The future of American Jewish life is less tied to the question of whether it will survive demographically than which subsections or segments will survive.

The issue of demographic survival must confront the question of qualitative survival. The unity of American Jewish life revolves around secular politics—national and international—rather than any cultural or social consensus, except perhaps for a vague, abstract commitment to Jewish survival. The more serious, complex, and divisive issues associated with the rationale for Jewish survival are not unrelated to the demography of

American Jews. It is important to emphasize the obvious point that Jewish demographics in America are voluntary and not imposed; the need to survive by choice and not only by ascription remains the key challenge and dilemma for American Jews. Undoubtedly if there was some clearer sociocultural consensus on American Jewish survival, there would be no apparent reason why the Jewish ethnic group in America should not be able to survive demographically. The absence of such a consensus among the disparate elements in the American Jewish community has been primarily responsible for a whole complex of social and demographic problems and has been the basic source of the demographic survival issue.

The demographic patterns of American Jews are one of the most obvious manifestations of their desires for survival and of the consequent choices that they make. Less appreciated is the fact that demographic patterns have implications for the structure and quality of American Jewish life. Not only are demographic patterns responses to and reflections of social structure and values, but they in turn have consequences for the Jewish social structure and values emerging on the American scene. It is this feedback mechanism from demography to quality that requires special emphasis. Rhetorical questions such as, Would the quality of American Jewish life be improved if there were an additional million Jews? or Would a 25 percent increase in total fertility have significance for Jewish quality? are irrelevant and meaningless. The central issues are how demographic changes reflect the qualitative choices in American Jewish commitments to survival and what the important implications are of demographic patterns for the quality of Jewish life in America.

POLARIZATION AND THE SHRINKING MIDDLE

The nature of the American Jewish community and the role of demographic factors in Jewish survival must be viewed against the background of the changing distribution of Jews on a general continuum of Jewish commitment. Descriptions of the strengths and weaknesses of American Jewry focus on the two polar ends of that continuum. The numerical and proportional distribution of Jews in categories that range from more to less Jewish commitment, the proportion of Jews who are in the middle, and the direction those in the middle are moving are the key issues. Over time, the proportion of Jews in the middle has narrowed significantly as a result of the clear shift among selected segments of the Jewish community toward assimilation and loss of Jewish commitment, and, of no less importance, because there has been some growth at the more Jewishly committed end of the continuum. As as result of the shifts in both directions, the size of the middle has diminished considerably in the last decade, and greater polarization and sharper distinctions among segments of American Jewry are emerging. Most important, choices in the future are likely to be less ambivalent, less ambiguous, and more decisively at one or the other polar end of the continuum.

The changes that have occurred in American Jewish life have been tied to the question of shifts in the level and extent of Jewish commitments and identity of the changing middle by generation.[4] There has always been a segment of the Jewish community that was traditional in its Jewish practices, identified strongly as Jews, and was committed to Jewish survival. On the other hand, there always was a segment among American Jewry that was secular in religious practice, assimilationist-universalistic in ideology, and marginal to Jewish survival. The relative balance of these two polar segments and the relationship of each to the stance of the middle has varied over time.

The major axis of change in American Jewish life in the present context relates to Eastern European Jews and their descendants. The Eastern European immigration in the four and a half decades beginning in the 1880s defines the dominant pattern of changes in American Jewish life. It drowned out, overwhelmed, and obscured the process of quantitative and qualitative assimilation evidenced by German Jewish immigrants and their descendants.

Although the evidence historically and for contemporary American Jews is incomplete, sufficient data and impressions are available to sketch in broad outline changes in the distribution of Jewish commitment to ethnic survival for the various generations.

In focusing on the level and distribution of Jewish commitment by generation, it is necessary to leave the definition of Jewish commitment as broad, vague, and unspecified as possible. It generally will refer to a wide range of Jewish activities, values, and self-definitions, including Jewish religious observances, synagogue membership and attendance, Jewish community and organizational membership and identification, ethnic self-identification, Jewish education, Jewish philanthropy, and socio-cultural-political activities that are Jewish-Israeli centered. The emphasis on any specific type of Jewish commitment obscures the problem of changing types of identity over time, the multiple ways Jews have responded in a variety of settings to these types of Jewish commitment, and the lack of detailed information on specific types by generation. Ideally what is needed is a composite measure of Jewishness that is highly correlated with Jewish survival—not only of the individual but of the next generation and the community. However, we do not know of the survival implications of the various dimensions of Jewish life. Hence, in this discussion, Jewish commitment will be used as if we were dealing with a set of indicators that has been correlated clearly with Jewish survival.

Among first-generation, foreign-born, Eastern European Jews were socialists and secularists, radicals and universalists who had already rejected ethnic-religious particularism in the urban centers of Eastern Europe. For many of these, America was the promised land where ethnic differences would be eliminated, and the melting pot goal was attainable as well as desirable. The size of this segment (even when added to the secularist-assimilationist segments of German-American Jews) was relatively small; the number of those at the opposite end of the continuum—those actively involved in committments to Jewish survival—was somewhat larger. However, the number and proportion of Jews of the first generation who were concerned about Jewish survival and continuity in America have always tended to be exaggerated. Perhaps the concern with economic survival and aspirations for the social mobility of children took priority over issues of ethnic continuity. More likely, the majority of first-generation Jews were Jewish by their very foreignness—in language, food, and habit—and there are no obvious signs that Jewish survival was a major issue to them. Perhaps three-fourths of the first generation were in the middle part of the continuum of Jewish commitment, concentrating, to be sure, in the direction of more rather than less Jewish commitment.

The second generation could not have completed the process of assimilation, even if that had been possible and desirable, for that would have involved a radical shift of the middle. The major change for it was a shift of the majority away from one part of the middle toward the other—away from leaning in the direction of more toward less Jewish commitment. While a small increase at the polar end of assimilation and minimum Jewish commitment occurred, the most dramatic change of second-generation Jews was a move toward less Jewish commitment, with the majority remaining in the ambivalent middle. Changes at both ends of the continuum took place—a dilution of the most committed and an increase of the noncommitted—but the majority retained parts of the world in which they were raised while becoming less Jewish and more American. The major characteristic of the second generation was the reduction of Jewish commitments while increasing American secular values. Neither their desire nor the receptivity of American society was conducive to total assimilation. The general pattern was that Jews Americanized faster than other ethnic groups with a retention of ethnic ambivalence. My guess would be that the decline at the more committed extreme was less than the increase at the less committed extreme; those in the middle who were toward the more committed end declined significantly, and those in the middle who were toward the less committed end increased sharply.

The third generation growing up in the 1940s and 1950s continued the shift toward the less-committed end of the continuum. The dominant move again was not toward the extreme end of zero Jewish commitment, although there was clearly an increase at that end at the expense of a declining middle. Moreover, the middle continued to shift toward less Jewish commitment. The retention of intensive ethnic Jewish identity among a small minority and the general continuity of the middle despite the reduction in level and type of Jewish commitments reflected in part the impact of Israel, the Holocaust, and, later during the 1960s, civil-rights and black ethnic movements.

The fourth generation, growing up in the 1960s and 1970s, exhibits patterns of continuity and discontinuity with previous generations. Consistent with previous trends is the clear increase in the less committed end of the continuum—representing perhaps one-third to two-fifths of the fourth generation. Moreover, the relative balance of the middle is toward the less committed end of the spectrum. But along with the growing proportion of noncommitted Jews of contemporary America and the continued secularization of the middle, two additional processes have emerged: first, the relative size of the middle has decreased significantly, encompassing for the first time less than a majority; second, a small but significant growth has taken place in the proportion at the more committed end of the continuum. The shrinking of the middle and the growth at both ends of the continuum suggest growing polarization and divisions among the new generation that were less clearly drawn previously. Moreover, within the Jewishly committed segment, there is a much wider range of Jewish commitments, which has resulted in growing fragmentation and differentiation among the committed.

Thus, the fourth generation has experienced continuity in assimilation, decreasing ambivalence among those in the middle, and growing polarization within the community as both ends have grown in size and heterogeneity. Jewishness has more and more become a matter of adult choice rather than a fact of birth. And that choice has tended to become an either/or choice—with a range within both extremes and with fewer options available to remain in the middle. How those choices will be made, which factors are likely to determine the nature of those choices, and how the children of the less committed will choose remain among the most important questions surrounding the nature of future Jewish survival in America.

My guess is that the proportion of Jews at the less committed end of the continuum has tripled in four generations—from 10 to 15 percent of the first generation to 35 to 40 percent of the fourth generation; at the more committed end, the proportions have fluctuated but show signs of increase to roughly one-fifth of the fourth generation compared to about one-tenth of the second generation. As a result of these changes, the middle has declined from about 70 percent of the first generation to around 40 percent of the fourth generation. Within the middle, the relative balance has clearly shifted in the less committed direction.

THE DEMOGRAPHIC ARGUMENT

It is against this background of the shifting middle and greater polarization in the 1970s that the quantitative argument takes on particular significance. The heart of the demographic argument is that there have been and continue to be revolutionary changes, subtle but of profound importance, in the size, growth, composition, and distribution of the American Jewish population. These demographic changes are critical for Jewish survival primarily because they reflect and have implications for the quality of Jewish life in America, and the quality of Jewish life is the key to Jewish survival. Population size is obviously a necessary but not sufficient condition for survival; the immediate Jewish future in America is tied to questions of quantity only indirectly. However, since demographic patterns are consequences and determinants of Jewish life in America, the analysis of American Jewish demography provides a context within which Jewish quality can be evaluated.

The evaluation of Jewish quality has always been ambiguous. The various dimensions of Jewish identity show no consistent, uniform patterns over time; there is no general agreement whether particular indicators reflect Jewish quality; and there is no clear consensus as to the implications of the trends that have been identified. However, there is little ambiguity among those committed to Jewish group survival in America about sharp increases in intermarriages, below-replacement reproduction, declining proportions of young people, and related demographic measures. These demographic patterns are among the most consistently reported and best documented.

The less disputed meaning of the demographic patterns and their clearer documentation and trend must be balanced by the fact that some of the demographic changes are more subtle, and it is often difficult to appreciate their longer-term implications and repercussions. While a decline in financial support for Jewish organizations may be immediately appreciated, declining birthrates, changing marriage patterns, and increasing population aging take a longer time to be documented and absorbed as social facts. Of primary importance, the demographic processes that affect population size, composition, and distribution are extraordinarily difficult to reverse unless some of the basic values, attitudes, and social processes change. Jewish demographic processes are integral to the social conditions of American Jewish life, not marginal or independent of social structure. Hence, to change, redirect, or channel population change, the societal context must also be altered. Jewish demographic patterns fit the pattern of American Jewish life and may be viewed as the price paid by American Jews for the level of commitments they have to Jewish survival. To reverse the demographic patterns, some of the major commitments of American Jewry have to be reordered in priority.

Both issues of quantitative and qualitative Jewish survival must be considered not only in the overall, national American Jewish context but also in the local Jewish community system where size and quality are more obviously correlated. Within this context, demographic variation and heterogeneity dominate; population size and population processes vary enormously among the variety of Jewish communities in the United States. Differentiation between communities is complicated by the critical question of how selected segments of the Jewish community relate to Jewish survival. Suburban residents, the college- and graduate-school-educated, professionals, the upper middle class, and Jews outside the major areas of Jewish population concentrations are among the subgroups that need to be examined in terms of differential Jewish commitments.

Hence the changing proportion of Jewish commitment by generation has to take into account three demographic considerations: the changing absolute size of various segments over time, the changing distribution of Jews within the United States, and changes in the relationship between Jewish commitment and types of heterogeneity within the Jewish community.

THE JEWISH DEMOGRAPHIC BALANCE

The three most important demographic factors shaping the continuity of the American Jewish community are rates of reproduction, marriage, and intermarriage.[5] Significant changes have occurred in each of these processes in recent years; in combination, they represent a serious challenge to the vitality and growth of the American Jewish population. Although fertility, marriage, and intermarriage will determine the future quantitative growth or decline of American Jewry, other demographic processes, in particular immigration, have influenced the evolution of the Jewish population in the United States. Moreover, population distribution and internal migration are significant determinants of local Jewish population size and composition.

Discussions of demographic survival among American Jews in the 1970s appear distorted to the historian. The concentration on the demography of American Jews during the last fifty years often obscures the most oustanding feature of American Jewish demography: the extra-ordinary growth of Jewish population in the United States. Considering that in mid-nineteenth century America the total number of Jews is esti-mated to have been around 50,000 while a century later Jewish population size had increased to a hundred times that number, a Jewish population explosion of impressive dimensions has occurred in America.

On closer inspection, however, the growth of the Jewish population in America has been uneven over time and largely the result of net immi-gration rather than natural increase. Mass immigration ended over half a century ago as a result first of immigration quota restrictions and sub-sequently because the potential sources of immigration—the large centers of world Jewry in Eastern and Central Europe—were eliminated in the Holocaust and its aftermath.

Immigration played a key role not only in Jewish population growth in America but in shaping the social structure of American Jewish life. Mass immigration from Eastern Europe converted American Jewry into a vi-brant, complex, large, and diverse subcommunity. For the past several decades Jewish immigration to America has been relatively small in absolute numbers and relative to the size of the American Jewish popu-lation. Jewish emigration from America has always been small and in-significant demographically. Hence, the role of immigration as a factor influencing American Jewish demographic growth has declined to in-significance. The well-developed community structure and size of Ameri-can Jewry preclude an important role in the future for immigration.

America has become the world Jewish demographic center as a result of the combined impact of the forty years of mass immigration between 1880 and 1920 and the destruction of European Jewry in World War II. In recent decades, Jewish population growth in America has been slower than growth in the total American population. Some have argued that Jewish Americans are not only in the forefront of zero population growth but show early signs of negative population growth or population decline.

Jewish mortality patterns in America are somewhat different from those for other white Americans, but the differences are too small to account for population growth differentials. To the extent that mortality and immigration are low, the analysis of the future demographic survival of American Jews can take these patterns as givens without further analysis. The variations that undoubtedly occur in the mortality level of Jewish communities reflect variations in age structure and Jewish popu-lation distribution.

The disproportionate concentration of Jews in particular metropolitan areas—in the Northeast, large urbanized areas, and suburban areas of metropolitan communities—is a well-documented feature of American Jewish demography. The differential impact of population distribution on local institutions and organizations has been noted in a variety of studies. In terms of the vitality of local Jewish communities, migration and population redistribution are of greater significance perhaps than any other demographic factor. The dispersal of Jews within metropolitan areas and in new communities throughout the United States is of critical importance since there are clear implications of differential Jewish density levels for Jewish survival—demographically and sociologically. Migration and population dispersal have increased among third- and fourth-generation Jews, particularly among those who are highly educated and in professional and salaried occupations. Changes in the occupational structure of Jews, the labor market, and the educational level of young Jewish men and women may result in greater mobility in the future. There are indications that the migration of Jewish Americans is greater than that of the total American population and that rates have increased in the last decade among third- and fourth-generations Jews.[6]

The nonrootedness of the young generations and the movement away from centers of Jewish concentration—regionally and within metropolitan areas—are among the major determinants of lower levels of Jewish commitment. To be sure, the willingness to move to areas of low Jewish population density already implies lower levels of Jewish commitment. Nevertheless, areas of low Jewish population density have had in the past important consequences for Jewish identity, Jewish community participation, intermarriage, and generally lower rates of Jewish continuity. Although the major centers of Jewish concentration probably will remain and new centers of high Jewish density will emerge, it is likely that significant proportions of fourth-generation Jews will be living in areas of low Jewish concentration. Their mobility and their residential environment imply a weakening of Jewish community ties and a challenge to Jewish continuity in these areas.

Of equal importance is the fact that Jewish communities and sub-communities are undergoing significant structural changes in age composition because of a combination of selective out-migration and low fertility rates. Neighborhoods of major centers of Jewish concentration have become heavily weighted toward the older segments of the age pyramid as have new retirement centers around the country. These areas have no potential for Jewish population renewal except through selective migration. Yet it seems less likely that fourth-generation Jews will decide to move to areas of Jewish concentration as they age and retire, given their pattern of residential integration throughout their life cycle. In short, areas of low Jewish density, as well as areas of high density with an older population, will decline in the next generation and then disappear. Jewish survival is likely to be most pronounced in the large metropolitan centers of Jewish concentration—old and new.

The aging of particular Jewish communities and subcommunities is the consequence both of selective migration and low fertility. For the American Jewish population as a whole, lower Jewish fertility is the key factor accounting for the greater aging of Jewish population than the total population. However, population aging is only one, and perhaps not the most important, consequence of low fertility. An examination of low Jewish fertility along with marriage and intermarriage patterns is critical in identifying the whole set of issues associated with Jewish demographic survival.

Three general questions serve as guidelines for our focus on reproduction, marriage and intermarriage: Are Jewish patterns different from non-Jewish patterns? Are Jewish patterns changing, and in which directions? How do these patterns vary for the different subgroups within the Jewish community?

REPRODUCTION AND DEMOGRAPHIC REPLACEMENT

Since the end of the nineteenth century, research in the United States has pointed to the unmistakable conclusion that Jews have lower fertility than the American population as a whole or other ethnic groups.[7] The major fertility studies undertaken over the last two decades have consistently confirmed this finding for a wide range of fertility and fertility-related measures. Measures of actual family size, fertility desires, contraceptive knowledge and practice, family size planning, and the timing of reproductive behavior all point in the same direction: Jewish couples want, plan, and have small families. Fertility among Jews is low in absolute level, as well as relative to other subpopulations.

Low Jewish fertility is not a new American pattern. As far as can be discerned from the available data, fluctuations around replacement levels have characterized Jewish marriage cohorts starting as early as the mid-1920s. No less significant perhaps is the fact that low Jewish fertility is not unique to the American experience. Jews in every other modern society, over the last half-century at least, have been characterized by low absolute levels of fertility and lower fertility than other ethnic or majority populations.

The available evidence on these patterns over time and in comparative context suggests that there might be a relationship between the position of Jews in Western societies and their fertility patterns. Certainly lower Jewish fertility is not a recent phenomenon; nor are there uniquely American features associated with Jewish fertility. Nor should we lose sight of the fact that Jews accentuate a pattern of fertility control and behavior that characterizes other segments of modern society. Jewish fertility levels are not deviant although they may be extremely low; patterns of Jewish reproduction should not be viewed as exceptional but rather as foreshadowing changes that may characterize other minority groups in the future.

This is not to argue that there are no substantial fertility differences between Jews and non-Jews in general or when socioeconomic, residence, and other variables are controlled. Differences between Jews and non-Jews in reproductive behavior, attitudes, and contraceptive practices are reduced but not eliminated when their socioeconomic characteristics are standardized. The central point is that Jewish fertility patterns are consistent with the position Jews occupy in modern society. Reproduction patterns are neither tangential nor extraneous to Jewish social life; nor are there involuntary factors that account for Jewish fertility patterns. The explanation of lower Jewish fertility and trends and differentials rests with the complex interaction of the peculiar socioeconomic characteristics of American Jews combined with their minority group status in American society. Reproductive behavior and attitudes are an integral part of the changing social situation of Jews in the United States, the attitudes of Jews toward themselves and toward the larger society, the changing importance of family values and cohesion, and the changing roles of men and women within the Jewish family.

Despite the fact that Jewish fertility has been relatively low for almost one hundred years in America and at replacement levels for about four decades, the problem of Jewish fertility has not been raised seriously until recently. Has there been such a long delay in appreciating the implications of replacement level fertility? Was it not known that Jewish family size was small and stabilizing at around two children per family on average? The major factors associated with the recent concern with fertility do not relate primarily to the lack of information available or to the absence of clear implications of replacement level fertility and small family size. Nor have any significant changes in mortality levels or net immigration among Jews altered the demographic balance in the last several decades to place fertility levels in special focus.

Three major changes have occurred placing low Jewish fertility in a unique demographic context in America of the 1960s and early 1970s: changing fertility experiences of Jewish women beginning in the 1960s; changing relationship of cohort marital fertility patterns to annual birthrates; and changes in net out-marriage rates among the fourth generation. These developments have renewed the whole issue of the future of Jewish demographic survival in America.

First, let us examine the fertility changes and experiences of Jewish women in simple cross-sectional perspective as well as in the more complex and sophisticated cohort view. For measurement purposes, the examination of family size changes among different cohorts of women as they pass through the childbearing cycle is essential. Another view examines annual birthrates—period measures—that relate to family formation and childbearing at particular time periods irrespective of the ages (or cohorts) of women giving birth or their previous childbearing experience. To oversimplify, we can examine births occurring in a given year. These births occur to women who are in a variety of stages of childbearing and from a variety of marriage cohorts. Included in an annual or period rate are women completing their childbearing, as well as those just beginning and those in the middle stages. Moreover, annual rates do not necessarily reflect eventual family size of ever-married women but may be distorted by changes in the tempo and timing of childbearing and the changing proportion of women who are married. It is obvious, therefore, that average family size among ever-married Jewish women may remain relatively stable while annual Jewish birthrates fluctuate greatly.

Jewish women marrying in the 1920s and 1930s had around two children by the end of their childbearing period. However, births occurring during the 1920s and 1930s were not only to women marrying during these years but to women who had been married for longer durations (older marriage cohorts whose fertility was higher). Most of those marrying were second-generation Jews whose family of orientation was relatively large. For these women, low Jewish fertility could not have been viewed as a special problem. The economic depression of the 1930s and the war years were periods of general low fertility in America and were viewed as transitory. In the immediate postwar era of the 1940s and 1950s a baby boom occurred among Jews as well as among the general American population. Although the baby boom reflected mainly changes in the timing of childbearing and the making up of postponed births and delayed marriages, the existential experience of this period was childbearing and early family formation. There is some evidence that small increases in actual Jewish family size characterized the immediate post-World War II cohorts. It was, however, not until the 1960s that both families of orientation and procreation were small in size; almost all Jewish women who were giving birth during this period were characterized by relatively small families, efficient contraceptive usage, and the planning of the number and spacing of all births. Thus, the problem of low Jewish fertility has been experienced only recently despite the fact that fluctuations around replacement level fertility have characterized cohorts since the mid-1920s.

A second set of factors calling attention to the problem of low Jewish fertility in recent years relates to the changing timing and tempo of child-bearing and to the question of nonmarriage. During the 1960s and 1970s some delayed marriage and nonmarriage began to emerge on the American Jewish scene, possibly accompanied by changes in the timing of childbearing among married women. If the proportion of married women declines significantly and delayed childbearing within marriage takes place, a family size of two or three children will not necessarily imply annual population replacement rates. While the long-run trend in Jewish fertility is toward the two- to three-child family, annual fertility rates during the 1960s and early 1970s may have been distorted by timing and marriage changes.

Further accentuating this pattern of the changing tempo of childbear-ing for the Jewish population during this latter period (rather than average family size for ever-married women) is the fact that the actual number of Jewish women of childbearing age was significantly lower in the 1960s. Most Jewish women marrying in the 1960s were born in the late 1930s and early 1940s when the number of Jewish babies born was significantly lower than in the previous period or the subsequent post-World War II boom. Hence, there are fewer Jewish women to have children. I suspect that a substantial part of the explanation of very low annual Jewish birth-rates in the last decade lies in these combined changes in the timing of family formation and childbearing and in the number of Jewish persons entering the childbearing period. Cohort family size has changed much less than period fertility rates and has remained around and not very much below replacement levels. Nevertheless, replacement levels for those who marry is not synonymous with replacement levels for the pop-ulation as a whole, particularly if a growing proportion of women do not marry or delay marriage.

Community planning, educational enrollments, and the general presence of children in communities are based not on a cohort view of childbearing but on the number of babies born in particular time periods. Delayed childbearing through nonmarriage, postponed marriage, and divorce, as well as timing changes within marriage, combined with the changing numbers of persons reaching childbearing age, must be con-sidered in evaluating changing period rates of reproduction. Add to these processes the general low replacement level fertility of Jews, the ability of Jewish couples to plan total family size, and the spacing of all children, and the results are clear: an impressive and conspicuous reduc-tion in the number of Jewish children born in the last decade.

Finally, when family size is low and marriage patterns, cohort age structure, and the timing of family formation and childbearing are all changing to push marital fertility rates below population replacement, a small minority group cannot sustain losses brought on by out-migration or out-marriage. Small population declines become problems when additional sociodemographic processes exaggerate that decline. For Jews in America, rates of intermarriage increased during the 1960s and early 1970s. Young Jews marrying in this latter period were largely third- or fourth-generation Americans, characterized by significantly less Jewish commitment. Even minimum net losses through out-marriage (and the actual number is well beyond minimum losses) combined with these annual patterns of below-replacement fertility raises the specter of the vanishing American Jew.

In sum, low Jewish fertility has been an issue that is often distorted and misunderstood. Cohort marital fertility among Jews remains low, probably averaging around two children. In the long run, by the end of the reproductive period for cohorts of women—there will probably be an adequate total family size for replacement of the married population. Annual reproductive rates, however, may reflect increasing rates of non-marriage, changes in the timing and tempo of childbearing, and population structural effects such as the changing number of women of reproductive age. The increased gap between cohort marital fertility rates and population replacement, combined with a higher rate of population losses through net out-marriage, has probably resulted in Jewish population decline in America in the last several years.

Given this overall pattern of low fertility desires and behavior among Jews, it is instructive to ask whether there are any subsegments or subgroups within the American Jewish population that have larger family size desires and higher fertility. On the whole, there are few significant differentiators of Jewish fertility in contemporary America. The traditional variables associated with higher fertility in America—rural residence, poverty, contraceptive ignorance, low education, farm and blue-collar occupations—are virtually nonexistent among Jewish men and women in the childbearing years. There is some variation in Jewish fertility by socioeconomic status, but the range is very small and not very significant.

The major sources of higher fertility ideals and larger family size are among self-segregated religious Jews in a few metropolitan areas of the United States. This segment of committed Jewry has rejected in a variety of ways the integrationist ideology and behavior of the vast majority of American Jews. In their emphasis on traditional roles for women, family and spiritual centrality, and general nonacculturation, large family size values and behavior have been retained and supported.[8]

In contrast, there appears to be no clear empirical relationship between measures of Jewishness (in the broad sense outlined earlier) and fertility that cannot be accounted for by socioeconomic factors. Little support has been found for the relationship between a variety of indicators of Jewish commitment and Jewish values on the one hand and fertility desires and behavior on the other hand.[9] However, among the heterogeneous category of committed Jews, a small proportion—largely those living in segregated religious communities—contribute a disproportionate share of children to the Jewish community. Indeed some of the growth of the committed third- and fourth-generation Jews can be attributed to this pattern of differential reproduction.

Reproduction for the Jewish group takes place mainly in a family context. Recent changes in family patterns and in women's roles within the family and the community may have important implications for the sociodemographic survival of American Jews.

THE DECLINE OF THE JEWISH FAMILY

The family functions to maintain group continuity. It is one of the key units of socialization and cultural transmission for the next generation. Demographic and cultural continuities have been primarily located in the family. This is no less true for ethnic subgroups than for total societies. Moreoever, because of the interdependence of the family and other aspects of society, it is not unexpected that as broader societal changes unfold, family patterns will be altered as well.

Until recently, American Jews have been remarkably successful in maintaining overall patterns of family stability and cohesion. They have held on to family centrality despite social and geographic mobility and general acculturation and integration. The persistence of almost universal and relatively early marriage patterns, low divorce rates, and general family solidarity has indeed been exceptional considering the radical social transformations of American Jews in the last three-quarters of a century.

Although there is no systematic empirical documentation of family changes in the 1960s and 1970s among Jews, a variety of indirect indicators suggests that a series of revolutionary family changes are unfolding among selected segments of fourth-generation Jews. For the first time in recent American Jewish history, significant proportions of twenty- to thirty-five-year-old men and women are not marrying. Moreover, the increasing proportion of the never married adds to the growing number of nonmarried, divorced, and separated Jewish women and men. Together these groups represent a new phenomenon in American Jewish life and are a challenge to institutional, organizational, and community structures that have in the past focused almost exclusively on the family as the unit of greatest significance.

The increasing proportion of nonmarriage, delayed marriage, and divorce among Jews has obvious implications for fertility and reproduction patterns and family values, as well as demographic and sociocultural continuity. The implications of these patterns of family and marriage are unmistakable even if they are only temporary responses to social and economic conditions, reflections of peculiar demographic limitations associated with the availability of Jewish mates in particular locations, statuses, or age categories, or are more deeply related to changes in marriage and family values, women's roles, and sexual behavior characterizing America of the 1970s.

If these impressions of changes in nonmarriage and high divorce rates are accurate, then the patterns of low fertility and high intermarriage rates will be further exacerbated among Jews. Changes in marriage and family behavior and norms have a direct impact on the timing of marriage, decisions not to marry, processes of separation, divorce, and remarriage, the number and timing of births, the relationship of children to their families of orientation and to their extended family networks, and mate selection.

In a broader sense, the sexual revolution, changes in women's roles, and in turn, changes in marriage and family patterns have special significance for Jews because of their tradition of family cohesiveness and unity, endogamy, and universal marriage patterns. As noted earlier, changes in Jewish fertility have been less in the direction of zero and one-child families and more in the direction of almost universal two- to three-child families. However, when fewer Jews are getting married, some are marrying at later ages, and still others are deciding to have no children because of career patterns for women, then two- to three-child families are insufficient to attain overall population replacement levels. A low average family size among married women cannot compensate for growing numbers of unmarried and childless women. Changes in marriage and the timing of childbearing may not have the effect of reducing marital fertility in the long run but may reduce current birthrates below replacement levels and place the burden of population replacement on a smaller group of married women.

Jews have tended in the past to be in the forefront of major socio-demographic revolutions. American Jews are located in social statuses and geographic locations that are the most responsive to changes in marriage and the family. The high proportion of Jews with college and graduate level educations, their disproportionate concentration in select metropolitan centers, and their middle-class backgrounds and values place them in the avant-garde of social change. For Jews, the decline of the family implies additional threats to Jewish social, cultural, and demographic continuity in America. When added to the empirical results of increasing rates of intermarriage and low levels of fertility, changes in marriage and the family are clearly in the direction away from Jewish demographic survival in America.

INTERMARRIAGE AND DEMOGRAPHIC SURVIVAL

Much more than fertility levels or changes in marriage patterns, intermarriage between Jews and non-Jews has called into question the possibility of quantitative and qualitative survival of a small religio-ethnic minority group in an open society. No other issue symbolizes more clearly the conflict between universalism and particularism, between the American melting pot and sociocultural pluralism, between assimilation and ethnicity. The unresolved dilemma for American Jewry revolves around traditional values of family cohesion, Jewish continuity, and endogamy on the one hand and the consistency between out-marriages and the structural-cultural features of American Jewish life on the other hand.

Until the 1960s, the Jewish group in America had been accurately described as the classic illustration of voluntary group endogamy. Social scientists hardly had a basis for questioning Jewish group continuity when their intermarriage rates were low, marriage rates high, and family patterns strong and cohesive. Demographic survival issues were rarely raised when intermarriage was a marginal feature of American Jewish life, even when Jewish fertility patterns fluctuated around replacement levels.

Evidence of increasing levels of Jewish out-marriages began to accumulate in the early 1960s, and intermarriages, conversions, and the intermarried have become more prominent features of the American Jewish situation. In the 1960s and 1970s, the demographic concerns of numerical losses through Jewish intermarriages were heightened since American Jewish population size was relatively small, dispersion more pronounced, growth through immigration insignificant, and natural increase low. Intermarriage rates indicating significant losses among the young pose a particular demographic threat to a small minority reproducing at replacement levels. In the particular American Jewish demographic context of the 1960s and 1970s, intermarriage rates have taken on additional significance.[10]

Clearly the concern of the American Jewish community about population reduction through intermarriage was not directed to macrodemographic issues that have rarely been understood fully or well documented statistically. Rather Jewish intermarriage has come to symbolize significant shifts in Jewish family life and Jewish group continuity.

Jewish intermarriage in contemporary American society is not the result of a specific desire to assimilate or a consequence of particular intermarriage norms. It is the direct result of the structure of American Jewish life and general values shared by American Jews. Indeed it is the structural integration of American Jews that results in higher rates of intermarriage among the fourth generation. These structural features include residential integration of Jewish and non-Jewish neighborhoods, social interaction between Jews and non-Jews, and public school and college attendance where Jews are a minority in a middle-class environment. A set of ideological commitments and value patterns reinforces these structural features. Conducive to high rates of intermarriage are the belief in the equality of all persons, an emphasis on liberalism, the faith in minority group integration, the rejection of ethnocentrism, and the commitment to universalism. These structural features and cultural values have come to characterize the Jewish ethnic group in America.

Intermarriage (and its sociodemographic consequences) can no longer be treated as marginal when it is the result of a deep-rooted sociopolitical ideology and value structure and a function of life-style, residential pattern, and educational occupational structure. It cannot be ignored within the Jewish community when few Jewish families have not experienced intermarriage directly or through friends and neighbors. Indeed the intermarriage issue has become one of the central axes around which revolve the internal struggles of American Jewry. For those who view intermarriage as a threat to Jewish demographic survival in America, the ultimate choice appears to be either to change the overall social structure and value orientations of the American Jewish community or to accommodate and accept the intermarried. There are no indications that the first alternative has been or will be selected by the majority of American Jews.

A brief overview of findings on changes and variations in Jewish intermarriage in the United States reveals the following patterns. Overall Jewish endogamy is high and intermarriage rates are low relative to larger American ethnic-religious groupings. However, given the specific demographic characteristics of American Jewry, the level of intermarriage represents a diminution in the size of the American Jewish population. No evaluation of the demographic survival of American Jews can ignore the centrality of Jewish intermarriages in absolute and relative Jewish population changes.

The general pattern of low rates of intermarriage based on a cross-section of the Jewish community obscures the effects of age and generation and confuses cumulative and current rates. The separation of period and cohort perspectives is no less required in the analysis of intermarriage than in fertility studies. An examination of intermarriage rates by age and generation as well as general levels of intermarriage between different time periods reveals an unmistakable pattern of increase in the volume of Jewish intermarriage. Some scattered evidence and impressions suggest that disproportionate shifts in the rate of intermarriage have occurred in the 1960s and 1970s among those currently marrying.

The systematic evaluation of the quantitative significance of changing intermarriage trends is incomplete since the level of conversions to Judaism is not well documented. Nor do we know the eventual Jewish commitments of the children of intermarried couples. The general impression from selected American studies is that the level of conversion to Judaism has increased, and some significant proportion of the children of intermarried couples are being raised as Jews. Although it is impossible with the data available to be precise, there is no question that the current rate of Jewish intermarriage reduces the size of the American Jewish population annually and has longer-term demographic significance for the size of generations yet unborn. It is also clear that not all Jewish intermarriages imply the loss to the Jewish community of the Jewish partner, the non-Jewish spouse, or the children of the couple. On the contrary, substantial evidence shows that for some select proportion of intermarried couples, the Jewish community gains rather than loses members through intermarriage, conversion, and Jewish identity and socialization of the children of intermarried couples. Moreover, some data show a tendency among those who intermarry and remain within the Jewish community to be more religious and more Jewishly committed compared to Jews endogamously married.[11] These important qualifications should not obscure the fact that perhaps only a relatively small proportion of those intermarrying are committed strongly to Jewish survival.

In addition to the question of changing intermarriage rates and their demographic implications are issues relating to differential levels of intermarriage among American Jewish communities and among subgroupings within the Jewish community.

The level of Jewish intermarriage varies considerably among communities and reflects in part social compositional variations. Communities and subcommunities (suburbs, for example) vary in the rate of intermarriage simply because of variation in the size of Jewish population and in generational and socioeconomic characteristics as well as related factors such as religiosity. It is not clear on the basis of the available information whether communities with higher intermarriage rates foreshadow what will come to characterize the Jewish American population as a whole or whether because of their size or composition these communities are exceptional.

There are some indications emerging from the literature that socio-logical differences between the intermarried and nonintermarried have diminished among recent cohorts. Analysis of changing patterns of age at marriage, fertility, socioeconomic status, and sex differentials suggests some convergence of the intermarried and nonintermarried in these characteristics. These tentative findings fit in with the general notion that intermarriage is no longer a marginal or deviant phenomenon in Ameri-can Jewish life. There appears to be much less selectivity in intermarriage processes among contemporary Jews, and the intermarried may become in terms of their characteristics, as well as subsequent behavior, not significantly different from those in endogamous marriages. In addition, the social background characteristics of the Jewish and non-Jewish part-ners to intermarriage tend to be quite similar among recent intermarried couples when compared to intermarried couples of previous generations.

Two social characteristics have been found to be related quite con-sistently to the probability of intermarriage: Jewish residential segrega-tion and Jewish education. An empirical relationship has been reported in a variety of studies between the character of residential neighborhoods and intermarriage rates. Jews living in areas of greater Jewish population concentration are more likely to be endogamous than Jews living in areas of low Jewish population densities. This may reflect the fact that con-tacts and interactions between Jews and non-Jews are integral processes determining levels of intermarriage. The more extensive and significant the interactions between Jews and non-Jews in schools, neighborhoods, organizations, and social and business activities, the greater the likeli-hood of intermarriage. It is, however, not clear whether residence in areas of low Jewish population density is a determinant of high inter-marriage rates or a consequence of selective migration patterns of intermarried couples.

A key finding of previous research has been that extensive and intensive Jewish education is generally correlated with Jewish endogamy. Again, the implications are less clear than a superficial examination might sug-gest. It is not obvious, for example, what the relationship is between Jewish education and residential segregation or the relationship between Jewish education and a variety of dimensions of Jewish identity and com-mitment. Nor does this finding specify the amount or type of Jewish edu-cation that clearly results in endogamy. However, the finding at the most simple level indicates at a minimum that commitment to Jewish survival either through Jewish education or through processes that are reflected in Jewish education is conducive to Jewish endogamy and continuity. Jewish intermarriage rates therefore tend to be highest among those who stand at the least committed end of the Jewish continuum.

A final point requires special reemphasis: it is not the level of Jewish intermarriages per se that challenges the sociodemographic survival of Jews in America. Nor are the patterns of Jewish reproduction, migration, family, or age structure exceptional in their individual and separate levels and trends. Rather it is the specific demographic context within which intermarriage rates operate in America that is of paramount significance. The combination of low fertility, geographic dispersion, minimum potential sources of population renewal through immigration or further mortality reduction, declines in family cohesion, and relatively high intermarriage rates pose the real threat to ethnic group continuity and vitality.

IMPLICATIONS AND POLICY ALTERNATIVES

There are few indications of demographic vitality and growth among the American Jewish population and no obvious sources of potential population growth in the near future. The patterns do not indicate the rapid decline of Jewish population in the United States nor an imminent disappearance. The analysis suggests, however, a shrinking middle, a smaller, declining national community, and a growth at the two polar ends of the continuum of Jewish commitment. Emerging from the investigation of change are the greater polarization and greater divisions within the American Jewish community between those who are more and those who are less committed to Jewish survival. To the extent that the children and grandchildren of those with less commitment have a low probability of Jewish survival, further population reductions and greater divisions may be expected in the future.

Are size and the potential for growth important for the future of American Jewry? How do we deal with the basic fact that Jewish communities in America and elsewhere, now and at previous historical periods, have been much more vibrant, vital, and Jewishly creative with many fewer Jews and smaller Jewish populations? The answer is complex and is tied to the total set of historical circumstances, national and international, associated with American Jewish survival. The American Jewish community represents the classic test case of whether ethnic survival is possible in a modern society characterized by universalism, equality, and openness.

More important, with the loss of six million Jews in the Holocaust, the American Jewish community has become the population center of world Jewry. Except for Israel, no other Jewish population concentration exists to compete with American Jewry as the standard-bearers of Jewish survival. The conditions of modernity in America are unprecedented in history, and the position of Jews in American society — in size, influence, and potential — is unparalleled.

Most important, the combination of factors characterizing the demography of American Jews is probably unique in Jewish history. High rates of intermarriage, replacement level fertility, population dispersal and high rates of migration, the absence of sources of population through immigration, an aging population structure, increasing rates of postponed marriage, nonmarriage, and divorce along with general declines in family cohesion and values all point in the same direction: declining population size and reduced commitment to Jewish survival. Jews in America are also characterized by a set of socioeconomic characteristics—education, occupation, and residence—that imply a continuation of these patterns. Hence, in a general and a Jewish context, the question of Jewish survival and the role of demographic factors is far from trivial.

The power of the demographic argument is strengthened, not weakened, when the whole issue of quality is raised. Clearly the demands of survival—the goals and objectives of ethnic particularism—do not necessarily emphasize more but better. It is precisely because demography and Jewish qualitative survival are not independent processes but are intimately related that the changing quantity takes on particular relevance.

Population size, composition, distribution, and the potential for sustained growth are critical for the continuity of a small minority group in an open society. The demography of Jews finds its clearest importance at the subnational level. Small Jewish communities that are aging in population and declining in size for a variety of reasons have to face their eventual demise since sources of population renewal are nonexistent. Jewish communal institutions and organizations along with the services they provide have already experienced the meaning of population change.

Moreover, demographic factors may be viewed as the ultimate indicators of the choices Jewish communities in America have made regarding Jewish continuity and survival. Jewish population decline symbolizes in dramatic ways the priorities attached to ethnic particularism and voluntary survival.

Given the importance of demographic factors in the survival of American Jewry, it is instructive to raise the question of policy and community intervention. Are there alternatives to population decline? What can be done to reverse the demography from decline toward stability, if not growth? It is beyond the scope of this paper to evaluate some alternative policies. Nevertheless, some general points emerge from our analysis.

1. Demographic factors are integral parts of the subsociety; patterns of fertility, marriage, and migration fit the social structure and values of American Jews. To alter the demography, the society has to be restructured and the values reordered. Societal processes associated with modernization, industrialization, and secular-

ism, as well as the occupational, educational, and residential characteristics of Jews, are conducive to low fertility, high rates of migration, and intermarriage.

2. Some demographic processes are more difficult to change than others, and some processes (for example, further mortality reduction and large-scale Jewish immigration) are unlikely demographic solutions to Jewish population decline.

3. Given the occupational and educational patterns of American Jews, the changing roles of women, the sexual revolution, and general sociopolitical values of Jews, it is not likely that the majority of Jews of the fourth generation will be attracted to residential segregation, highly concentrated Jewish neighborhoods, or a return to a strong family cohesion and stability.

4. There is the general issue of how policy is implemented for a minority group that lacks a central authority structure or a general sociocultural consensus. There is also the question of which segments of the Jewish community policy recommendations are addressed to. To be effective, the target population should be mainly those who are committed to Jewish survival. However, neither below-replacement fertility nor high rates of intermarriage characterize the more committed end of the Jewish continuum. The lack of general consensus among American Jews and among Jewish organizations and institutions is at the heart of the Jewish survival issue.

5. Of the wide range of demographic factors discussed, the most significant in quantitative terms for Jewish population decline is intermarriage. It does not seem any more reasonable to reduce the level of Jewish intermarriage without changing the structure and value system of American Jews than it would be to increase fertility or encourage residential segregation. Nor is it any less difficult to reduce intermarriage among the less committed than it is to implement other "Jewish" policies among that Jewish segment. However, the acceptance of the intermarried not as a loss but as a challenge might stem the decline in demographic growth. Undoubtedly the creation of a climate of acceptance of intermarried couples and their children within the Jewish community involves some radical changes in the ways committed Jews think of themselves and their future. But in this case the policy is directed to changing the attitudes of those most Jewishly committed — not an easy task, but less problematic than defining those who have minimum commitments to Jewish survival as the target population.

The demographic conditions of American Jewish survival are only in part unique in recent history or particular to Jews. The issue of whether modern society based on universal values, integration, and equality is consistent with the growth and vitality of ethnic particularism is still open. To what extent can we learn about ethnic group survival and demographic factors from comparative and historical analysis? Are there clues and suggestions about policy alternatives that may be obtained by examining other attempts at demographic intervention? In short, can we gain insight about the relationship of demography and American Jewish survival from examining other subgroups in America and around the world at various points in time? Perhaps the examination of the relationship between demography and the survival of American Jews can provide important clues for other minority groups in America and in other countries. In many ways Jews in America exemplify in accentuated form a whole range of issues associated with minority group survival in modern society.

NOTES

1. See, for example, the discussion in Calvin Goldscheider, *Population, Modernization and Social Structure* (Boston: Little, Brown and Co., 1971), chapters 8 and 10.

2. A systematic analysis of many of these features for seven ethnic groups is presented in Frances Kobrin and Calvin Goldscheider, *The Ethnic Factor: Family and Mobility Processes* (Cambridge, Mass.: Ballinger Press, 1978).

3. These perspectives have been presented in somewhat exaggerated form for emphasis. The literature upon which this discussion is based is much less categorical than my presentation. See, for example, M. Sklare, *America's Jews* (New York: Random House, 1971); M. Sklare (ed.) *The Jew in American Society* (New York: Behrman House, 1974); Arnold Dashefsky and Howard Shapiro, *Ethnic Identification Among American Jews* (Lexington, Mass.: Lexington Books, 1974); Sidney Goldstein and Calvin Goldscheider, *Jewish Americans* (Englewood Cliffs, N.J.: Prentice-Hall, Inc., 1968).

4. This is a major theme in Goldstein and Goldscheider, *Jewish Americans.*

5. Some of the basic demographic materials appears in Sidney Goldstein, "American Jewry, 1970: A Demographic Profile," *American Jewish Year Book, 1971,* vol. 72, pp. 3-88.

6. See Kobrin and Goldscheider, *The Ethnic Factor,* chapters 9 and 10.

7. See the reviews in Calvin Goldscheider, "Fertility of the Jews," *Demography* 4:1 (1967): 196-209; Calvin Goldscheider and Peter Uhlenberg, "Minority Group Status and Fertility," *American Journal of Sociology* 74:4 (January 1969): 361-372; Sidney Goldstein, "Jewish Fertility in Contemporary America," in Paul Ritterband (ed.) *Modern Jewish Fertility,* forthcoming.

8. See, for example, the studies by George Kranzler, *Williamsburg* (New York: Philipp Feldheim, 1961); Solomon Poll, *The Hasidic Community of Williamsburg* (New York: Schocken Books, 1962).

9. See Calvin Goldscheider, "Ideological Factors in Jewish Fertility Differentials," *Jewish Journal of Sociology* 7 (June 1965): 92-105; Bernard Lazarwitz, "Jewish Identification and Jewish Fertility in the Chicago Jewish Community," in U. O. Schmelz (ed.). *Papers in Jewish Demography 1969* (Jerusalem: The Institute of Contemporary Jewry, The Hebrew University of Jerusalem, 1973).

10. For a review of Jewish intermarriage, see Sklare, *America's Jews,* chapter 6; Goldstein and Goldscheider, *Jewish Americans,* chapter 8; Arnold Schwartz, "Intermarriage in the United States," *American Jewish Year Book 1970,* vol. 71, pp. 101-121.

11. See, for example, Schwartz, "Intermarriage in the United States;" Goldstein and Goldscheider, *Jewish Americans.*

6 Dialogues

GROUP FERTILITY: FACTORS AND TRENDS

CHARLES WESTOFF

If we seriously wish to predict fertility rates for the next generation, let us ask what the probability is that fertility is likely to increase as a consequence of changes in fashion or social trends or whatever. It seems unlikely. I think we ought to take a look at what is happening to marriage in this country. One of the big factors affecting fertility, as we well know, is not just contraception but changes in nuptiality patterns. Consider particularly what is happening in Sweden; it is quite amazing. Between 1967 and 1973, the number of marriages in Sweden dropped by 50 percent. The number of remarriages has also dropped, and the number of divorces has increased tremendously. Illegitimacy, as a consequence, has gone up. Fertility continues to go down.

Last year, for the first time, the same thing was beginning to happen in the United States. Marriage rates went down, remarriages have stopped increasing, and illegitimacy continues fairly high, especially among young teenagers. I would be willing to bet that we are lagging about a decade behind what is happening in Sweden. This could be the beginning of a rejection of marriage among young people, or at least a massive postponement of marriage, which seems to me to be quite inconsistent with the notion that high fertility will recur.

NATHAN GLAZER

I want to throw in a small piece of information, which suggests to me that at least at some point in modernization and development, one does have an increase in fertility. I am thinking of the work on the age of menarche, which shows that the age drops. Thus, in developing countries there seems to be evidence that the increase in growth rate is not only because of a mortality decline but because of an actual increase in fertility. And this seems to be a regular process with a surer food supply.

I think one should not expect a substantial increase in the birthrate in developed societies. On the other hand, very often we ignore the transition, which may last a long time. One forgets how long a generation is and how significant in the life of a nation thirty or sixty years may be while a transition to zero growth is occurring. The mere fact that there may be a general tendency toward convergence does not answer the question, When? Next year or in seventy years?

I don't see how developed countries can go back to big families. Two things have intrigued me in the recent literature. One is the research on intelligence and how it declines with the number of children in a family. I don't know how widespread or substantial this knowledge is, but certainly it seems quite clear that in larger families, the later children on the average have lower IQ. It seems related to the capacity of adults to interact with children and so forth.

A second thing is a similar hypothesis by a sociologist or demographer at the University of Wisconsin who argues that the size of families also affects social mobility. I think the deficiencies of large families in society, caused by the competition in advanced societies, are going to be so substantial that I find it hard to see much reversal.

DANIEL CALLAHAN

I want to get one factual question clarified. I assume the prediction of converging fertility rates presumes a convergence of socioeconomic conditions. Is the convergence of fertility rates caused by things happening independently in ethnic communities, or is it because people begin sharing a more common general culture, which affects fertility?

FREDERICK S. JAFFE

If you look at the situation in the United States in the last fifteen years, socioeconomic conditions between the poor and the rich or between blacks and whites and Chicanos or any of the other groups have not equalized. Yet the convergence in fertility is very striking, much more so than any other socioeconomic indicator.

If you say that everybody in America shares a common American culture in a vaguely defined sense, I suppose that is true to some degree. But in terms more specifically of socioeconomic conditions, there is much argument about whether the improvement of conditions among minority groups in the 1960s was rapid or slow. Yet the convergence in fertility preferences, practices, and behavior is quite striking.

It seems to me that the black fertility experience in the United States is very paradoxical from the point of view of American social science. I invite you to go back ten or fifteen years and look at the statements in the social science literature on what the norms were among blacks and what the expectations would therefore be. Then look at what happened in the last fifteen years. I don't think you find much congruence between what was in the literature fifteen years ago and what actually happened. I particularly invite you to go back six or seven years and look at the literature on attitudes toward abortion. You will find four or five psychologically oriented studies or attitude polls, and in every one of them the blacks came out less favorable to abortion than any other subgroup, with the black poor most opposed. Then look at the abortion rates in New York City, in Maryland, in California, and in every other state or city where statistics are reported on a racial basis. You will find that blacks utilize legal abortion, when it is made available, at rates per thousand women two or three times greater than whites.

I wonder when social scientists are going to face up to the fact that the paradigm they are working with is not exactly predicting the reality of the world they are living in. The discussion we are having here about the larger social context is based on that paradigm. But there are important changes in patterns taking place that are not comprehended by what we are saying.

It is time we looked at the black experience and found out, as far as we can, what caused the changes. As far as I can tell, the blacks are still black, they are still discriminated against in the United States, they have not become rich, they have not become college graduates, they still live in ghettos. You can't explain the changes in fertility norms, in family-planning practices, or in childbearing outcomes on the basis of marginal changes in the socioeconomic position of blacks. One thing that did change substantially was the availability of effective fertility control services to low-income persons generally, including the black poor. Utilization of such services by blacks increased dramatically in the past decade.

The fertility decline among blacks has been not only among professional middle-class blacks but among the black poor as well. And the people who are having abortions in New York City are not only middle-class black women, they are the patrons of the municipal hospitals and they are the black poor. And in fact, the abortion rates in the poorest black geographical areas of New York City are higher than those of any other area.

Few social scientists would have predicted this five or ten years ago. Charles Westoff might have, because his findings showed that the proportion of unwanted and unplanned births among blacks was much higher than among whites. Based on those findings, it could have been predicted that if abortion became legal, available, and accessible, a very large number of blacks would utilize it. But I don't think many other social scientists gave very serious attention to these findings. In fact, they mostly spent their time discounting them.

I wonder when they are going to start paying attention. It is a serious question. I have been observing this process for a long time, and I don't see any regeneration of theory from reality. The reality continues to exist on one level and the theory continues on quite another. There is not much congruence between the two.

HARRIET PRESSER

It is hard to predict trends. If you look at survey data you find that people's own answers about what they are going to do in the near future may not be good indicators of their future behavior. In the case of attitudes toward abortion, for example, the pattern of responses changed considerably after abortion became legal.

In studies on family size preferences in New York City, we found that people's preferences are not very stable, and the variations have nothing to do with ethnic group. Even over a period of a year, 50 percent of the respondents may change their minds about preferred family size, despite the fact that the most popular desired family size is two children. Even though the range of variability has narrowed, people still shift between wanting two and one, two and three, one and three, or none. There are some people who say they regret having had any.

There is another point that should be emphasized. When we talk about differential fertility, we compare groups, but there are also variations within groups. We are really talking about the average number of children in a family, and that "average" averages out a great deal. Blacks may have higher fertility than whites, but there is also more childlessness among blacks.

Education affects fertility patterns, but we don't know the exact relationship. Perhaps there is an educational threshold beyond which fertility behavior converges sharply. Maybe high-school graduation is the threshold in the United States, and in Latin America it might be eighth grade. Perhaps as the population passes that educational threshold, the marginal effect of education on fertility becomes quite small.

BERNARD BERELSON

Just as the Jews today are a special case of low fertility on the American scene, the Mormons are a case of high fertility—despite their low mortality, high level of education, affluence, urbanization, and membership in the social mainstream. Why are they so distinctive? The full answer apparently is not in, at least not to the satisfaction of specialized scholars, but there do appear to be some doctrinal themes that underlie their relatively high fertility. Mormons believe in a preexistence and an afterlife surrounding this earthly existence, and in the theology the millennium cannot come until all the latent souls have gone through the earthly form. Thus the individual Mormon has an obligation to participate in, even expedite, that necessary process. Accordingly, abortion is much disapproved, and even contraception not quite approved. Without much question, their residential concentration in and around Utah helps to keep the doctrine strong and operative through social reinforcement. In addition, there may be a particular valuation placed on male children since the entry keys into heaven are believed to be held only by men. Will the Mormons converge toward the lower fertility norm of the mainstream? Well, they have not yet—and on the other side of the issue, the Jews have maintained low fertility within their societies of residence for a very long time. So in the Mormon case, it may be that the doctrinal distinction carries more weight than the socioeconomic similarity.

CHARLES KEELY

If there continue to be differentials in fertility among groups and even some very extreme cases, for example, the Mormons, I wonder if the distinction that Etienne van de Walle made in types of groups and certain structural characteristics of groups might explain these differentials.

For example, it seems to me that we can conclude that territorial groups probably have less of this "survival instinct" than, say, religious groups or language groups. I wonder if we can isolate characteristics, perhaps subtle characteristics, of groups that may lead them to higher or lower fertility during and even after this transition and convergence?

JUDITH BANKI

I would like to know whether there is some available information or data on the relationship between fertility and catastrophe—not about long-run, long-range mortality, but a specific regional, national, ethnic, or group catastrophe. For example, I believe something like fifteen million Russians were killed during World War II. My understanding is that after that period, the Russian birthrate went up significantly and then came down with the replenishment of the population.

I don't know what the statistics are for the Jewish community in the period immediately following the Holocaust. Statistically, is there not some relationship between a particular catastrophe and a change for a period thereafter in the birthrate? Would this not be consonant in some sense with a desire for group survival? It may also be that with the loss of so many men, there may have been larger families. There may have been fewer men, but the men that were there may have fathered more children.

SAMUEL BAUM

The data show no consistent relationship between the number of casualties suffered by European and North American countries during World War II and the extent of the baby boom that occurred after the war.

The postwar baby boom was the most impressive in the United States and Canada where there were no civilian war casualties, whereas some European countries (England, Germany, Italy) with heavy civilian war casualties experienced only a moderate increase in birthrates in the postwar period (1945-49).

Among blacks in the United States, fertility rates declined during 1960-1970. Between 1960 and 1970 fertility rates declined not only for blacks but also for Spanish-Americans and American Indians. The decline in birthrates between 1967 and 1970 (the period for which fertility data for minorities are most adequate) was larger for each of the three minority groups than for urban whites. American Indians had the largest decline, followed by blacks and Spanish-Americans.

ETIENNE VAN DE WALLE

The Mormons are an interesting case. They keep coming up in the discussion, and someone might also have thrown in the Hutterites, who have such a high fertility that they should have conquered the United States by now, but many of them abandon the Hutterite creed and join the mainstream. As for the Mormons, they represent the classical example of a people deciding: "We are going to step out of the mainstream; we are going to an isolated region where we shall be able to have a place of our own, a kingdom on earth for the Lord." And they have done so. But they have escaped the demographic transition only for a while. Mormon fertility is on its way down, and they don't have the large families they used to have any more. Similarly, if you look at pockets of high fertility in Europe — obscure little valleys in the Alps and so on — the fertility is coming down everywhere. Everyone is converging, although not necessarily right to the bottom, and there will be some differentials left. But it is safe to say that the past fertility norms of the Mormons (and others) are not actually determining their numbers of children today and that their fertility norms are in turn affected by their actual reproductive performance and their ability to influence it by resorting to birth control.

Now I shall do my best to justify what may well be a somewhat heretical point of view. First, from talking to Charles Westoff and Norman Ryder, I understand that fertility norms are hard to define or measure because of the invincible tendency of parents to readjust them toward their actual number of children, or toward the number of children that they presume they will not be able to avoid. Second, there may have been changes in norms in the last century, but if so they have tended to converge toward the small family in all Western populations. Under the circumstances, I see the large fertility differentials existing in the West in the past, and the differences in growth rates that have resulted and are of concern to us here, essentially as a temporary phenomenon, explained by lags in the contraceptive revolution. If various groups are at different stages between the beginning of their long-term fertility decline and the time when they hit the bottom, then large differentials will be obvious in cross-section. These will gradually be attenuated after all groups have completed the transition. Increased effectiveness in controlling fertility, rather than changing norms, should contribute toward even greater convergence of family sizes in the future.

I agree that the distinction between norms and means is a weak one, since both keep interacting. Norms readjust themselves when contraceptive means become available, which will permit lower family norms to become effective.

I disagree with the view that there has been no convergence in fertility performance. I am even predicting—perhaps out of ignorance—that it is going to converge even more. Obviously every country or nation has started from a point in the past where women had an average of perhaps seven or more births. We are now close to an average of two in all the countries that have gone through the population transition. The fact that most groups in developed countries are near the average of two children is not an accident; it reflects the convergence.

Obviously there were many fluctuations of fertility in the recent past—the baby boom, for instance—and there will be more in the future. We may well have a bottoming out and rise of American fertility in the next few years. What I am arguing is the irreversibility of the long-term decline from seven to two children. There is no historical experience of such a reversal.

As for the baby boom, it was a small ripple in the secular fertility decline, which it interrupted for reasons that are poorly understood. It was perhaps an accident, but it did not represent a long-term change in the desired family size of American women.

NORMAN PODHORETZ

Must the decline in fertility be viewed as an irreversible process? Might the trend not bottom out and then change? One could argue that there are some signs in contemporary culture pointing toward precisely such a reversal, given certain conditions. One might anticipate, for example, a rebellion against the contraceptive pill for reasons of health or for other reasons. We may not be justified in extrapolating the downward trend into the future.

Look at the development of modernization. One could hardly have predicted a few years ago that there would be an ideological rebellion against the idea of growth generally in modernization. One could just as well have projected that there would be support for infinite technological and economic growth. The paradox is that the rebellion against growth that one now sees everywhere is accompanied by an opposite reaction with respect to population. Many of the people who are against technological growth are for doing exactly what comes naturally, and in fact they have a bias against contraception. This tendency has not yet expressed itself statistically, but I would not be surprised to see statistical expression of it under certain conditions in the coming years, precisely in the more technologically advanced industrial societies like our own.

MILTON HIMMELFARB

I too am bothered by saying that a trend is "irreversible." By "irreversible" I suppose one means "unreversed so far." But was there, for instance, a rise in the birthrate of the bourgeoisie in England between the infidel eighteenth century and the evangelical nineteenth? That is to say, the movement has not always been from superstition to enlightenment. It has fluctuated. There have been religious revivals. And with religious revivals, to the extent that they are serious, there is a transformation of the outlook on life and on the world.

Now the new mysticism among young people is in part a body mysticism. You must do what is natural. Contraception, let alone abortion, may increasingly come to be seen as unnatural and therefore to be rejected.

In answer to the question about catastrophe, the last issue of the newspaper published by the Jewish displaced persons—the survivors of the death camps—boasted about the extraordinarily high birthrate among the people in the DP camps.

DOV FRIEDLANDER

I don't think that the fertility of Jewish death camp survivors was unusually high. A retrospective fertility survey covering the different population subgroups in Israel provides family size estimates among Jewish women immigrants from Europe during mass immigration (1948-51), many of whom were survivors of death camps. There is no sign of increase in fertility over and above "making up" for the time in death camps. Their fertility experience does not lend support to the hypothesis that the urge for group survival tends to affect fertility levels in general and for the American Jewish community (because of "leakage") in particular.

It seems to me that discussions and statements concerning the relationship between the spread of contraception and levels of reproduction or those emphasizing the change in societal norms and family size are not very useful. Indeed if we agree that the number of children in the family tends to be functional with respect to other familial and societal aspects (and not all demographers agree on that), then it is the change in the functions that tends to affect both reproductive behavior and the norms concerning reproduction. It may therefore be hypothesized that it is the conflict between levels of reproductive behavior on the one hand and other societal processes on the other that should be examined to explain changes in fertility and family size. This seems to me a more promising approach. Since nineteenth-century England has been mentioned, I would add that it may indeed be a good illustration. It can be shown that differences in the functions of children between agricultural communities and coal-mining communities at that time can explain differences and changes both in nuptiality and in marital fertility.

Turning to the future, the question of whether fertility levels of the Jewish community in the United States (or for that matter of any other population group) may be expected to increase can be answered only if we can project what kind of a society it is likely to be. Is it going to be a society for which a return to the large family may be expected to be functional and appropriate? My intuition leads me to reject such a hypothesis. This is based on my belief that in the coming decades the conflict between rapid population growth and the welfare of the family and the individual will not diminish and that the cost of raising children will further increase, to mention just two reasons. It seems to me very unlikely that Jewish fertility in the United States may be expected to increase dramatically in the future. Indeed, further declines in the future may be even more probable.

GARY SCHIFF

There is now a differential fertility pattern among Jews in the United States as well, for example, in the Orthodox community. While the Hasidim and other traditional groups have maintained a consistently high rate of fertility, only recently has this pattern begun to have an effect on the fertility behavior of the modern or neo-Orthodox Jews, by setting minimal standards in this area as in other forms of religious observance and behavior. On the basis of personal observation in various modern Orthodox suburban communities, it is clear that these modernized but still traditionalist Jews are thinking of having the third, fourth, and even fifth child, whereas one generation earlier the two-child family was the accepted norm. Thus, there is an emulative factor within an ethnic group that may operate independently, and at times in reverse, of the macrotrends.

Jews have also emulated the endogenous fertility trends of the non-Jews among whom they live. A patent example of this phenomenon is pre-World War I Poland. Since Poland had been divided into Russian, German, and Austrian sectors, the Jews living in each area conformed to the prevailing non-Jewish fertility behavior rather than to any indigenous Jewish pattern. Thus, for example, the Jews of the Russian empire exhibited extremely high fertility patterns, and those of the German empire showed extremely low patterns. Their fertility behavior, therefore, was a function of their desire to assimilate to the surrounding culture and their perception of the receptivity of that culture to them.

CALVIN GOLDSCHEIDER

It seems to me somewhat inappropriate to talk about fertility norms and contraceptive usage and the interaction between them as "determinants" of fertility differentials. Changes in specific fertility norms and contraceptive usage are clearly means to attain certain goals and not the explanation of differential fertility patterns. Moreover, the emphasis on a "transition" model implies convergence of fertility differences. The implication is that there is a beginning and an end to the transition from high to low fertility and a "lag" among various groups who are responding to these changes.

Rather than conceptualizing the processes of fertility change and fertility variation in terms of transition and lags, it seems to me more appropriate to conceptualize the processes involved as adjustments in fertility that are made in response to a wide range of social and economic conditions. These conditions include ideological and cultural factors that have been operative in the past and will continue to operate in the future as determining factors in fertility differentials. To discuss convergence and disappearance of fertility differences as lags rather than adjustments is in a sense to assume the convergence and disappearance of all socio-cultural differences. This is essentially arguing a demographic melting-pot theory of fertility differentials and is no more accurate than general melting-pot theories. As long as fertility is a response to the total set of socioeconomic cultural conditions of subgroups, I would not expect the disappearance of fertility differences any more than I would expect these conditions to be equalized.

Certainly differential fertility is not solely a function of the availability of the means to control fertility. Fertility is a response to the total social situation of minority ethnic or social groups, and to ignore the power of that "fit" or adjustment is to miss a central point with regard to ethnic group differences. I would not expect convergence of fertility differences in the near future any more than I would expect convergence of all ethnic differences.

Let me clarify my basic argument. The position that I have taken does not argue that there has not been convergence in fertility levels. Rather I am saying that if the explanation of that convergence is in terms of the availability of contraception and the convergence of fertility norms rather than in terms of adjustments to sociocultural conditions, then one would predict the elimination of all fertility differences. Fertility will obviously vary around low levels in modern societies just as it varied around higher levels in the past. I don't deny the convergence of fertility difference, but I do challenge the conclusions arrived at when differences are explained in terms of contraceptive usage and fertility norms. The societal factors that operate to move fertility toward lower levels tend to affect all subgroups. Nevertheless, fertility differences will not be totally eliminated.

Often we treat ethnic and social subgroups in very broad terms as if these were homogeneous groups. Blacks, Jews, Catholics are hetero-geneous populations within the United States, and there are segments within these communities that are characterized by very high and very low fertility. In national terms, and in a practical sense, the impact of these segments is marginal in affecting overall fertility levels. These sub-strata differences are nevertheless important in terms of the demography of ethnic groups.

As for mortality and fertility, although these two factors are linked as demographic variables to population growth, the distinctions between them as processes are obvious. Fertility relates to norms; questions of individual decision making and goals are important components of fer-tility processes and are irrelevant to mortality. Why use the mortality experience as the model for fertility change? Indeed, that is what demographers have shown repeatedly: the analysis of fertility patterns involves different processes from those of mortality, and hence the analytic analogies made between them are most limited. When dealing with future fertility patterns, we have to focus on changing norms and not only the availability and efficiency of contraception. And normative changes are much more complex to deal with in terms of the future.

Now, I have been asked to summarize this part of the discussion. Perhaps I might begin by indicating that a large number of the critical issues have been discussed previously in a variety of forms, but I know of little research that has been addressed specifically to the question of population and intergroup relations. The evidence that has been brought to bear on the issues has been gathered for other purposes, and it is often inadequate, it seems to me, to test out directly some of the relationships that have been examined. One consequence of discussing the issues and focusing on this topic is to encourage research in this area.

The discussion here has focused on two major themes. We first examined the question of differential fertility. Then we discussed the problem of small group demographic survival.

First, on the question of differential fertility, two major items emerged from that discussion. There was general agreement that convergence of fertility behavior has occurred. Modern societies have reached the point where family size is relatively small and fertility differences between groups are much smaller now than they used to be. Fertility differences are narrower than they were when the transition toward lower fertility was just getting under way, and some groups responded much more rapidly than others to social change.

Although much convergence has occurred, fertility differentials continue to exist. We have not reached the point of uniformity in fertility attitudes and behavior among all subgroups in modern society.

The possibility that in the future greater uniformity in fertility may emerge was discussed, as was the possibility that some fertility differences might remain. Clearly fertility differentials exist in contemporary society although the range of variation is smaller.

The argument about future fertility rates centered on the question of whether fertility differentials merely reflect temporary cultural lags. The point was strongly made that there are factors in modern society preventing the return to large family size. In fact, these factors force the variation in fertility or the differentials in fertility around very small numbers. The differential discussed is between two and three children, and there appears to be no reasonable basis to suggest a return to a differential between two and seven children. In the context of modern society, social and psychological forces operate to encourage small family size.

The difference in views with regard to future fertility patterns results partly from the different types and levels of explanation that one brings to bear in accounting for these differences. Some speakers viewed contraceptive usage and birth-control technology as the dominant intermediate variables affecting fertility differences. Others emphasized that social and economic factors are the underlying determinants of these intermediate variables. Differential fertility has to be understood in a functional context. The low fertility of Jews and the relatively high fertility of Mormons, for example, have to be seen in a context of the socioeconomic conditions of Mormons and Jews. It is not that Mormons do not have access to modern contraceptive technology while Jews do. Everyone wants the smallest number of unwanted children, but some may want more children than others. That reflects the functional adjustment of fertility to a variety of societal or social, economic, or cultural conditions.

It seems to me that the range of family size may be less significant than the range in the timing and tempo of childbearing. In this regard, it is not sufficient to look at broad groups such as blacks or Jews or other ethnic, social, religious, and minority groups as if they were homogeneous, cohesive units characterized by common fertility patterns. There may be a greater variation within groups than between groups.

ATTEMPTS TO ALTER FERTILITY RATES

BERNARD BERELSON

There appears to be a judgment in the air that dictatorial countries have been more successful than democratic countries at influencing fertility—not necessarily because they have more impact directly on people's behavior but because once the policy is adopted, the totalitarian government can make the bureaucracy work harder at it and disregard any kickbacks from the field. China as against India is the obvious example—China with its exhortation in the name of the revered leader and its use of the political apparatus to make community norms dominant over individual desires. On the pronatalist side, the child-assistance programs of Western Europe have not seemed to increase fertility very much, but we do have the dramatic example of something like a 60 percent increase in fertility in Rumania over a period of a decade or more from the single governmental action of suddenly withdrawing permission for a legal abortion. It is worth noting that the Rumanian curve is one of the sharpest in recent fertility history. Another was the Japanese downturn, also directly related to the availability of induced abortion. If those are the two most dramatic instances of recent years, they both derive from technological change, not social or cultural movement—that is, the technology shifted, not the norms.

Decisions on family size, however imperfect they may be, are best left up to the individual family. The parents know better than anybody else how many children they want to have—and those decisions cumulate into what their community—the nation as a whole or some subgroup—will have. But that leaves a key question unanswered: What if people are not satisfied with the outcome? Some of us, for example, think that the Indians have too many children and some of us think that the American Jews have too few. How is that, and is there anything in common here? With regard to India, the advocate would say that he favored full availability of the means of fertility control Surely American Jews have that but village Indians do not. Now that can be supplied to them, but even then the outcome is not satisfying, so the position is amended to say that people have to have full information about consequences of their fertility behavior, both individual and collective—the children won't get educated, there will be too much unemployment twenty years from now, and so on. There again the American Jews are surely advantaged: If they do not have full information about consequences, nobody does. But not so for the Indian villagers, so an educational job has to be done there. So what if the outcome still does not seem right by some standard? Then we have to conclude that the fertility market is not working very well, that what economists call the negative externalities are not being taken into account in either of our two illustrative populations. The Indians may suffer economically from too high fertility maintained over time, and American Jews may not appreciate the impact of low fertility upon their collective position, spiritual and otherwise. That raises a whole set of instrumental questions that are not easily handled, but short of something like Chinese persuasion, the channels of strong influence and impact are not many, promising, or attractive. Inform and propagandize, fine, but will that have an effect here? Change life conditions, fine, but how to do that there?

Beware of the philosophical traps in this argument. Having another child for the fatherland has been and is abhorrent to most of us. What about having another child for the survival of a special group? In one case, it is the bad guys and in the other case the good guys, but what is the structural difference in the argument, not to mention the perceptions of other subgroups in the society, when one seeks to maintain or develop a competitive advantage through differential fertility?

ERNEST ATTAH

The Black Muslims are probably the main group of blacks that have systematically opposed birth control. They have made much of the possibility of genocidal designs being executed through encouragement of fertility limitation. Their newspaper has repeatedly carried reports and commentary with dramatic headlines, dealing with such cases as the sterilization of two young girls in Alabama. However, we do not know if the Muslims themselves actually undertook to increase their own fertility. Thus it might be interesting to study the recent trends in the fertility levels of the Black Muslims specifically, and possibly also other particular groups of blacks. There is the individual case of Dick Gregory, for example, who has undertaken, to breed as rapidly as possible; but we have no evidence right now as to how widespread this pattern has been. Since we do know that black fertility levels on the whole have decreased substantially over the last decade and a half, I would guess that this pattern has not been very widespread.

There is a difference between the rhetoric that gets printed in newspapers and thereby finds its way into occasional quotations in the social-science literature and the real structure of attitudes and practices across the community as a whole. Although the genocide argument may make news headlines and cause a stir when some prominent black person or perhaps a media-appointed community leader says something about it, the actual atmosphere in the community may be quite different from what one might suppose from listening to the rhetorical statements of such headliners. For example, in Pittsburgh, Dr. Charles Greenley was very active against birth control clinics being installed in the black ghettos and took it upon himself to engineer the closing of a particular clinic. However, the black women who lived in that area organized themselves and had that clinic reopened because they wanted the services.

I would also like to note a possible limitation of the data. Typically social science surveys are conducted with people whose residences can be identified and who, for their part, can be caught up with and convinced to donate the time to answering questions. One then trusts that the responses are straightforward and motivated solely by the religious or other moral and ethical principles that direct the frame of the respondent's attitudes and behavior. My question is this: Having found widespread opposition to abortion in sample surveys, what are we to make of the large numbers of abortions that take place at the same time? What segment of the black population is represented by the respondents in these surveys, and from what segments do the people who have abortions come?

MARY M. KRITZ

I have a question about Fred Jaffe's paper. What is the usage of the term *power* in his paper, and what does it derive from? Supposedly, greater power results from occupying higher status positions, but is this to be interpreted as a benefit to the individuals—improved income—or to the ethnic group? If the latter, does this mean that members of ethnic groups will perform tasks differently from members of the dominant white group or of other minority groups?

Toward the end of Mr. Jaffe's paper he mentioned that between 1960 and 1970 there was a convergence across all U.S. ethnic groups in fertility behavior. One article by James Sweet noted some contradictory evidence on this point. Sweet found that for three groups—blacks, American Indians, and white rural farm—there was a convergence in that their fertility rates declined faster than those of the native white population. However, for Japanese- and Chinese-Americans the fertility gaps with native whites remained constant and for a third group, Puerto Ricans, the gap widened. Thus, at least one article provides evidence that questions the claim made by several speakers to the effect that convergence in fertility rates was inevitable.

FREDERICK S. JAFFE

For a definition of power, I simply used a common-sense definition of a group's ability to enforce its ends or secure its survival. I looked at what the scholars say are the determinants of power. There is relatively little discussion of these questions at a group level; the literature is more extensive at the national level. The consensus seems to be that there are multiple determinants of national power, of which size is one, but only one, of the elements. Of the other elements, I find particularly applicable the concept of human capital or human resources development, however expressed—basically the same notion of how much a group invests in its future generations.

The underlying concept of my paper is that it is very difficult for a society or a group to intervene in fertility processes in any direction. We start with this difficulty. Then the question becomes, Is it easier to increase fertility or reduce it? In the literature on population decline in the 1930s in Europe, there was an almost naïve assumption that the decline could be reversed if the conditions of maternity or motherhood were made a little more attractive, really very little more attractive. They did not put very much into making motherhood terribly attractive. And they were surprised when they found out that births did not increase. Even when de Gaulle later increased the level of family allowances, things still did not change.

Against that background, in the last ten years I believe the rate of change has been more rapid in the less-developed countries that have initiated family-planning programs designed to reduce fertility—not rapid enough, perhaps, but more rapid than occurred in European nations that were attempting to increase fertility. I imagine that these considerations underlie Bernard Berelson's conclusion that it is easier to reduce fertility than to increase it.

I relied mainly on Sweet's article, but there are, I think, others. Nonetheless the expectation would have been quite the other way. The fact that fertility has been dropping faster among blacks, American Indians, and Mexican-Americans than other urban whites is therefore a very remarkable finding.

The case of the black composition in major cities is very interesting. The concern and anxiety that blacks are going to take over American cities has been a dominant theme of American political life for the last twenty years. Associated with it automatically in the minds of most publicists, media, and influentials has been the relationship with higher black fertility. Has anybody studied the relative contributions of fertility and migration to the racial composition of American cities?

If it is migration, then it is not a function of differential fertility; it is a function of American farm policy, which began after World War II to get rid of the family farm and develop agribusiness, without looking at the implications for the political composition of cities. The point is that most of the discussion centers around fertility and there is very little discussion of the other factors, which may have been more important.

In general I take a dim view of exhortation as an effective means of inducing behavioral change. In terms of differentials between types of societies, we had the experience with the Nazis and fascists in the 1930s and the Soviet Union. I do not think they did much better than democratic countries did in effectively exhorting their people to have more children. That is what the literature I have read on that experience appears to say.

The one case that is provable is Rumania's action to illegalize abortion. The birthrate went up very fast and then began to taper off. Researchers like Michael Teitelbaum and Nick Wright, who have looked at Rumanian data, expect that the rate will probably dwindle back down toward something close to what it was before 1967. They interpret this to mean that the illegal abortion industry is now functioning again. Now that is an effective means. When the government changes that kind of policy, something happens, at least in the short run. There is a whole literature on positive inducements, and the arguments get to be almost theological, to my tastes. I do not know how other people would want to add up what they have seen in the literature of the effectiveness or ineffectiveness of those programs. I add them up as not very effective. Canada introduced a family allowance program right after World War II, and the changes in the Canadian fertility curve are identical to those in the fertility curve in the United States, a roughly comparable kind of society. But we had no family allowance program.

Our conventional notions of the relationships between a group's leaders and members are under sharp attack almost universally, and not only within minority groups. In the last fifteen years, young people in this country have been challenging in fundamental ways the traditional concepts of leadership and authority. The concept of an elite that knows best what needs to be done compared to members who know least and are to be led — that is under very great challenge.

One point is implicit in my paper that should be made explicit: there are different requirements in the translation from the knowledge base to policy making. The uniformity of policy response across ideologies suggests that there are deep-seated assumptions that have not been challenged by the social-science community. In effect social scientists allow the assumption to continue by not challenging them. I was looking for the knowledge base to support those assumptions. I could not find it. You can read the research and argue about it and have different opinions as to how to interpret it. But I do not think it can support the kinds of assumptions that are invariably reflected in all kinds of groups and all kinds of societies. Those assumptions are little different today from what they were a hundred years ago, and that is depressing. With the increase in knowledge, we would have hoped that the form of the argument would have changed at least. A little more enlightenment should have been shed and a little less heat.

It seems to me what we really have is a problem at the level of underlying assumptions, which are inherently broad-brush assumptions. To deal with them, we have to sweep with another kind of broad brush that says, "You really can't make that assumption." Maybe you can't make the opposite assumption either, but in terms of what we know, your assumption is untenable. Social scientists don't feel comfortable using that kind of broad brush, and that is one reason they don't seem to contribute often to many policy debates.

A most interesting question that lies buried in all of this is the relationship between the individual and the group, whether the group is defined as a subgroup or a nation, how the respective claims are adjudicated, and how we conceptualize their interpretation. The ways in which they have been conceptualized have not been very satisfactory. The conceptualization is very selective in terms of focusing on only certain factors and leaving out large chunks of human experience. The latest omission to which we now are (or should be) sensitized is the experience of women. But that is only the latest one, and I am sure there are many more yet to come. Five years from now, or ten, we are going to ask, Why didn't we put that into the calculus, too? We don't put it into the calculus because our conceptualization begins with biases and those biases constitute our assumptions which are rarely challenged directly.

There is also a point about the Chinese situation that I would like to emphasize. I can conceive of a process of social decision making as described in China as being acceptable in a society where presumably they do a lot of social decision making about everything. I find it very difficult to see that it would be acceptable in a society such as ours where we do almost none of it, where nobody has experience with social mechanisms to deliberate about how many cars we should buy, how many acres we should live on, how much income we should strive for, or any other major aspects of our existence. In such societies, I just don't see how one can expect to establish communal committees to decide who can bear a child.

DAVID L. SILLS

Fred Jaffe has adopted a classic social science analysis position. He has examined the policy proposition that minority groups seek to increase their size and, instead of moralizing about this position, instead of attempting to design a utopia around it, he has tried to analyze the trade-offs that are involved. In the course of the discussion of his review of the trade-offs, there were a number of questions and objections raised by participants in the discussion. These are not very large, but in the following summary I will make the best of them.

Jaffe's position on the problem of minority group survival can be summarized by four statements. First, the problem of minority group survival is not new. Second, minority groups or sympathetic do-gooders can't do much about a declining birthrate. Third, if they do try to do something, they are likely to bring about unanticipated and negative consequences. Fourth, it does not matter much in any case, since culture, rather than numbers, is what counts from the point of view of minority group survival.

Jaffe's paper describes three assumptions of pronatalist leaders. The first assumption is that size brings power; Jaffe says this is not true. He provides as his major illustration the relative power of the twenty-four million blacks in this country versus the six million Jews.

I am reminded of the problem of right-of-way in sailing. There are very elaborate rules about who has the right-of-way when two boats approach each other. Commercial boats have the right-of-way over recreational boats; sailboats have the right-of-way over powerboats; and sailboats that are sailing into the wind have the right-of-way over boats that are sailing with the wind. There are many more rules than these. It is all very complicated, and since I am a compulsive law abider, I have internalized these rules and have even developed a mnemonic device to remember them. But there is one rule that is not written down in any of the dozen or so sailing books that I have read: larger boats have the right-of-way over smaller boats. And if you don't believe that, just go sailing on Long Island Sound in a small boat on a Sunday afternoon in July.

In a certain sense, in spite of all of the obvious reasons for deprecating population size, bigger does have the right-of-way. Nigeria, far and away the largest country in tropical Africa, has more influence in African meetings than does any other African country.

The second assumption of pronatalist leaders is that lower fertility brings lower relative size, but all this depends upon a very long time frame. In short, the time frame of demography is much longer than the time frame of political discussions. I don't think anyone argued very much about this; we were basically so put off by anything involving more than forty-five years that we did not have very much to say on the topic.

Milton Himmelfarb has told me a very informative story abut the revival of the Hebrew language. About a hundred years ago, Hebrew was a dead language, as Latin is today. But a man named Ben Yehudah proposed that Hebrew be revived. He was laughted at by everyone, but he persevered, and, of course, within the next forty years Hebrew was in fact revived and is today a living language.

Himmelfarb's point is that Hebrew is the only dead language that has ever been revived, and yet if you can demonstrate that you can in fact revive one dead language in the course of forty years, why can't you revive the decline of a people within forty years? There is certainly a problem here of improper analogies between language revival and demographic revival, and the problem hinges on the time frame of demographic processes.

The third assumption of pronatalist leaders that Jaffe attacked is that higher fertility is all good and has no negative consequences. His cost-benefit analysis led to a number of unanticipated consequences of higher fertility. He mentioned higher dependency ratios, educational and occupational penalties, higher infant mortality, genetic defects, lower status of women, and other social consequences.

A FERTILITY POLICY FOR JEWISH SURVIVAL?

MILTON HIMMELFARB

I was struck by the example near the end of Bernard Berelson's paper. It shows that another child per Jewish family in the United States would produce twelve million Jews in a mere forty-five years. That is only one or two generations.

The Jews are survivors of survivors. The historian Salo Baron has estimated that two thousand years ago, during the Roman Empire, there were perhaps ten million Jews in the world. Now here we are two thousand years later, and there are not many more than that. At about the same time, someone has pointed out, there were ten million Chinese, too, but now there are rather more than that. Presumably there are as many biological descendants today of those ten million Jews of two thousand years ago as there are biological descendants of those ten million Chinese of two thousand years ago. The difference is that most of those descendants of Jews are not Jews, for well-understood historical reasons. Those who are Jews are the survivors of survivors.

It is altogether reasonable to assume that for a group that is quintessentially the minority group in the Western world, and that furthermore likes to send its children to the universities, the forces of attrition, erosion, and leakage will continue to operate even more strongly. From a cold, body-count point of view, if you are expecting an attrition rate of say 33 percent, you are dead if you average two children per famiy, but you are still in business if you have three children per family.

Why is quantitative calculus important qualitatively? Because there is the matter of critical mass. Unless you have a given number of warm bodies, you can't have institutions. You can't have a Jewish religious school unless there are enough kids in a neighborhood to fill the seats. You can't have a synagogue unless there are enough people to attend. You can't have a Jewish Theological Seminary, which is a distinguished scholarly institution, unless there is a base upon which it can rest. There is the question of demoralization, as well. What happens when your whole community is a kind of vast old folks' home, and there are signs of death all around, with far more funerals than circumcision celebrations or other signs of life?

Obviously one can use the migration or the national-population analogy, where immigration, emigration, fertility, mortality all enter into the account. I suppose the analogy in the Jewish community would be conversion (or entry) to Judaism, to offset, at the very least, departures from Judaism. Though I personally am in favor of conversion for nondemographic reasons, as a practical or demographic matter I don't know how useful it is. As an ethical proposition, I don't know how ethical it is to reason that if we are too effete to breed our own children, we will depend on others to do our breeding for us.

There was a nineteenth-century French aristocratic poet, Villiers de l'Isle Adam, who once had a marvelous line, "Vivre? Nos domestiques font cela pour nous." Live? Our servants do that for us! It is neither right nor healthy to let others do our living for us, and that includes letting them do our birthing for us. Jews need a fairly respectable fertility behavior to offset the losses that can reasonably be expected.

There are various devices for keeping fertility high. There is the isolation device. You withdraw within your own boundaries, and you don't send your children to school, and certainly not to college. The Amish use that. Amish don't go to college, almost by definition. You pull in, you isolate yourself. Most Jews don't do that. I don't. My children go to college. But knowing this about ourselves and knowing that a romantic-love ideology is regnant, and all the rest of it, how can we not expect a great amount of—let me use that word again—leakage? Consequently, from the point of view of community policy, things ought to be done that would encourage those parents who are going to send their children to college to have not two but three children.

The Jewish community is engaged in huge educational enterprises. But the world in which we live is one where universalistic ideologies appeal: "I am a citizen of the world. I am a human being first. You parochial Jews with your parochial problems, dont try to hold me back." If you send your children to colleges where that is the unchallenged ideology, how can you expect its appeal to diminish? It is no secret that in the past two hundred years the world has become less religious and certainly that classical institutional religion has been greatly weakened. All these things being so, are we not deluding ourselves if by a self-denying ordinance we rely for our survival on the appeal of particularist ideology and culture alone?

It is a question of simple arithmetic. If I'm going to lose 33 percent and I start with three, I end up with two, which is the same number as my wife and I. But if I start with two and lose 33 percent, for every thousand couples, or two thousand adults, with a 33 percent loss rate and a modal two-child family, in one generation you'll be down to something like 1,300, in the next generation down to fewer than 900, and in the next down to fewer than 600.

Let me give you a science-fiction scenario. I have all the money in the world. Suppose I offer a bounty, or guaranteed free tuition through age thirty-four, for every Jewish child throughout the world. Now, obviously, this is science fiction. But in principle, it is only an application of the carrot and the stick. When you don't have much stick to apply, you have to use a lot of carrot. But we haven't reached the point where we can discuss this kind of thing.

Milton Friedman believes in a free market, and one essential of a free market is information and knowledge. If the *New York Times* or the *Village Voice* could publish announcements, "Wanted: Jewish children for adoption," with the present inflation, Jewish children might go for, say $20,000 each. If there were such a free market, some of that demand might be met by increased supply.

Obviously situations differ. As a matter of fact, this discussion does not mirror the real world. The great population problem of the world today is the existence of a population explosion. What I am speaking of is an exceptional, maybe even unique, situation of population implosion. It does not seem to me necessary that measures adopted to cope with implosion should have to meet the same requirements as those applicable to explosion. They are two different situations.

When the ordinary American medical practitioner is asked to give nutrition advice, he is normally faced with people who are overweight. He tells them to consume fewer calories. This does not mean that when patients who belong to the minority of the severely malnourished come to him, he is ethically obliged to tell them to cut down on their food intake also. You have to make your prescription appropriate to the problem it is designed to cope with.

I greatly regret that Thomas Sowell is not here with us, because I have just finished reading his *Race and Economics,* and I wanted to tell him how good I think it is. Sowell makes the interesting point that status, position, security do not follow attitudes of like or dislike; on the contrary, it is achievement that comes first—Irish political power, for instance. Attitudes adjust to realities. This was first mentioned by Warner and Srole in their classic, *Social Systems of American Ethnic Groups.* The Yankees of Yankee City had had a contemptuous attitude toward the Irish, and then one of them is quoted as saying, "Well, something happened. They became more powerful and then we had more respect for them."

I am only trying to suggest that a group's growth in numbers need not necessarily elicit a growth in hostility toward the group that will be socially and politically significant. On the other hand, of course, that is possible. Others may ask, "If you, why not we? What gives you the right to do this while you deny us the right to do it?" It may be that if American Jews ever come within striking distance of twelve million, I will no longer have the moral right to ask for our exemption from ZPG duty. At this stage, I think I have the right because I can say that ZPG is for exploders and I am speaking for imploders.

I return to the Mormons. They are interesting precisely because they are anomalous. Implicit, or even explicit, in all that has been said here is an approved individualism. For us, government leaders and chauvinists can tell the people to have more children, but fortunately the people shrewdly consult their own needs and interests and decide they are not going to have more children. People can be urged to have that patriotic third or fourth child, but the patriotic third or fourth child does not get born.

Now the interesting thing is that the Mormons do have their patriotic third or fourth child, according to what Dr. Berelson says. Mormons, who are so educated, know contraceptive technology. Part of the reason for their having as many children as they do is that they want to keep the Mormon enterprise flourishing and growing. So here you have an example of people responding to an ideological appeal for a high birthrate when they are perfectly capable of ignoring that appeal if they wish to. It is a patriotically high birthrate for the Mormon homeland.

Exposed to the same amount of cultural erosion, the same centralizing, gallicizing influences, the Bretons with their high birthrate survive as Bretons — in the face of all the cultural assimilation and all the emigration. With a low birthrate, there are no Aquitanians left. Both Aquitanians and Bretons were subjected to the same assimilatory forces. If there are Bretons now and no Aquitanians, the independent variable is natality: low natality in the Aquitanian peasantry, high in the Breton.

As long as the French Canadians were having their "revenge of the cradle," they did not need to enact authoritarian language laws. As soon as they started having as few children as the others, they felt the need for language laws. If there had not been that differential birthrate, there would be no French Canadians today. Therefore it is totally wrong to say that fertility by itself is unimportant. Fertility is central.

The anomaly of the Mormons should tell us something about Fred Jaffe's statement of the opposition between quantity and quality. Apparently the Mormons have been able to achieve both. They have large families. The maps show them living in counties where there are more than four children per family. Perhaps one way in which they managed to reconcile quantity with quality was to settle for Brigham Young University. That is, four children at Brigham Young, possibly, cost no more than one and a half at Brown. The question is, is Brown absolutely necessary for human-capital development, or can Brigham Young be a reasonably adequate substitute?

When I was younger, I heard about a J-curve in fertility. That is to say, there is an upturn in fertility rates for families above a certain income level, so that Mr. Rockefeller has six children. If the J-curve phenomenon still exists in fertility behavior, then I could imagine that if Garrett Hardin's advice were taken and you imposed a crushing tax burden on parents to make them pay for their parentage, that would be very effective in dissuading people from childbearing. Garrett Hardin doesn't fool around with democracy; he wants results. Now suppose that were reversed. Suppose you imposed a crushing tax burden on childlessness. Would that work? Would the birthrate rise?

As to exhortation, I find that ambiguous. Many people in the pews like to be exhorted not to be guilty of their favorite sin. A Jew can go to the synagogue to hear the rabbi denounce him for violating the Sabbath. If the rabbi stops denouncing him for violating the Sabbath, he won't like that rabbi. He continues to violate the Sabbath, but he wants his rabbi to tell him not to because that is what he pays the rabbi for. So the discrepancy between exhortation and behavior does not necessarily lead to dysfunction. On the contrary, the relationship may be highly functional. It may very well be that Catholics could have continued to combine birth control with going to church. That is not hard to do. Maybe they stopped going to church because they preferred the Latin mass to the new vernacular. And maybe they only used their disagreement as a rationalization for not going to church. I would not myself take the perils of a clerical exhortation at odds with lay behavior too seriously.

But linked to exhortation is something you could call community tone—the ethos of a community, the positive and negative supports. Obviously, it operates with the Mormons. It operates not merely because having children is good doctine. It operates because if a family has children it is approved of, and if it does not have children significant others look at it askance. That has something to do with exhortation, at least in a broad sense.

I have often speculated on the possible marginal effects of a conceivable symbolism. Fifty years ago the Jewish community used to support birth-control clinics. Most Jews did not go to Jewish birth-control clinics in order to get their birth-control information, but those clinics said something to them: "Birth control is good; it is how a proper Jewish person should behave." Concurrently eyebrows were lifted, and the mother of a married woman was embarrassed, when her daughter became pregnant for that third time. It was too—too Catholic. Everybody was terribly embarrassed.

Suppose that symbolism were reversed. Again, with no expectation that Jews would use Jewish communal institutions for the actual service, but only as a symbolic statement, suppose the Federation of Jewish Philanthropies in this city were to establish fertility clinics. The symbolic discourse, the signals emitted would change. I don't know what would happen then. By itself, it probably would not be enough. But to the degree that the change in symbol implied or encouraged a change in ethos, we should expect some change in behavior. I don't think it is all that easy to distinguish between exhortation and change in ethos.

I am convinced that in this, well-informed American Jews have used their cleverness to avoid facing a central issue. There has been a huge exaggeration of the extent to which this question of the Jewish birthrate occupies the attention of Jews generally or even rabbis specifically.

Fifteen years ago Erich Rosenthal wrote an article about Jewish fertility, or rather infertility, for the *American Jewish Year Book,* of which I am an editor. It sank like a stone to the bottom of the well. It was never heard from again. Two years later we published his study of intermarriage. It may be the most widely discussed and influential article ever to appear in the *Year Book.* I think an argument can be made that fertility may be as important, to say the least, as intermarriage. Question: Why do Jews want to hear about one and not about the other? Answer: We all know that we use our intelligence to rationalize our follies, to help us be silly in clever ways. American Jews have deliberately averted their eyes from what I consider to be our central problem.

You can make information available to people, but if they don't want to hear the information, it is remarkable how easily they can avoid hearing it or how easily they can distort what they hear. Your posing of the question is thus a great advance, because in fact the discussion has not even begun. What I have tried to do is to help get the discussion started.

I think the most important point has been totally ignored: How do potential Jewish mothers feel about this? I repeat, the Jewish community itself has been so deliberate about ignoring the question that it has not even begun to ask itself a simple thing like this: What in the way of re-organizing our services can we do to make it less difficult for Jewish women simultaneously to realize themselves as people with ambitions and to bear children? Shall we emphasize child-service agencies, nurseries? I don't know what the answer is. The question has not even been asked, let alone discussed.

A few years ago I spoke at Purdue University, to a general university audience, on "Zero Population Growth: For Whom?" I said what I have said here: exploders should stop exploding and imploders should stop imploding. I said that population was a problem with differential impact on groups having different needs and requirements and desires. My impression was that I was rather well received by the non-Jewish side of the audience, but that the Jews were acutely uncomfortable, when not actually rebellious and resentful, at what I had said. In my experience there is more objection among Jews to this proposition than there is among people generally. People can understand that different people have different needs. Most Americans should eat less, but some Americans should eat more. That is not so hard to understand.

I believe there would be opposition, but not from ethnic groups. It would come from the educated elite, whose universalist ideology dictates that if it is wrong for Bangladeshis to increase their population, then it must be wrong for Jews too—or even for Jews to think about it. The resentment would come most strongly from some professors, especially the Jewish ones. (Paul Ehrlich has said that one American baby is worse than fifty Indian babies.)

ERNEST ATTAH

You seem to be referring to the effectiveness of encouraging increases in fertility in order to maintain the population in the face of ongoing decreases. For my part, quite apart from the effectiveness of the means advocated, I question the advisability of advocating such means. Consider the full range of components of the ongoing decreases in the population of the community: mortality, fertility, and out-migration. The historical experience has included extremely high mortality among Jews such as during World War II, but I do not know how much of this one may reasonably expect for the future. I would guess that at least for the Jewish community in America, there is no clear basis for expecting their levels to become extraordinarily greater than the levels for other groups in the society. Jewish fertility levels have been lower than average compared to those of other groups, but they have been at a level to ensure at least continued replacement—that is, survival—of the group as a whole. Before, then, adopting your preferred solution of stimulating higher fertility to counteract the losses to the community, I would look closely at the third component, out-migration. For example, what part of the leakage from the community that concerns you has been occasioned by people moving away from old neighborhoods and adopting less traditional ways of life? Similarly, how much has resulted from a detraditionalization of life-styles through increased contact with alternative life-styles such as at educational institutions? How much of the decrease in the size of the traditional Jewish community has also resulted from out-marriage or conversion to other faiths? I should like to know the record on these issues because if, as I suspect, it should be the case that these various forms of out-migration from the group hold the key to the leakage from the traditional community, how advisable would it be to encourage increased fertility among those that have remained faithful to the traditional ways as a means of maintaining the group, rather than, say, trying to find ways of keeping faithful those that are inclined to leave?

The question as to whether it is moral for the Chinese government to encourage more births among the ethnic minorities in China is actually very complicated in that it is difficult to ascertain precisely what motives underlie such policy. To take a cynical example, might it be that the government knows that (in Kurt Mayer's words) "attempts to influence fertility have hardly had any noticeable effect, regardless of whether their goals have been to increase or to reduce population growth"? Thus the government would succeed in convincing the minorities as to the sincerity of its concern for them without really having to worry, from a planning standpoint, about any additional population growth.

But let us suppose instead that the Chinese government seriously expects to stimulate increased growth of the minorities. We still need to know to what end it desires this in order to determine how well the means is suited to the end. Lacking such information, we can only decide as to morality by assessing the likely consequences of increased fertility among the minorities. And in this, our fundamental orientation is of paramount importance for the direction of our decision. That is, the predicates of morality will determine the judgment.

My views are predicated on the orientation that we should do our best to avoid increasing the numbers of people on a finite earth having ultimately limited resources. Such global scope is admittedly substantially removed from the sectionalism that rules at present, but it affords the freedom to make independent judgments in all cases without prejudice. And from that standpoint, it is immoral to advocate any increases in fertility, under any possible range of what may be agreed to as normal conditions from now into the foreseeable future. The personal and collective fulfillment of individuals and peoples should be sought otherwise.

NATHAN GLAZER

How small can a group be and still remain vital? Look at the Parsis in India. As I recall, Kingsley Davis in *The Population of India* says there are 150,000 Parsis. That seems too small, given how important they are in that country of six hundred million. But they maintain cultural institutions, they maintain educational institutions, a significant position in economic life, and so on.

I have been having some interesting conversations with a philosopher turned ethnic scholar at Harvard named Iso Camartin, who is Romansch, a professor of philosophy at Nuremberg. He became interested in Romansch history, and the Swiss government has sponsored his study. It seems there are only fifty thousand Romansch left, roughly, divided into four linguistic communities. They publish books and magazines, and they study Romansch literature. Now that is a little small, but it is an interesting question to ponder. Suppose there were only four million Jews?

And now to make another contrast. We have recently heard references to the Greek-Americans. There can't be more than a million of them, yet they have recently shown great political influence. Just recently we have had an interesting example of cultural vigor among Ukrainians. There is a Ukrainian student group that decided it would fund six professorships of Ukrainian studies at Harvard—something Jewish organizations of students would never dream of doing. Now there are not more than a few hundred thousand Ukrainians in the country, and not many of them are students.

You may recall that there have been arguments about the future of the Jewish community among the Orthodox. They say, Why do you need all those Jews? They are not very good Jews anyway.

I think the general conclusion is that—and Fred Jaffe's paper makes this clear—demographers don't really see how you can affect fertility decisions upward, but they say you can affect them downward. Even to do that you have to have very strong forms of social control, such as in China. I just don't see how effective demographic policies can be introduced by a voluntary community. American Jews are a voluntary community, voluntary in terms of their membership, voluntary in their group organizations. If that is so, you are left only with exhortation or information. That is the only element we have. One cannot change the overall circumstances that affect fertility. American Jews are not particularly desirous of changing those circumstances by, let us say, moving to Montana, or isolating themselves, or not sending their children to Harvard, or whatever it is they might do to increase their fertility.

I would suggest that for certain stages of social development, and for certain types of groups, we may underestimate the significance of information. Reference has been made to the antigrowth movement. Now, obviously, there have been many reasons why there has been a drop in American fertility. And yet, I cannot believe that one reason is not the widespread information about what higher growth rates mean, not only for the individual but for the society—crowding of the parks, the destruction of natural resources, all the things mentioned by the advocates of zero population growth. I am sure that in some ways it affects the way people behave. For instance, the way they talk when they're in child-rearing ages is reflected in the ease with which young people today resist parental pressure to get married. Social pressure has dropped greatly. There are now excellent arguments against having children. "We don't need more people. The more people the worse. Look how badly off India is," and so on. I don't know how to find the impact of this information, or, if you will, exhortation, but I believe it has had an impact.

Now it certainly would not have had that impact if it was radically against personal or familial interest. If everyone knew that by not having children they would starve in their old age, then no matter how much information you gave them, they would not avoid having children. They would feel that children were insurance, as in India, or whatever. And in the same way, if information has had an impact in reducing the birthrate—I mean general information, what it means to have all those people, what they do to Yellowstone Park, the suburbs, and Westchester, and so on—isn't it conceivable that information might affect their behavior the other way, too? It is conceivable. And it is really the only mechanism that exists for such a group as Jews in such a situation. For example, how many children do you need to run the Jewish school system? Or, what is the impact in terms of employment for young people as teachers? Or, what does it mean for political weight? Jews are concerned about what it means for Jewish neighborhoods, or for the maintenance of synagogues, congregations, organizations, or aid to Israel, and a lot of other things. If people really do not know, because there is no discussion—not only is there avoidance of discussion, but literally people just do not know how many Jews there were in 1950 and how many there are in 1970, what the Jewish birthrate is (that is, below replacement)—then information may have at least a marginal effect. Obviously it would not affect everybody, just as ZPG does not affect everybody. Knowledge of Jewish numbers could become part of a milieu of discussion, become some kind of influence at some remove on behavior. I think that is not unlikely.

Now it is true we have examples of presumably much better efforts at information, exhortation, which failed. You can't possibly compare what a few Jewish communities, or Jews individually, might be able to do about changing the tone of discussion about the need for more Jewish population, to what was done in Italy or Germany with dominance, and total dominance, of mass media, and so on. The only difference might be that for a group at a higher level of education, even less information might have more consequences. An unlikely result, but a possibility. It is true that a lot of information in Germany did not help. But it might have been against individual interest. It might have been a situation where people were unconvinced of the argument. Conceivably, in another circumstance, information may have some kind of marginal consequence.

CHARLES KEELY

In this whole discussion about fertility and the policies of group survival in Jewish communities, it seems to me we have been talking about two levels. One is the survival of the Jewish community in the United States in general, and the other, which I have heard more of, is the more localized question of the survival of individual Jewish communities in certain areas of the country because of the problems of mobility. I am not sure whether there is merit to educational propaganda, or whatever you want to call it, to increase fertility, since I question whether that same mechanism would work on both levels: to increase the security of survival as a group in general and increase the probability of the survival of local, small groups.

Another item was brought up that I think is extremely important. We have avoided it. That is the question of the perception and reaction of other people and other groups in the United States if it became public knowledge that Jews are adopting, or at least a segment of organized Jewry is adopting, a program to increase fertility. What effects would this have on perceptions of Jews, as well as relationships between Jews and other groups in the United States? Would that lead to various sorts of opposition of one sort or another? Would it be perceived as, for example, not so much trying to ensure the survival of Jews as a group, even though that might be the stated goal, but as a ploy to increase and enhance the power of the Jewish group? Might it be perceived not as maintenance but as an enhancer, of sorts, and would it not have boomerang effects, and in fact worsen relationships because people would fear increased Jewish power?

DOV FRIEDLANDER

The American Jewish community is not the only one to be concerned with what seems to be too slow a growth rate with respect to survival (because of leakage). There are other examples, one of which is Israel. It has been claimed for years that Israel's survival among one hundred million Arabs in the Middle East depends, among other things, on numbers. None of our leaders has yet suggested that we should beat the Arabs in terms of population size or growth. Nevertheless it has been suggested that fertility in Israel should be encouraged to achieve an average family size of four or five children. That would certainly add to numbers, particularly in the long run. Is such a change feasible? It is obviously not, because people do not seem to be willing to reproduce for the sake of a nation. And even if it were feasible, would it automatically increase Israel's chance of survival? What kind of a society would this increased population be? Would it be strong—economically and otherwise?

It seems to me that the kind of problem the American Jewish community is facing (because of leakage) and the Jewish community in Israel because of its hostile neighbors probably has no demographic solution.

As for the suggestion that one solution may be to raise immigration to the maximum extent, immigration is, of course, a much more effective means to increase the Jewish population in Israel (and perhaps the American Jewish community) than to increase fertility. However, it is much more problematic than it may seem. Even if Israel's economic situation were much better, it would still be very hard to absorb a large amount of immigration (say more than 1 to 1.5 percent a year).

ETIENNE VAN DE WALLE

As a member of a minority group of Belgian Americans, I really have nothing at stake in the survival of the Jewish group, except as a conservationist, to the same extent as I want to preserve the American eagle. Something would be lost if the American eagle should disappear, although I would not want to have American eagles all over the place. For cultural diversity, I would find entirely acceptable any propaganda campaign that would aim at ensuring the survival of the Jewish group.

Regarding the bribe that you want to give to a woman so that she will have a child; the child will be supported through college and receive all he needs, and eventually he will marry a non-Jew and the story will start all over again. The point is that you cannot guarantee that your bribe will have the desired effect. All you can do is buy a child. And if you educate him properly—give him a broad, universalistic education—you will jeopardize the Jewish identity.

There is another argument, which stresses the qualitative element. We must not think in terms of numbers only. The qualitative point of view involves the Jewish woman and the Jewish child as individuals. Very soon it may involve all of us to the extent that there is a need to ensure a proper distribution of the load that accrues to parents. Children are a burden to individuals in the community, and we may all have to devise ways to ensure the survival of another endangered species, the child. The Commission on Population and the American Future published a table showing the cost of a child to individual parents; the amount was mind-boggling. Fathers everywhere experience that this is true, and for the sake of the quality of child and family, the community at large (and not only Jewish communities) will have to consider means to make reproduction possible by relieving the burden to individuals.

I find the comparison with the Chinese fascinating. If we have to judge which of the two groups was more successful, assuming that they both started with ten million persons at a given date, I vote for the Jews. Weight in terms of human bodies does not count. What counts is the contribution of Jewish religion, traditions, artistic mentality, and so on to mankind. And this stands the comparison with the Chinese contribution very well. The Jews have even passed the ultimate test of success, which is to survive as a nation without a territory. We identify the Chinese because they live within certain borders, which have been arbitrarily designated as China. The Jews have proceeded beyond such a criterion.

American Jews are not a typical minority because they are a highly successful, dominant kind of group, part of the urban population and the intellectual elite. In a way, the Jews are like other urbanized groups, such as the Parsis in India (also a low-fertility group) or the Chinese colonies in much of Asia. They are minority groups if you like, but they provide the merchants, the civil servants, and so forth. These groups belong to the mainstream of modernity and in that sense are part of the majority.

It seems to me, by the way, that the low fertility of the Jews in the United States is largely the result of the fact that they belong to socio-economic positions where fertility is low: they are doctors, have high incomes, live in cities, and it is hard to distinguish the effect of Jewishness from that of being a doctor living in a city and having to pay for an expensive education for one's kids.

HARRIET PRESSER

For a woman the decision to have another child has generally implied a decision to forego four or five years of work outside the home. Now if Jewish families are to have more children, one alternative might be for Jewish men to take more time out for child rearing. This kind of issue is probably an important one for Jewish couples right now. The question of traditional sex roles is being raised explicitly among the most educated segment of society.

BERNARD BERELSON

Are the Jews less integrated into American life than the Mormons? Would their fertility increase if they were widely dispersed throughout the United States or perhaps became less urban and less eastern or even New York-ish? And if so, what would that do to their intellectual or political importance in American life? Even if you assume that the fertility of Jews would be higher if they all lived together in Idaho, next to the Mormons in Utah, what would be lost in the process and what side of that trade-off would you choose? As for the leakage of Jews through assimilation into American life, the community has to take the responsibility as well as the consequences. To the extent that there is such leakage, Jews do not feel so Jewish any more, and then it is difficult to say that the remaining Jews have to have more children to make up the difference. It gets down to the question of what the community means to itself—its integrity eventuates in its fertility, not the other way around.

FREDERICK S. JAFFE

I remember that many Jews went to the synagogue to be made to feel guilty about what they were going to do on Saturday afternoons. How many Jews did you lose in that process? Do you know? Does anybody know? Jews are concerned about leakage. One of the more important sources of leakage from the Catholic church appears to be the position of the church on fertility control and divorce. I suspect the church may compound the problem now by its position on abortion. In the few places where anybody has looked at religious data on abortion recipients, it is just as it used to be with birth control—the religious composition of abortion patients tends to be similar to the religious composition of the community's population. If the church ever shifts its position on fertility control and somebody does an intensive analysis of what happened to Catholics in the transition, I suspect they will find that the church's position on these issues was not exactly functional from the point of view of the church's survival.

Finally, on incentive programs, a professor in California did a piece in *Social Biology* around 1969, estimating what the cost would be of a program in the United States to offer an incentive for people to remain childless over time or to have fewer children. I don't remember his assumptions exactly, but I think that a woman would be paid twenty-five dollars for every month she was not pregnant. He calculated that it would have cost something like $19 billion a year. The only problem was with the incentive of twenty-five dollars a month, because you really couldn't expect to buy anyone in the United States to do anything very serious in 1969 for that much. So I asked, what might a reasonable bribe be? Let us assume that $125 a month would begin to get interesting. That would have meant a cost of a hundred billion dollars, which at that time was more than 10 percent of our GNP. I came to the conclusion that if anybody was seriously going to advocate such a policy, they could not advocate it and justify it on demographic grounds alone. They would be advocating a policy of basic income redistribution, which might be meritorious in its own right but would have to be justified on larger grounds than demographic ones. I believe that the numbers would work out in a similar way in practically any other group or nation.

The World Population Plan of Action says each nation should decide its own demographic goals in terms of its own demographic situation. Virtually no one denies that each nation or group has the right to make those decisions. The question is not really who has the right. The question is how wisely the right will be exercised. In that context, you have to confront the paradox that every group thinks its situation is unique. We have heard expressed, in eloquent terms, some aspects of the uniqueness of the Jewish situation in the United States and in Israel. Yet the burden of the papers by Dr. Van de Walle and Dr. Berelson essentially is that the same kinds of feelings are expressed all over the world, in all kinds of multiracial, multiethnic societies. Everybody seems to look at this kind of problem in very much the same way. What is more, they always seem to come out advocating very much the same sort of solutions, and the solutions don't work.

If the issue, then, is what would be the wisdom of one or another policy, what science can offer a group's policy makers is an assessment of the historical record. We had some discussion earlier about the

Mormons. They seem to be different; nobody quite knows why. Maybe somebody ought to go study why, and then we might find out some of the keys to the problem of increasing fertility and status concurrently. But there are very few such groups in the world.

CHARLES WESTOFF

If you are going to take seriously the idea of a propaganda campaign, it seems to me that one of the essential ingredients is good information. As we have said repeatedly, nobody really knows what the Jewish population is, what the birthrate is, at what levels the different segments of the Jewish population are reproducing. As you all know, the problems of taking sampling surveys are tremendous because of the geographic distribution of the Jewish population.

This year I am chairman of the U.S. Census Advisory Committee on Population Statistics, and I just proposed (to see how it would go over) the possibility of asking about religion—not on the census, which I think, politically, is out of the question, but on a current population survey, particularly the one that is coming up in June 1978, concentrating on fertility and marriage. It would be of great use in this discussion if we had that information right now. The Census Bureau looks upon this as something of a plague because they feel the substance of the issue makes them more vulnerable to criticism from the outside, and it may cost them something else they would like to do. I will remind you that in March 1957, when we had the one example in this country of a current population survey that did include this question, there was a great political hullabaloo. Organized Jewish groups were in the avant-garde of those who were opposed to it, for reasons which may or may not be any longer valid. I would think that perhaps things have changed. As a matter of fact, the secretary of commerce impounded the punchcards; they were released a few years ago. It is going to resurface as a proposal. I would be delighted with the endorsement of the AJC. I realize this may create internal political problems for you.

JOHN SLAWSON

I think that while I agree with Milton Himmelfarb's view with respect to the need for increased Jewish population, I am not too sure about his program, that is, how to go about doing it. I don't believe that people would increase the number of children they would have for the sake of the needs of the group. I do think that if Jewish group life had more meaning for the Jewish individual, the attitude toward increasing the family might improve, but not as a result of a specific program for increased population.

I would like to make an observation on the macrolevel rather than on the microlevel we've been talking about. There is a correlation between size and power. You take the Jewish group in the United States, and I am reminded of, I think it was Rudyard Kipling, who said, "The bleating of the lamb incites the tiger." In other words, the weakness of a subgroup represents a danger for its survival. The Jewish group, of which there is a concentration in large cities, has had a certain political strength that has been very important. And because it has that kind of strength, I think politicians tended to listen to some of its demands.

Now I am not always sure that what is good for the group is good for the total nation. It is said that what's good for America is good for the Jews, and what's bad for America is worse for the Jews. But you can't always tell about the reverse. And I think this business of smallness and power is a theoretical concept, which has to be related to the situation, especially in the case of a subgroup in the larger society.

Consider, for example, the black situation in the United States. I think we know that blacks comprise more than 40 percent of the population in the forty largest cities of the United States. This creates an intergroup struggle of a special nature, not only from the point of view of inundation because of density but also in relation to political power. This is particularly true since the Voting Rights Act was extended beyond 1965 with the federal government taking a responsible role in certain states where registration was actually prohibited or prevented.

But with respect to numbers, I can believe that if the Jewish group continues to decrease in size, it will occupy a much weaker position in the United States than it does now.

If you studied the trend of the Jewish group in the past three or four decades, considerable status and power have been gained. I believe it would never have happened if the numbers had become considerably smaller each year.

I agree with Milton Himmelfarb with respect to the question of size, but I believe the effects of concentration in large centers presents a special consideration.

CALVIN GOLDSCHEIDER

Most of the evidence about lower Jewish fertility in Western European countries and in the United States is solid, beginning in the twentieth century. There is scattered evidence suggesting lower Jewish fertility in the middle to late nineteenth century. Some have argued on the basis of the weak evidence available that Jewish fertility in eighteenth- and nineteenth-century Eastern Europe was quite high. The argument, presented most forcefully by Roberto Bachi in recent years, is that population growth among Eastern European Jews was very high during the nineteenth century. This population explosion was the result of high stable rates of fertility in a period of rapid mortality declines (falling more rapidly and earlier among Jews) and immigration.

The argument about the relative level of Jewish fertility is partly speculation for the pre nineteenth century period. I don't think fertility levels were stable or higher (or lower) for all periods. I would argue that Jewish fertility patterns were responses to the location of Jewish communities within European and American social systems. The particular minority status of Jews combined with the social characteristics and high rates of social mobility and mobility aspirations resulted in lower Jewish fertility.

Evidence on Jewish fertility is available up to the late 1960s, but my guess is that low Jewish fertility in the United States and in Western European countries has moved to even lower levels—below replacement—in the last five or six years. This reflects, and here I am guessing, increasing rates of nonmarriage and childlessness. Jews have been characterized as one of the groups of almost perfect contraceptors in the United States. Add to this the changes that I suspect have occurred in family structure (such as the proportion married and divorce rates) in the last decade or so, and I think you have a real deemphasis on family life. These changes, where a large proportion of more secular-modern Jews are not marrying or delaying marriage, where higher divorce rates are common, are indications of the real break in the cohesiveness and centrality of American Jewish family life that has taken place in the last five to ten years. These changes, I suspect, will have a real impact on Jewish fertility and reproduction rates.

There have been guesses and estimates suggesting population increases in Europe during the late eighteenth and nineteenth centuries, particularly in Europe. Although I don't think one can rely too much on these data, the estimates are that Jewish population size increased from fewer than 4 million in 1825 to 7.7 million in 1880 to 16.6 million by 1939. Most of this growth was concentrated among Eastern European Jewry in Eastern Europe and America. It is a reasonable hypothesis that Jewish fertility in Eastern Europe remained higher for a longer period of time than mortality and that population growth was rapid during the period of slowly declining fertility.

One point in this connection contradicts the view that majority populations generally responded earlier to fertility changes. That argument is probably incorrect empirically with regard to Jewish population. Jews, as a minority group, probably first experienced the decline in mortality and fertility in Europe and America. These patterns have been the result of their social characteristics and their minority status within European and American societies.

The Jewish population figure of fourteen million is plus or minus two or three million. I don't think there is any good demographic evidence on the major Jewish populations in the Soviet Union or the United States. For example, the 1971 Soviet census lists two million Jews; the *American Jewish Year Book* lists three million. Demographers have shown quite convincingly that the two million figure is more accurate. We don't know the Jewish population size in the United States. We have some guesses, but there is no way to determine the exact figure. So I think fourteen million plus or minus two million to three million is as accurate as we can be at the moment.

The only other comment I would like to make in this regard is that the migrants to Israel who had been in the major Jewish communities characterized by high levels of fertility have experienced a fertility decline of 40 percent in about a generation.

Going beyond the question of Jewish fertility, I think it is important to talk about the total amount of exiting and entering with the Jewish group, and that includes not only Jewish fertility and natural increase but in- and out-marriages as well. The central issue therefore becomes one of quantitative demographic survival rather than solely the question of changing patterns of fertility. If there is a quantitative demographic problem among Jews, I think it revolves less around the isolated fact of low Jewish fertility than the total complex of factors resulting in the reduction of Jewish population size. In this respect, out- and in-marriages are of much more quantitative significance.

I would like to return to a point that relates to the very important question of minimum demographic survival. Treating the Jews or any other ethnic group as a homogeneous group is inaccurate in fertility as in other matters. The question might be raised as to which subgroups among the Jewish population tend to have lower fertility; that is, in general Jews are characterized by lower fertility but certain groups within the Jewish population accentuate this pattern.

With the Jewish population those subgroups that are characterized by extremely small families are those that are less Jewish. Although there are few data on the problem, scattered evidence and some observations suggest that those who are committed Jews, particularly those living in segregated Jewish communities (such as Hasidic and other extreme Orthodox groups) tend to have somewhat larger families. It is not to these groups that the question of increasing fertility levels is addressed but precisely to those Jews who are most alienated from Jewishness—the most non-Jewish among the Jews. I think that the question of the Jewish demographic problem cannot be asked for all Jews in the United States. Rather, we must raise the questions, What are differential fertility patterns among Jews in the United States, and what subgroups within the Jewish population are we addressing when we want to intervene and influence fertility behavior and attitudes? This is no different from the question of fertility problems among the black population. We also must take note of the fact that there are some segments of the black population who do not have large families and who do not have a high proportion of unwanted births.

Therefore, our questions should be addressed more specifically to differential fertility patterns within ethnic subgroups. In this sense the issue of residential segregation or integration and vitality of ethnic community life is not focused on "American" Jews but on more localized Jewish communities. There are Jewish communities within the United States that are demographically vibrant because of population growth through replacement-level fertility and net in-migration, and there are also other Jewish communities in the United States that are losing population through out-marriages, out-migration, and low fertility. The latter are the "less" Jewish-committed—the smaller Jewish communities in various areas of the United States. In these communities the problem of population size is most acute; I am not sure that fertility levels are lower, but clearly out-migration and out-marriages are higher.

I would like to make two additional points. First, we subscribe to the principle of universalism—that residential segregation is not good on principle—yet that principle conflicts with the fact that those groups that have retained higher fertility are the most segregated. I am not sure you can have the principles of integration and universalism, as well as strong group identity involving higher fertility. Comparisons with Mormons and the Amish and other segregated groups are not helpful once you have argued for the integrationist-universalistic position.

More important, there are very real differences between leadership roles and power in minority groups and leadership in government. A government might reach a decision with regard to fertility programs that may or may not require the agreement of the population. The machinery of implementation is clearly available. The lack of central authority and the absence of consensus among Jews represent real obstacles for policy agreement and implementation. There is some truth to the notion that two Jews produce three opinions. Disagreements and competition among Jewish organizations, secular and religious, are so pronounced that I cannot see an effective consensus emerging at the policy level. The voluntary nature of Jewish communal life and the heterogeneity of organizational objectives seem to be powerful arguments against the possibility of reaching agreement that it is good for the Jews to have more children.

Let me summarize the discussions of group survival. The discussion revolved around what role differential fertility plays in the total complex of factors that determine the survival of groups. There are those who argued that differential fertility is the most important component and, therefore, low fertility has certain implications for policy, that is, low fertility is the reason that some groups fail to survive demographically or tend toward nonsurvival or are in danger of nonsurvival.

Another view was expressed, that differential fertility is one component affecting the population size of groups and that there are other processes that influence the size of groups. Because of problems associated with the practicality of influencing fertility and perhaps simply because one should take the total picture into account, it seems much more reasonable to look at all the factors involved in group survival rather than just differential fertility.

The central question in that discussion was about the special circumstances characterizing one minority group with replacement-level fertility and high leakage, which is really another term for high rates of out-marriages and low rates of in-marriages or conversion to that minority group. The discussion centered around the problems of the Jewish minority within the United States.

Since Jewish fertility has been very low and Jewish population size small as a result of historical circumstances, the question was raised whether it would be desirable to raise the level of Jewish fertility to ensure demographic survival. I am not unbiased in my reporting of that particular discussion, but it seems to me that what emerged was the question of whether universalistic, integrated communities that are characterized by social and economic levels associated with lower fertility can change these very strong tendencies because of the need for survival, which is defined demographically.

I think some serious doubts were expressed in the discussion about that possibility. Moreover, looking at variation within the group, patterns of assimilation and the role of fertility make the fertility component not the most problematic element in demographic survival. Of the total range of factors influencing population size, growth and patterns, and demographic survival, it appears that the fertility component is not necessarily the most critical problem involved.

Again let me come back to the initial point that I made. With regard to Jews, and I imagine with regard to other groups that might be examined, the available data and the existing studies of the relationship between these demographic unknowns and intergroup relations are very under-developed. Assuming that these are important issues, both in theoretical terms and in terms of practical programs and policies, it seems to me that a first step is to attempt to examine more systematically the data avail-able and gather directly the type of evidence that would more clearly shed light on some of these problems.

IMMIGRATION AND POPULATION CHANGE

MYRON WEINER

Charles Keely's paper deals mainly with the United States, but the policy issues he raises are relevant for Europe as well. The common policy prob-lem, to put it rather simply, is this: in Western Europe and in the United States, manpower needs are increasingly met through migration policies that affect the ethnic composition of those populations.

These manpower needs are related to the fact that in Western Europe and in the United States, we no longer have the large rural population that provided the manpower for our urban industries and for other de-velopments in our economy. Increasingly we have had to turn to Mexico and to Puerto Rico to provide employees for low-skilled industries and for service trades. Many Puerto Ricans, for example, work in marginal industries, such as the shoe industry in New England, or take on jobs that the indigenous population is no longer prepared to take. This has been a major phenomenon in Europe as well. The French, for example, do not like working night shifts so they bring in Algerians to work nights. We also import manpower to maintain certain agricultural industries, as in the Southwest.

Now, as I say, this is a general problem, not just in the United States, but in Europe, too, and it is related partly to our own demographic de-velopment, the fact that we are moving toward ZPG. Also the kinds of people we need for some jobs are not available in the United States. Paradoxically, in the United States we have a manpower need even at the same time that we have large-scale unemployment.

In an effort to meet those needs, migrants are brought in, largely from low-income countries. In the case of Western Europe, the migrants are brought in from southern Italy, Greece, Yugoslavia, Turkey, and North Africa. In the United States, a large part of the labor force is brought in from Mexico, Puerto Rico, and other parts of Latin America.

International migration clearly has important effects on the ethnic composition of populations—with significant political consequences. Western European governments adopted a policy of bringing in workers for short-term periods. The temporary guest-worker phenomenon was a device to fill manpower needs without affecting the ethnic composition of the population. The United States, following its historic traditions of bringing in a labor force for permanent settlement, did not opt for that kind of solution except, as Mr. Keely indicated, for the Bracero program, but that was a program we have always felt uncomfortable with. The American notion is that we make it difficult to come to the United States, but once someone comes, he can stay permanently. In Western Europe, they make it easy to come but difficult to stay permanently.

In Western Europe the migrations have increasingly resulted in a substantial permanent settlement, despite the fact that the governments intended to make it temporary, with the result that there are ethnic conflicts in a number of countries. There have been a nativist backlash movement in Switzerland and tensions in France in relation to Algerians. In Germany there are tensions over the Turks. And in the United States, there are problems with the Hispanic population.

In considering alternative policies, I consider it a mistake to think exclusively of the question of how to satisfy manpower needs by seeking a temporary or permanent labor force through migration. An alternative is to think about the jobs and the structure of the job market for which migrants are being employed, and there you get into a whole new set of policy issues. Do we want industries for which local manpower is not available? Or should we encourage such industries to relocate abroad? Can we eliminate some kinds of jobs through technological changes? Can we make greater use of sections of our population that are not now fully employed? Can we, for example, make greater use of women in our labor force? Or young people? Or the disabled? Or the elderly retired? Perhaps we should "export" certain industries. We may want to let the shoe industry in New England die or let certain agricultural industries in the Southwest disappear as a means of reducing our manpower requirements and minimize some of the ethnic issues that are becoming major problems in both the United States and Western Europe.

One thing we can predict with certainty is that the consequences for intergroup relations of present and future migrations will not be the same as the consequences that earlier migrations had for intergroup relations in the United States. The circumstances under which the current wave of migration is taking place are substantially different from those that took place earlier. The ethnic composition of the migrants is now different, the areas of the country to which they are going are not the same as in the past, the structure of the labor market and the opportunities for labor mobility are different. The experiences of the second generation of migrants are different, and the extent of ethnic awareness and the acceptance of the legitimacy of political organization of ethnic groups is different. Even the legal rights and benefits for minorities have changed.

We need to know more about the changing circumstances under which our migrants deal with the problems of adjustment into our labor market and into our political structure. I think the adjustment process can work more easily in a closed labor market when the economy adjusts through changes in the wages of the labor force or changes in technology. The United States has traditionally not operated with a closed labor supply. We have not only had a policy of bringing in migrants, but we have also allowed a substantial amount of illegal migration into the country. I say "allowed" because most European countries penalize employers for the hiring of illegal migrants; the United States does not. European countries have registration systems, which have given them the capacity to close or open their labor market as they choose. Migration is a matter of explicit policy control. In the United States we have in effect allowed individual employers to make manpower policy decisions for us. This has made illegal migration possible.

Let me add one additional item to the research agenda. We have had no paper on the question of the internal distribution of minorities within our society as it affects their survivability, their political power, and intergroup relations. We also need to examine the changing forces at work that affect the redistribution of ethnic groups in America.

ALAN SWEEZY

The concept of need is one that bothers economists a great deal. As far as manpower goes, I think there are two different aspects. One is the overall manpower need, so-called, or general labor shortage. The other concerns particular types of labor.

As to the overall aspect, it is a fallacy to think that there can be such a thing as a general need for more manpower. An apparent shortage is actually a function of fiscal and monetary policy. We notice that in wartime there is always a labor shortage. And why is that? Very simply because we are trying to expand our total output faster than our resources allow us to.

Germany and other European countries were operating under forced draft in the period of the 1950s and 1960s. Our economy was also operating under forced draft in the late 1960s. You may remember that there was an overall manpower shortage in the late 1960s because we were allowing stimulation to occur at a very high rate. When we slowed that stimulation down through restrictive fiscal and monetary policy in the early 1970s, the manpower shortage turned into a manpower surplus. You can always do that.

Now the other aspect is particular shortages. This is what Myron Weiner is talking about, and those are a matter of the adjustment mechanism in the economy. People who worry about these shortages are really saying they have no faith in the adjustment mechanism of the economy; because a particular group of employers experiences a shortage of labor, we should do something to provide them with the labor they want. That would mean perpetuating the existing structure of jobs, and there is no good reason for that. It has often been pointed out that we could grow silkworms in this country if we wanted to supply the enormous quantities of labor that would be necessary. I understand that for a little while in the depression of the 1930s, there actually was some silkworm growing in southern California. When the economy improved, of course, there was a terrible shortage of labor for that occupation. But from the policy point of view, it would be completely stupid to try to meet that shortage by importing cheap labor or in any other way providing cheap labor. So it seems to me that while it is not a conscious policy, the U.S. policy of ignoring manpower has been sound. Basically we should not import labor in order to satisfy labor shortages. We should let the adjustment mechanism, rising wages, and other shifts in product markets and in the labor market take care of the problem for us.

It seems to me that Myron Weiner almost said what I was going to say. That disappointed me a little because I wanted to say it. But I was arguing, basically, that no nation, no country needs more people than it has, because people are both producers and consumers. Now, that's oversimplified, and consideration of diminishing returns, and possibly of increasing returns to scale, would modify that. There are particular occupations rather than the overall supply of manpower. You may find that at a point in time, in particular occupations there is an experienced shortage, or scarcity, which the people employing labor would love to see repaired without an increase in wages. But if we have faith in the adjustment process—and here it is rather strange for me to be talking like such an orthodox economist, but I do have that much faith in the adjustment process—changes in wages and other changes will pretty much rectify things. Remember once upon a time we had two people working on every bus? One drove the bus, and the other took the fare. Well, that went the way of a lot of things without our bringing West Indians in to take fares on buses for us.

About five or six years ago there was a great to-do about a labor shortage in Japan. In *Science* magazine there was an exchange, and some of the Japanese, particularly Japanese employers, were saying that that was a dreadful siutuation; they were going to have to do something to increase the rate of population growth, increase the birthrate, because, it seemed, they did not want to talk about immigration. Well, that has pretty much evaporated. There really was not anything to it. Japan was in the process of readjusting to a higher level of productivity, and a higher standard of living, and in that process some of the low-paying occupations, the low-productivity occupations, were victims of a shakedown. But Japan has gone ahead and prospered very greatly without any notable increase in the birthrate.

Another beautiful case is Switzerland. In the early and middle 1960s, there was a big debate in Switzerland about the influx of foreign manpower, which they felt was becoming somewhat dangerous from the social point of view. The argument against reducing the influx was that the economy would suffer. They did impose very severe restrictions and brought down the rate of increase practically to zero over the period of the late 1960s. Instead of going down, the productivity per man actually rose at a faster rate, which is what classical economics would tell us should happen in an economy that already has enough people to occupy its land and its capital adequately. In Switzerland it actually went up over this next period.

MILTON HIMMELFARB

Mr. Keely's is the first paper that squarely poses the question of ethnic conflict.

Let me ask whether there isn't something in addition about Hispanic immigration to the United States, and let me ask also about another immigration that he did not mention, black West Indians. In two different ways, their immigration complicates the situation and may intensify ethnic conflict.

Under various affirmative-action programs, people with Hispanic names and black people are entitled ipso facto to certain advantages. The result is that people coming here from any part of Latin America or from Spain proper, and black people coming here from the West Indies, have certain advantages. For certain important purposes it's better to be an immigrant from Santo Domingo with a Spanish name than to be a native-born non-Hispanic. On the face of it, this raises a question.

Then there is the question of ethical and moral obligations. Take West Indian black people. Now the basis or justification for preference for black people in the United States is that American black people have certain claims upon the society as a consequence of the history of black people in America. There's a real question whether the same claim may be made by someone from Jamaica. Perhaps an argument can be made that it may be. But certain questions must be raised in that regard.

But in addition, there is this. Earl Raab has told me that there's a group of Hispanic people in San Francisco who say that because the United States has been the imperialist oppressor of Latin America, the United States has obligations to all Latin Americans in so far as they are Latin Americans—legal immigrants, illegal immigrants, Puerto Ricans, other

Latin Americans. For these people, the United States has obligations to Latin Americans as such. In a way, the United States continues to be the enemy.

There are parts of the world, including Latin America, where the dominant ideology is an anti-American ideology, of a much more clear-cut and intense kind than, say, most European anti-Americanism. There is anti-Americanism in Europe, but generally immigrants from Europe don't come here carrying an anti-American ideology in their baggage, whereas from Latin America they may very well do so. From the very viewpoint of policy, there's a real question, it seems to me, whether immigration should be encouraged precisely from parts of the world where people are likely to have animosity against the country and who, to put it crudely, may continue to be troublemakers over the course of generations, having settled in America with an anti-American ideology.

I'm worried about the issue of bilingualism that Mr. Keely raised in such a thought-provoking way. A year ago I was in Chicago a day after there had been a fight between two factions in a high school which was predominantly Puerto Rican. The majority faction supported a Puerto Rican candidate for principal who was an accommodationist, an integrationist—a believer in Spanish as the school language to tide students over until they could enter the mainstream. The other faction was smaller, but more militant. Its members supported a woman basically opposed to English. The two factions came to blows, and the police had to separate them.

The point has been made here that immigrants now are like the older immigrants. That's true, in the sense that the older immigrants certainly retained their language for some time, and many tried to bequeath it to their children and grandchildren. But this insistence on an exclusive or official status for the language is new. It is this new thing, the insistence not merely on a tolerated position, which the United States has always given to minority languages, but on an official and indeed exclusive position for the language—specifically, Spanish—which raises questions for the future.

CHARLES KEELY

I doubt that the Spanish-speaking immigrants in this hemisphere come with an anti-American ideology. I'm wondering whether many of them perhaps come with the same kind of ideology as a person from Europe or Asia. They are perhaps like most immigrants, economically motivated.

Further, when we talk about U.S. imperialism and the anti-American feelings and so forth, I think again, as in all these things, we have to distinguish. I think the Puerto Rican case is very different from the Mexican case, and that's very different from the Colombian case, and so on. Whether and for what reasons these groups share anti-American feelings, to whatever extent they do exist among the immigrant communities or the descendants of immigrants, to what extent they can all get together on that basis, I think this is open to question. On the particular question of the West Indian blacks, one of the problems is that U.S. Immigration does not collect information by race. We can only make estimates.

The next question is what effect the size of the West Indian group has in terms of the intrablack relationships, as well as intergroup relationships involving blacks. Would that increased number of West Indian blacks just maintain the West Indian part of the black population at current proportions or not? Apparently the West Indian blacks are of high socioeconomic status and probably could well have less fertility and so forth. Migration could therefore be very much a replacement mechanism in terms of keeping the proportions the same.

I would also point out, as I mentioned in the paper, a black West Indian group that has become extremely important in New York: the Haitian group. There are whole areas in Brooklyn where French is as common as Spanish in the rest of the city. The Haitian situation has the added dimension of the political situation in relationship to this government and the Haitian government.

There may be an intensification of the ethnic identification of Hispanics, especially if our Census Bureau collects data and publishes information on Spanish-speaking or Spanish surnames and especially if we have affirmative action dealing with Spanish surnames, making no country distinctions. If our identification system, or our legal dealings with groups treat the people as one, they in fact do take on a common fate and may identify. They may, in fact, add Hispanic to their other identities.

We are not particularly encouraging Western Hemisphere immigration in the United States at this point. The wait for visas is now somewhere in the neighborhood of two and a half years. There are also administrative ways of cutting back on immigration from any area, the easiest being to cut down the consular staff, and the State Department has not been unknown to do that.

There are different sets of restrictions for obtaining a visa. The world was divided for U.S. immigration purposes into the Western Hemisphere and the rest of the world. And there are different conditions that one must meet to get a visa. The situation results from the history of the United States' not having any quotas on the Western Hemisphere. The 1965 law imposed a ceiling on the Western Hemisphere and levied different regulations for visas for natives of this hemisphere and the rest of the world. It takes longer in the Western Hemisphere because the number of applications and the number of visas does not mesh as well as in the Eastern Hemisphere. It is a technical problem in terms of legislation, but there are political reasons for the current system. Senator Sam Ervin was afraid of our being inundated by Spanish-speaking people from Latin America, to put it in a nutshell.

The only thing that bothers me about manpower analysis is that in all of my reading of congressional testimony and talking with people who are or were involved in lobbying and so forth, nobody in the United States ever talked about immigration policy as manpower policy. As a matter of fact, they make a very clear distinction between the United States and the Canadian situation, which they often bring up. The point system in Canada is supposed to be a fine-tuning mechanism for the labor market. Immigration is not used as a fine-tuning mechanism in the United States. Whether in fact there are attempts at achieving these functions underlying government actions is another question. But on the phenomenological level, shall we say, on the level of experience, decisions don't get talked about in that fashion. That kind of information does not get brought into deliberation. I never see data on the labor force or on a use of immigration as a fine-tuning or even a "gross-tuning" mechanism.

There is labor certification, but this was a sop for the support of organized labor in the United States. The Labor Department says it is a waste of money. I think if you got the people in labor, like Howard Samuels, in a corner, they would say it is a waste of money. However, labor is not going to give it up. They want to preserve that symbolic idea that they are protecting American labor. But it is not a fine-tuning mechanism. It affects less than 12 percent of immigrants.

As for the distribution of immigrants within the United States, I am quite sure one of the papers for the Population Commission addressed the question of the feasibility of requiring them to stay in a certain location. There are many constitutional questions. Another approach is to give a person a benefit similar to the Canadian point system for saying he will locate in some area. Again, there are constitutional questions about enforcing that. How long do you have to stay, and so forth? It has been looked at, but I do not think anybody in the immigration field wants to really face up and develop a policy on that because of other constitutional implications concerning the rest of the citizens of the United States.

There are three points I would like to make. The first is on the question of amnesty for illegal immigrants. In the current bill, there is a proviso for amnesty for anybody who has been physically present in the United States continuously for seven years. Such persons would be allowed to adjust status. This is in the bill that passed the House, and there is support in the Senate for it. The Kennedy format of the bill is similar. It may not be quite as "liberal" as it sounds because continuous residence means you have never left the country at all, and having to prove that may present some difficulty.

The second point relates to the question of illegal aliens. All sorts of people suggest that we ought to do something about it. I am not so sure that unilateral police action on the part of the United States is going to stop illegal immigration. I think it is part of a population redistribution and that unilateral action on the part of any one government is not going to stop it. This is not just in the United States. It is a worldwide phenomenon. I think we would have to take close to draconian measures to close the Mexican border. As it is, there are any number of ways of getting in and out.

And the third point is how we make the decision about what is good for us as a society. That question is being raised not so much in terms of the composition of immigration but in terms of volume. Do we have enough immigrants because of population growth? The question really comes down to, Who is us? Different organized groups have different opinions about the problem. Just as an example, the Jewish community in the United States is very supportive of the current "liberal" immigration policy. When I say the Jewish community, I mean a lot of the organized groups, the AJC being one of them. The "liberal policy" support is now partially due to the idea of having a sanctuary for Soviet Jewry. That is very clear in the statements and discussions that I have had with people connected with organizations about whether the United States should be a place for refuge and so forth.

But then the question is, What is a refugee? From one point of view, and it is an arguable position, there is no inherent difference between a political refugee from the Soviet Union, deprived of his life and occupation and being persecuted in other ways, and an economic refugee from Mexico who leaves because the opportunities are not there. That is a debatable point. When does one decide that political persecution gives one a quasi-right greater than that of an economic refugee or a refugee from a natural disaster? Why is the political one, but not the victim of an economic or natural disaster, considered qualitatively different so that he may be given a right? There are people who talk about Mexican immigrants, legal and illegal, as economic refugees.

It really comes down to a question of values, because none of those issues are going to be decided by some set of irrefutable facts. I do not think we can ever decide whether a political refugee has more inherent right to asylum than a refugee from economic or natural disaster.

One quick remark on the language question. Fred Jaffe was pushing me a bit to include some information and analysis in my paper on the numbers of people coming in to the United States of Hispanic background. Are they increasing proportionately and can we project that, at a certain point, in the past or in the future, we have tipped the scales so that biculturalism will become important? I am not so sure that that is a demographic question. In a sense, I think it is more a question of the organization and the goals of the group. I think there are enough Spanish-speaking people in the United States now so that they could make a real question of biculturalism and bilingualism if they decide to push for it. At what point that happens, I don't know. It is obviously impressionistic, but I think we are approaching that point. That is the only group that could challenge the Anglo-Saxon dominance of the culture, the law, and so forth in this country. Bilingualism may be more important in local areas, such as New York, the Southwest, or Dade County, Florida. Perhaps at first we will take a federalist approach and vote bilingual state by state.

Probably no country has a more "liberal" immigration policy than the United States. The United States is generally the most open-handed in terms of making visas available and particularly making available permanent immigration. There are people in the United States who say we make our decision on our country's needs, but our country's needs are defined differently. Our country has had a tradition of welcoming people, and our major reason for letting people in is family relationship. People who support immigration say the economic need in the United States is not the paramount reason for immigration, and it should not have paramount importance in terms of policy goals. And that is where I think the basic dilemma comes in. Some people say we ought to have immigration because it has been good for the country in the past and we ought to reunite families. Other people say that these reasons are not as important as our own growth problems or other needs, and we ought to have other goals.

It would be nice if we could predict changes in volume or composition of immigration as a result of changes in our immigration legislation. Very briefly, the quality of data available does not allow us to do that. A colleague, S. M. Tomasi, editor of the *International Migration Review,* and I just finished a study on the quality of U.S. immigration data. Our conclusion is that there is absolutely no basis to make any prediction about what effect the proposed changes in legislation currently before Congress would have on the composition of the immigrant population. If Congress were presented with estimates by the State Department, the Immigration and Naturalization Service, or anybody else, they would be misleading. The reliability and quality of the immigration data and supplementary data collected by the State Department are not equal to the task of projection. Current legislation proposes to unify immigrant selection into a world-wide system of 300,000 people and to make the same provisions applicable to the Eastern and Western hemispheres, which means introducing the present preference system to the Western Hemisphere, changing labor certification criteria for the Western Hemisphere, and a number of other technical changes. The State Department obviously does not collect data on the possible relatives in the Western Hemisphere who might qualify under such changes. So the demand created by the introduction of the preference system is unknown. In addition, the quality of the data that do exist—for example, the labor-force data—is extremely questionable. So our conclusion is that there are problems with the data. All demographers say that. We try to state clearly what those problems are. On the question of prediction, our conclusion has to be that any estimates of size or composition of future immigration based on current data are probably misleading.

NATHAN GLAZER

This is a wonderful perspective for consideration of immigration, a perspective that does operate on part of the European continent. But it involves a different attitude toward planning, and it involves different kinds of national traditions. Even in Europe, if you go to England, immigration policy never operated that way. While postwar immigration of Indians, Pakistanis, and West Indians has filled labor needs, it has not been considered in the context of satisfying labor need. In that sense, England is more like the United States. We share common traditions, and our immigration has always been seen in the context of who has the right to come rather than who we need—at least since the quota system. The quota system said you have a right if you represent a group; your right depends on the contribution of your group in the making of the American population. That was the form of right given. You don't have a right if you haven't contributed enough. Obviously there were other things, too—racial aspects and so forth.

In 1952 there was still a question of right, and even in 1965. In other words, the best claim you have for coming to this country is that you are related to someone in it in some way. That has nothing to do with manpower needs. That is the way it is thought of. So our immigration policy is thought of in terms of various rights, and basically they are family connections, either family connections in the large (one represents the group) or family connections in the small (one is a relative).

The second point of view about immigration is that there should be a rational model based on manpower need. But this is a very peculiar problem in the United States because we do have high rates of unemployment. How can you justify immigration by manpower needs? After all, in the case of Europe the huge immigration occurred in a very tight labor market. I think one can still think in terms of manpower needs affecting immigration because all the illegal immigrants come in to work and are working for the most part. But this means we must think about American unemployment in ways that are still not widespread. People look at gross unemployment rates and ask how we can afford immigration. They don't look at how much of that unemployment is created by new forms of rights, such as unemployment insurance, or by choices based on welfare, or by the special role of the student and the role of people who come into and out of the labor market, such as women in certain stages of life. So, in effect, we speak in terms of a gross unemployment rate and don't realize that really there are labor shortages even when unemployment is high. Take agriculture or the work to make up beds in New York hotels or something of that sort.

Milton Himmelfarb raised a third set of justifications I've not seen raised before. We had the familial relationship connection or group connection. We had the economic justification. Now he has raised the question of political justification for immigration. In a way it has been raised before, for example, in the notion that you should not let Communists into the country. We have always had that kind of modest political control. Now you have raised the question of who is going to make a good American. I suspect that's a very complicated issue. I think that most illegal Latin American immigrants come out of work motivation; they want to make a living and they want to get ahead, and they become very patriotic. I am thinking of the long account of an illegal Colombian family in New York, in the *New York Times Magazine,* by a young man who writes for the *Village Voice.* It seems like a legal immigrant family even though it is breaking the law.

The ideology of immigrants does play a role in immigration policy. It plays a role in the policy of Israel toward the Arabs. That is a much more extreme case of deciding whether to let a people come in who want to destroy your country. If one thinks of Latin American immigrants, I don't think you have such attitudes. It may be found among Latin American students, but I don't think it is important among immigrants.

I don't know the views of the ordinary Puerto Ricans, and on a certain level I suppose they are anti-American, but the Puerto Ricans who attend the Harvard Graduate School of Education are very definitely anti-American. They have posters up, "Defend the political prisoners of 1950." It took a while for me to remember that these were the prisoners who tried to kill Truman and succeeded in almost killing five congressmen. Of course, their views are not so different from the point of view of many native-born Americans. The question of the political level of justification of immigration seems too difficult to deal with. We have not even solved the economic issue, let alone the political one.

A final point, and this is suggested by the exchange on the Hispanics. It was a mistake to make one category of Spanish surnames for purposes of affirmative action; everybody knows that. It is convenient to put Mexican-Americans and Puerto Ricans together into one category, but it got terribly confused. There are Cubans; there are now a lot of Latin Americans. You create categories not only out of inner-social development, like creation of the Italian mentality out of provincial village mentality, but you also create political forces. You decree that a group is all of one group, and it is to its interest in many ways to act as one group. It is to the interest of the Puerto Ricans and all the other Hispanics, even if they don't like each other in New York, to make one great Hispanic union for certain purposes, like the election of the next mayor. It is to the interest of the Spanish surnamed in general to make sure that their category does not disappear from affirmative-action rules and regulations. In that sense, it was, you might say, a perfect example of the reverse of divide and rule.

CALVIN GOLDSCHEIDER

There is a strong relationship between immigration, residential segregation, and internal migration within the United States. In general we deal with immigration policy in terms of the consequences of immigration for intergroup relations on a national basis. It seems to me that the implications and consequences of immigration patterns and policies on intergroup relations vary within the United States. The implications are not uniform by area and by the degree to which social and geographic mobility occur within the United States. Some immigrant groups are more mobile; others are residentially and regionally concentrated. The relative social and demographic conspicuousness of ethnic groups within regions generates group conflict.

Assuming that the consequences of immigration for intergroup relations provide an important component in designing policy, I wonder whether some consideration might be given to the specific question of the geographic location of ethnic groups within American society. Perhaps just as regional manpower needs ought to be considered as part of immigration policy, so should the question of regional ethnic concentration.

BERNARD BERELSON

The secretary general of the World Population Conference, a Mexican, suggested to the Population Association of America a couple of years ago that if illegal Mexican immigrants did not get into any trouble in the United States for a period of seven years, then that would show they were making some sort of productive contribution to this society, and a statute of limitation ought to be invoked so that they could then take up citizenship instead of remaining illegal immigrants forever. The numbers are large. There are at least as many, and perhaps twice as many, illegal Mexican immigrants in the United States today as there are American Jews—who are, of course, the result of legal immigration decades ago. Now some advocates of zero population growth are urging that the United States restrict immigration on demographic grounds—that is, on the ground that the demographic costs are greater than the political, cultural, and economic benefits. Do we need them or do they need us? Are we allowing immigration because it is good for them or good for us? Note that the United States still has a relatively open-door policy, though less than formerly, as compared with most of the other industrialized countries of the world, which are becoming somewhat restrictive—even Australia these days. In this respect, the United States and Israel are two of the very few exceptions to the normal practice (that is, with regard to permanent immigration, not transitory labor flows).

ETIENNE VAN DE WALLE

An interesting side issue was brought to my attention by one of our students who is studying the Filipino community in Philadelphia. Many of them are medical doctors and nurses, and the economics of the medical profession have been totally modified by the existence of a second class of citizens with high skills, although not as high as those of their American counterparts. Although no conscious policy has been operating, it has completely transformed the supply curve of medical education by relieving the need for auxiliary medical personnel trained in the United States. There are about as many doctors entering the United States from abroad as are educated in American medical schools. Also, the economic position of the American doctor has been transformed. He can settle in the suburbs and treat clients who make his material position very comfortable, while the large, bankrupt hospitals in the city are staffed by foreign doctors who feel exploited by the system.

DOV FRIEDLANDER

I would like to pose a hypothetical question. Suppose that, as has been demanded in the United States, Israel, and elsewhere, the Soviet Union were to let one million Jews out in a very short period. What would be the official U.S. policy toward the possibility of mass immigration of Soviet Jews? And if many Soviet Jews were admitted to the United States what would be the effect upon relations between Jews and other ethnic subgroups? And what would be the effect (perhaps long-term) upon intergroup relations within the Jewish community? Precisely the same questions may be directed toward Israel, but the implications are much more critical because of differences in scale. I think such a hypothetical change in Soviet emigration policy could create a major crisis in Israeli society, as a result of a conflict between the ideology of immigration and population growth on the one hand and Israel's limited absorption capacity on the other. It may sound strange that small, poor Israel of 1948 could absorb an annual immigration rate of over 30 percent for a few years, while a much stronger Israel of 1971-72 with a population five times as large could hardly cope with 1.5 percent per year. Immigration into Israel today and probably in the future affects intergroup relations very strongly. The veteran population in Israel, particularly the socially deprived sections (mainly of Afro-Asian origin), would view large-scale immigration with hostility because they feel that immigration competes with the chances for an increase in their own welfare. A good illustration of this was the hostility toward immigration from various groups in Israel during 1970-72 when annual immigration was around 50,000. Apart from internal conflicts that might arise in Israel as a consequence of a hypothetical large-scale immigration, a more obvious conflict may develop between Israel and its neighbors. I wonder what would be the reaction to a large-scale Jewish immigration into the United States.

ELLIOTT ABRAMS

On the labor certification question, Dr. Keely said that only 12 percent of the immigrants actually get labor certification. It is really even a less significant factor than that because so many immigrants change jobs so quickly after receiving their labor certification. This is perfectly proper, and the law permits it, but it makes the labor certification program even less effective than it appears to be.

Now the immigrants are working. This is an interesting thing. They have to work because in many cases they cannot get, or are afraid to seek, public support. And they find work. Now that is interesting not so much for what it tells about immigration as for what it tells, I think, about the composition of American unemployment. These jobs are there, but for some reason Americans do not wish to take them. With some forms of public assistance, and from many other points of view, we have distorted the job market. There is high unemployment, but there are also some sorts of jobs—such as domestic service—going begging.

An interesting thing about the new immigrants is that both politically and economically, and despite ethnic differences, there are very close comparisons between them and the old immigrants. My impression—and I think the evidence can be only impressionistic—is that the new immigrants come here for economic reasons. They work very hard and take many of the poorest jobs; and they have the same feelings about this country and its economic opportunities and political freedom that old immigrants had. I suppose there is a little bit of social Darwinism here. Who, after all, are those who take the trouble to come here?

We think we have isolated two separate areas of immigration policy: the question of volume and the question of composition. Both independently and together, these certainly have an effect on intergroup relations. If volume is low enough, composition does not become a matter of great public concern; but it is also clear that as volume goes up and new ethnic groups start to be formed or reinforced greatly, the question of immigration can become a significant one for ethnic group relations.

As to the question of composition itself, it seems to me that we have identified three possible bases of selection of new immigrants: the economic or labor market basis; the family unity basis; and a suggested third, the political, based on the kinds of values and beliefs potential immigrants hold.

Our own history in the United States has been of what was called settlement as opposed to labor migration, and we have focused on family unity as the basis of our immigration policy. This is reflected, first of all, in the present immigration law, where virtually all immigrants are admitted on the basis of family ties without having to go through the labor certification process.

Nonetheless, we do see at least a reflection of the manpower policy that we might have adopted, in that for various classes of immigrants, there is a labor certification process. I think one might view it more as a symbol than as a working screen for keeping out various classes of immigrants. It has been pointed out, I think rightly, that there is a very interesting comparison here between the present European model of admitting immigrants easily, but not to settle, and our model of attempting to have higher standards or different standards for admitting immigrants, but being much more likely to allow those who are admitted to stay.

One of the questions that was raised returned us to the problem of volume. This was the question of how important are any questions relating to composition if there is not a very large volume. As Professor Keely mentioned, the social meaning of the immigration composition figures is in many cases larger than their pragmatic effect on the U.S. economy or on the composition of the population from the religious, racial, or ethnic viewpoint.

Thus, in a practical sense we may see in questions regarding such problems as illegal immigration more than is really to be found there. Nonetheless, immigration policy raises questions of values. What kind of a society do we think we are or should be developing? These are questions that are worthwhile addressing even if current immigration policy does not tell us what the answers must be.

Although current U.S. immigration does not necessarily determine the way population trends or ethnic group relations are going to develop, certainly we have identified three problems in this area that are very real today. The first of these is bilingualism. Prior to the new immigration law, there was already a sizable group of Spanish-speaking people in the country. Puerto Ricans are, of course, American citizens by birth. With a significant amount of legal and illegal immigration from Latin America over the past ten years, bilingualism has become a question that it will be necessary to confront more and more in the future.

The second problem was that of regional concentration of immigrants. It may well be that although a particular group seems small when compared to the total U.S. population, or even against total immigration, if the group concentrates in one area, questions such as bilingualism and absorption policies are raised.

A third and related problem was that of economic concentration— concentration of immigrants in particular professions or industries. The story of the medical profession makes a good example. One might make a strong case that the entire medical manpower situation in this country has been very significantly affected by American immigration policies. In fact, the case seems so obvious that it would be hard to deny its strength.

Given these three problems, it seems clear that if there are not intergroup conflicts about immigration policies today, there is certainly a potential for such conflicts. One such potential conflict was raised in our discussion—whether disadvantaged minorities in the United States might take the position that our nation's resources should be devoted more to helping native-born Americans than to bringing in immigrant groups and helping them. For example, it has been argued, though not here, that if America simply excluded all foreign doctors from immigrating, we would be forced to expand the number of medical schools and of American medical graduates because we would soon perceive a shortage of doctors.

In any case, there is a clear potential within any given volume of immigration for head-on conflicts between various ethnic groups, each of which wishes to see more immigration from groups with its own background.

Finally, let me add one or two brief notes about where we ought to go from here in discussing immigration policy. First, I think international comparisons are very helpful, and one that comes to mind is the case of Canada. The argument has been made that Canada is moving away from a very liberal immigration policy because Canadians were surprised to find a large group of nonwhites coming to Canada, and they wished to limit that group. That argument is disputed by some Canadians, but in any case, the experience of Canada raises the question of bilingualism and the question of the effects of immigration policy on ethnic relations within a country. It would help us, in our own decisions, to know a little bit more about the experience elsewhere.

Second, though it is an old story, we badly need much more information about immigrants to this country. The statistics in some areas are not so good. We know little about matters such as geographical dispersion and employment dispersion. We do not, for example, know in what labor markets the immigrants are to be found five years after they arrive. The matter has been getting some attention recently from Professor Keely and others, but certainly it is an area about which we need to know a great deal more.

And finally, as we begin now to reform the immigration laws once again, we must make a greater attempt at predicting the practical effects of the changes that are proposed. This is true of the effects both on ethnic group relations and on American labor markets. And I should add that we must attempt to predict whether the new laws will create, or will limit, illegal immigration. Few attempts at prediction were made when the 1965 law was passed, and few of those were accurate. One would hope that more attention might be given this time to predicting what effect the proposed reforms will have when they are put into effect.

Appendix:
Conference on Population and Intergroup Relations, October 27-28, 1975

POPULATION AND INTERGROUP RELATIONS: PERCEPTIONS, REALITIES, AND CONSEQUENCES

A conference to be held October 27-28, 1975, under the sponsorship of the American Jewish Committee, 165 East 56th Street, New York, N.Y. 10022.

It is a generally accepted truism that population will have to cease increasing. There is a growing body of opinion, in both developed and developing countries, that a slowing down of population growth now would contribute to the economic and social progress of the Third World and to more rapid solutions of pressing social and environmental problems in developed countries. In a recent United Nations survey, nations with a majority of the world's population described their current growth rates as "excessive"; many have adopted policies intended explicitly or implicitly to reduce them. At the U.N. World Population Conference in Bucharest last summer, a World Population Plan of Action was adopted which, while leaving up to each nation the responsibility to set its demographic objectives and decide its policies, presages greater international attention to population matters in the years ahead.

At the same time, even a cursory reading of history reveals that differential rates of growth have long been viewed with concern by group leaders and spokesmen. Such concerns have related both to differentials between religious, ethnic, and racial subgroups *within* nations and to differentials *between* nations. The focus of these concerns typically has been some notion of differences in size and growth rates as factors affecting the distribution of power between and within nations. Leaders of nations and majority groups have frequently expressed fears that they would ultimately be overrun or submerged by minority groups or other nations; not infrequently, these concerns have reflected racist, eugenic, and social Darwinist doctrines and nationalist and imperialist ideologies. Minority group leaders have often responded in mirror-image terms, advocating increased growth rates to increase their group's power or enhance its chances of survival in hostile settings. Within Jewish communities in various nations and the black community in the U.S., for example, there are those who advocate increased fertility in response to their concern about group survival.

These tendencies are likely to exacerbate intergroup tensions unless an improved understanding is developed of the perceptions of group leaders in regard to the relationships between population change and group survival and the underlying demographic realities. To address these issues, the American Jewish Committee is sponsoring a small planning conference, of 20 or 25 scholars. The purposes of the conference are:

1. To assemble available information on intergroup problems related to population changes.

2. To assess the demographic realities underlying these problems.

3. To explore the need for, and feasibility of, a broader program of activities (e.g., conferences, research, publication) to be undertaken by AJC and/or other organizations.

4. To yield an AJC publication, based on the prepared papers and the conference discussion, which would focus attention on these problems and their solution.

CONFERENCE ON POPULATION AND INTERGROUP RELATIONS   OCTOBER 27-28, 1975

Elliott Abrams	Washington
Ernest Attah	W. E. B. DuBois Institute, Atlanta
Judith Banki	American Jewish Committee
Samuel Baum	International Division, Bureau of the Census
Bernard Berelson	Population Council
Daniel Callahan	Institute of Society, Ethics and the Life Sciences
Dov Friedlander	Hebrew University
Nathan Glazer	Harvard University
Calvin Goldscheider	Brown University
Sidney Goldstein	Brown University
Oscar Harkavy	Ford Foundation
Gertrude Himmelfarb	CUNY
Milton Himmelfarb	American Jewish Committee
Selma Hirsh	American Jewish Committee
Frederick S. Jaffe	Alan Guttmacher Institute
Charles Keely	Fordham University
Mary M. Kritz	Rockefeller Foundation
Norman Podhoretz	*Commentary*
Harriet Presser	Columbia University
Geraldine Rosenfield	American Jewish Committee
Seymour Samet	American Jewish Committee
Gary S. Schiff	Jewish Studies, CUNY
Seymour Siegel	Jewish Theological Seminary
David L. Sills	Social Science Research Council
John Slawson	American Jewish Committee
Alan Sweezy	California Institute of Technology
Etienne van de Walle	University of Pennsylvania
Myron Weiner	M.I.T.
Charles Westoff	Office of Population Research

Index

ABOUT THE CONTRIBUTORS

Victor Baras was assistant professor of political science at the Graduate Faculty of the New School for Social Research in New York. He wrote on Eastern European politics for *Soviet Studies, Current History,* and *Commentary.*

□

Bernard Berelson, senior fellow and president emeritus of the Population Council, New York, has written extensively on population and family planning issues.

□

Calvin Goldscheider is an associate professor of demography at the Hebrew University, Jerusalem, and an associate professor of sociology at Brown University, Providence, Rhode Island.

□

Milton Himmelfarb, director of information and research services for the American Jewish Committee, author of *The Jews of Modernity,* an editor of the *American Jewish Year Book,* and contributing editor to *Commentary,* has taught at the Jewish Theological Seminary and Yale.

□

Frederick S. Jaffe, vice-president of Planned Parenthood-World Population and director of the Center for Family Planning Program Development, served as an adviser to the President's Committee on Population and Family Planning and has coauthored *Planning Your Family* and *The Complete Book of Birth Control.*

□

Charles B. Keely is an associate professor of sociology, Fordham University, New York City, and the coauthor of *Whom Have We Welcomed?* His articles on immigration policy and its demographic effects have appeared in *Science, Demography,* and the *International Migration Review.*

□

Etienne van de Walle is a professor of demography and director of the Population Studies Center, University of Pennsyvania, Philadelphia. His writings include *The Demography of Tropical Africa* and *The Female Population of France in the 19th Century.*